THE MAFIA'S PRESIDENT

ALSO BY DON FULSOM

Nixon's Darkest Secrets:

The Inside Story of America's Most Troubled President

Treason: Nixon and the 1968 Election

THE
MAFIA'S
PRESIDENT

NIXON AND THE MOB

DON FULSOM

THOMAS DUNNE BOOKS

St. Martin's Press ≈ New York

THOMAS DUNNE BOOKS.
An imprint of St. Martin's Press.

www.thomasdunnebooks.com
www.stmartins.com

Designed by Kathryn Parise

The Library of Congress Cataloging-in-Publication Data is available upon request.

ISBN 978-1-250-11940-7 (hardcover)
ISBN 978-1-250-11941-4 (e-book)

Our books may be purchased in bulk for promotional, educational, or business use. Please contact your local bookseller or the Macmillan Corporate and Premium Sales Department at 1-800-221-7945, extension 5442, or by email at MacmillanSpecialMarkets@macmillan.com.

First Edition: November 2017

10 9 8 7 6 5 4 3 2 1

To my daughter, Beth Willett,
and my son-in-law, James Willett

CONTENTS

AUTHOR'S NOTE

I was a member of the White House Press Corps during the Johnson, Nixon, Ford, Reagan, and Clinton administrations, but it was covering the entirety of the Nixon presidency up close that left me with a lifelong determination to uncover all the truths I sensed were hidden.

In Timothy Crouse's classic *The Boys on the Bus*—about the reporters who covered President Nixon's 1972 re-election race against Senator George McGovern—I was praised as one of the few White House reporters who took a highly skeptical view of Nixon's Watergate denials and those of his eventually discredited spokesman, Ron Ziegler. I was the first reporter to connect the break-in at the Watergate complex to the Committee to Re-Elect the President.

Until his death in 1994, Richard Nixon fought the release of all White House tapes that had not been put out during the Watergate scandal. But a lawsuit led to a 1996 settlement with the Nixon estate that brought the new tapes to light. I had been avidly following their now-complete release—listening to history and listening for news.

I have found that the best source for information on Nixon is Nixon himself—the real Richard Nixon, a chief executive whose haunting tape-recorded schemes and rants still resonate through earphones at the Nixon Library in Yorba Linda, California. There, earlier at the National Archives in College Park, Maryland, and now online, I have made several important discoveries, including the placement of a Nixon loyalist in Senator Edward Kennedy's Secret Service contingent in order to, in Nixon's words, "catch him in the sack with one of his babes."[1]

I chronicled many of Nixon's capers and criminalities in my 2012 book, *Nixon's Darkest Secrets: The Inside Story of America's Most Troubled President*. I have written articles about America's thirty-seventh president based on the newly released tapes for the *Washington Post*, the *Chicago Tribune*, *Esquire*, *Los Angeles*, *Regardie's* (a former Washington political and business magazine), and *Crime Magazine*.

The first inklings I had that Richard Nixon was somehow mixed up with the Mafia came during the 50 or so trips I made to cover the candidate, president-elect, and then president at his Key Biscayne, Florida, home. I got to know many of the residents of that lovely little island just south of Miami, and through them I heard rumors about Nixon's best friend, Bebe Rebozo, who ran a small bank on Key Biscayne. One story was that the bank was suspected of being used as a laundromat for funny money skimmed from Mafia gambling casinos in the Bahamas, but the bank was never charged with wrongdoing. Another was that Nixon and Rebozo had secret shares in, and split profits from, a Mob-run bridge in the Bahamas that carried tourists to those casinos.

At the time these were just rumors, not evidence that I could actually report on. But they whetted my appetite for more.

For the past eight years, I have taught courses at American University on Watergate and on the John F. Kennedy assassination, and I have done considerable research on Nixon's possible ties to both the Mob and the assassination. The result of my research is this book, *The Mafia's President*, a fresh compendium of the secret deals, favors, and payoffs Richard Nixon forged with leading Mafiosi over his long political career, and the role Nixon's Mafia and CIA connections might have played in President Kennedy's death.

TIMELINE OF EVENTS

November 1946: Nixon wins House seat with financial help from Meyer Lansky and other Mob leaders. Nixon's campaign manager, Murray Chotiner, has top Mafia figures as legal clients. Author Jim Marrs says Chotiner "had connections leading back to reputed New Orleans Mafia chief Carlos Marcello and Teamsters leader James Hoffa."[1]

1947: Congressman Nixon intervenes to get gangster Jack Ruby excused from testifying before a congressional committee investigating the Mafia, according to an FBI memo discovered in the 1970s. (The FBI claims the memo is fake.) But the fact of a Nixon-Ruby association has now been verified by a devoted Nixon friend, and right-wing political strategist, Roger Stone.

1947: Nixon strongly backs legislation establishing the Central Intelligence Agency. Around this time, Nixon first meets CIA agent (and Watergate burglar) E. Howard Hunt.

Late 1940s: As a young congressman, with considerable help from the CIA and FBI, Nixon helps expose State Department official Alger Hiss as a likely Soviet spy.

1950: The Senate Kefauver committee staff learns that Jack Ruby was "a Syndicate lieutenant who had been sent to Dallas to serve as a liaison for Chicago mobsters," according to a former staffer.

November 1950: Nixon is elected to the Senate from California after suggesting his opponent is a Communist sympathizer. Hollywood gangster Mickey Cohen is a generous contributor to Nixon's campaign. One of Cohen's cohorts in L.A.'s crime empire at that time is none other than Jack Ruby.

November 1952: As Dwight Eisenhower's running mate, Senator Nixon is elected vice president, despite a scandal over a secret slush fund put together by wealthy California backers. Ike also knew—but the public did not—that Nixon had accepted a $100 million bribe from a wealthy Romanian exile, according to CIA evidence revealed many years later.

Early 1956: Mob- and CIA-connected billionaire Howard Hughes reportedly furnishes Nixon with a secret $100,000 to help the vice president fight a dump-Nixon move by fellow Republican Harold Stassen.

November 1956: President Eisenhower and Vice President Nixon are re-elected.

1958: The Mafia puts a $5 million dollar price on Fidel Castro's head because his guerrilla activities are hurting tourism in Cuba. This was revealed in the diaries of newspaper columnist Drew Pearson. Other sources say Meyer Lansky offered $1 million for a hit on Fidel.

1958: Nixon meets Hunt again in Montevideo, Uruguay, during a vice-presidential goodwill tour of South America. Hunt was the CIA's station chief in Montevideo. The meeting gave the agent an opportunity to tout his leading role in a CIA-aided coup in Guatemala. Hunt later recalled, "Shortly after the Nixon tour left, I received a cable from Washington" saying the agency needed him "for an important new project" similar to the Guatemalan operation.[2] Hunt would soon be working for the vice president on a secret Mafia-CIA plan to assassinate Cuba's Fidel Castro.

1959: The FBI recruits Jack Ruby as a PCI, Provisional Criminal Informant.

1959–1960: Vice President Nixon and CIA agent Hunt are key figures in secret CIA efforts to overthrow Cuban leader Fidel Castro. Nixon is the chief motivator behind an associated Mob-CIA plan to murder Castro. Hunt later admitted his role in such plots. Nixon's onetime informant Jack Ruby was also active in anti-Castro operations.

Summer of 1960: The CIA asks Nixon crony Robert Maheu—a former FBI agent with top Mob contacts—to find mobsters who might be able to assassinate Castro.

September 1960: Louisiana crime boss Carlos Marcello reportedly contributes $500,000 to the Nixon presidential campaign through Jimmy Hoffa and his associates. Within a few weeks, the vice president manages to stop a Florida land fraud indictment against Hoffa.

November 1960: Senator John F. Kennedy defeats Nixon in a 1960 nail-biter; after his January 1961 inauguration, the new president goes ahead with secret Nixon-Hunt plans for a CIA-backed invasion of Cuba.

April 1961: The amphibious invasion at the Bay of Pigs is a monumental failure; Nixon, CIA, Mob, and Cuban exile leaders blame Kennedy for withholding planned U.S. air cover.

Kennedy privately blames the CIA and threatens to dismantle the agency and "splinter it into a thousand pieces."

November 1961: The Bay of Pigs disaster causes Kennedy to release Nixon/Hunt buddy Allen Dulles from his position as CIA chief. (Hunt is often credited with ghostwriting Dulles's "autobiography.")

November 1962: Nixon is defeated in the race for governor of California after a secret $205,000 "loan" from Howard Hughes to Nixon's brother becomes a major issue. The loan is never repaid, and some believe Richard, not Donald, Nixon, pocketed Hughes's money. Nixon moves to New York and becomes a corporate lawyer.

1962–63: Angered by CIA incompetence during the Bay of Pigs, President Kennedy moves to limit the agency's power.

Summer of 1963: Lee Harvey Oswald and the CIA- and Mob-linked David Ferrie are seen together in Clinton, Louisiana; the House assassinations committee later learns this from testimony of numerous witnesses.

July 23, 1963: Teamsters boss Jimmy Hoffa tells his lawyer, Frank Ragano, "Something has to be done. The time has come for your friend (Santos Trafficante) and Carlos (Marcello) to get rid of him, kill that son-of-a-bitch John Kennedy." Ragano disclosed Hoffa's statement in a 1994 book.[3]

October 27, 1963: Jack Ruby reportedly receives a $7,000 payoff in Chicago from Hoffa associate Allen Dorfman.

November 7 and 8: Ruby is in telephone contact with Barney Baker, Hoffa's "enforcer."

November 8: Oswald allegedly writes a note to a "Mr. Hunt" asking for "information." Could it have been intended for old Nixon friend E. Howard Hunt of the CIA?

November 21: Hunt is spotted in Dallas at the same agency "safe house" also visited that day by Jack Ruby and Frank Sturgis, according to testimony in a 1985 Florida court case.

November 21: Ostensibly in Dallas to attend a Pepsi Cola convention, Nixon asks the city to give President Kennedy a respectful welcome. Interestingly, he also predicts JFK will drop LBJ from the 1964 ticket. Ruby visits the Pepsi convention to pass out free tickets to his strip joint. (Did he and Nixon meet?)

November 21: Chicago Mob boss Sam Giancana meets with Nixon in Dallas to discuss the planned Kennedy assassination, Giancana later tells relatives. (Giancana also claims to have met Vice President Johnson in Dallas—but LBJ was with the presidential party in Fort Worth at that time.)

November 22: Former vice president Nixon leaves Dallas, ostensibly before Kennedy's arrival.

November 22: President Kennedy is slain in the downtown streets of Dallas.

November 22: A Dallas FBI Field Office paraffin test on alleged JFK killer Lee Harvey Oswald's right cheek finds no traces of nitrates, indicating he had not fired a rifle. Oswald is seen in the second-floor lunchroom of the Texas School Book Depository 90 seconds after the assassination—not in the sixth-floor sniper's nest.

November 24: With scores of police providing security and a national audience watching on television, onetime (and still?) Richard Nixon informant Jack Ruby shoots and kills Oswald in the basement of the Dallas police jail.

November 25: A Secret Service analysis of Dallas businessman Abraham Zapruder's home movie of the assassination indicates there were two shooters in Dealey Plaza, according to a CIA document pried from the agency in 1982.

1963: Titular GOP leader Richard Nixon recommends Congressman Gerald Ford for a spot on President Lyndon Johnson's Warren Commission. Ford quickly becomes FBI chief J. Edgar Hoover's spy on the panel.

1964: Nixon lies to the FBI in denying he was in Dallas on November 22, 1963. He later tells several different stories about where he was when he learned of the assassination.

1964: Ford drastically and clandestinely revises a previous compromise arrangement just before the commission's report is issued. Ford's changes make its preposterous "single-bullet" assassination theory slightly more believable, according to documents released in 1997. The Ford rewrite holds that one of the bullets struck Kennedy in the back, came out his neck, and then somehow critically wounded Texas governor John Connally, taking a sharp dogleg turn after it went through President Kennedy. In his own handwriting, Ford altered the description of the back wound and placed it higher on Kennedy's body.

1964: In advance of the issuance of the Warren Commission Report, Nixon and Ford write articles in popular magazines endorsing its anticipated conclusion—that Oswald alone was responsible for Kennedy's assassination.

September 1964: The Warren Commission finds Oswald fired three shots from the sixth floor of the Texas School Book Depository, killing the president and wounding Connally. It says Oswald had no co-conspirators and "was not an agent of the U.S. government."

November 1968: Just before the election, President Johnson amasses solid proof of Nixon's illegal interference with Vietnam peace talks—but he remains silent on what he privately calls "treason." In an extremely tight race, Nixon is elected president with near-solid support from the Teamsters union and the Mob.

1971: After a Mob payoff of at least $300,000 (and perhaps as high as $1 million or more), Nixon grants clemency to Hoffa—who had been jailed for jury tampering in 1967. In a generous gesture to Nixon's new best Teamsters pal, the more malleable Frank Fitzsimmons, the president prevents Hoffa from regaining union office until 1980.

June 1971: Former CIA agent E. Howard Hunt secretly joins the Nixon White House as the president's chief spy.

Summer 1971: Nixon repeatedly orders a break-in at the left-leaning Brookings Institution, where he thinks LBJ's papers on Nixon's Vietnam "treason" are being held. Those plans are eventually abandoned after a Nixon agent scopes out the building and finds it too secure for the break-in Nixon envisioned.

June 17, 1972: A group of burglars working for Nixon's re-election is caught by Washington, DC, police while breaking into Democratic headquarters at the Watergate complex. E. Howard Hunt and former FBI agent G. Gordon Liddy are soon identified as the group's supervisors.

June 23, 1972: To gain CIA help in the Watergate cover-up, Nixon tries to blackmail CIA chief Dick Helms over the secrets that Hunt might blab about the CIA's links to "the Bay of Pigs"—which Bob Haldeman later reveals to be Nixon/CIA code for the JFK assassination.

November 1972: In a landslide, Nixon is re-elected president with the help of a reported $1 million Teamsters contribution.

January 1973: Former members of Nixon's staff, G. Gordon Liddy and James W. McCord Jr., are convicted of conspiracy, wiretapping, and burglary in the Watergate scandal. Five other men also pleaded guilty, but at the time their names were not released.

April 1973: Top White House staffers Haldeman and John Ehrlichman resign due to the fallout of Watergate. Nixon's attorney general Richard Kleindienst also tenders his resignation.

May 1973: Haldeman reminds Nixon that he—Nixon himself—had informed him that the CIA was hiding big "Bay of Pigs" secrets—though this was not disclosed until 1996, when the National Archives released a new batch of Watergate tapes. Sections of numerous Nixon conversations on the tapes dealing with "the Bay of Pigs" remain deleted for "national security" reasons.

July 1973: In a few intense summer weeks, Watergate prosecutors become privy to the fact that Nixon recorded all conversations in the White House. A few days later, Nixon orders that all taping systems be disconnected, and when asked for the tapes from previous years, he refuses to give them up.

October 1973: In an event known as the "Saturday Night Massacre," Nixon not only fires the special prosecutor but abolishes the office altogether. His next attorney general, as well as the deputy attorney general, also resign.

1973: Nixon picks Congressman Gerald Ford to succeed the disgraced Spiro Agnew as his new vice president.

December 1973: The White House fails to explain an almost 20-minute gap in the tapes released to prosecutors.

April 1974: In a supreme act of deception, Nixon pretends to comply with the House Judiciary Committee's demands and releases 1,200 pages of transcripts of the tapes from the White House. Unsurprisingly, the committee finds the transcripts to be heavily edited and redacted.

August 1974: After Congress starts the impeachment process,

Nixon is forced to resign the presidency over the Watergate scandal.

September 1974: President Ford grants Nixon a preemptive pardon for all crimes Nixon might have committed in the White House.

1975: When Senate investigators uncover the Mob/CIA murder plots against Castro, Warren Commission lawyer David Belin condemns as "inexcusable" the CIA's failure to tell the commission about the plots.

2007: In releasing selected parts of the agency's "Family Jewels," the CIA finally admits it worked with the Mob to kill Castro. The number-one "jewel" on this list is completely censored. Could it somehow deal with the JFK assassination?

2007: In a "deathbed confession," E. Howard Hunt claims to have been a "benchwarmer" in the JFK assassination plot (which conflicts with earlier stories that he turned down a chance to take part). Hunt says President Johnson led the murder conspiracy; that many top CIA agents were involved; and that a French sniper fired on Kennedy from the front of the Dallas motorcade.

2008: In a foreword to a collector's edition of the Warren Report, former president Gerald Ford says the CIA destroyed or kept investigators from locating critical JFK assassination secrets. A Ford family spokeswoman confirms to this author the authenticity of Ford's quotes.

2013: Nixon associate Roger Stone (and in 2015, a top political adviser to Donald Trump) confirms the Nixon-Ruby connection, saying: "Richard Nixon told me in 1982 that he immediately knew who Jack Ruby was when he saw him shoot Oswald." But Stone contends Nixon believed that Lyndon Johnson headed a conspiracy to kill President Kennedy.[4]

2014: Nixon's chief Watergate accuser John Dean reveals that death threats prompted the feds to put him in the Witness Protection Program instead of prison. Watergate investigators told Dean they feared Nixon associate Bebe Rebozo might order a hit on him. But Dean stresses to this author that he himself has no firsthand knowledge that Rebozo had such inclinations or capabilities.

2016: Pulitzer Prize–winning reporter Pat Sloyan discloses that even Gerald Ford—the biggest public booster of the Warren Commission—privately did not believe the "magic bullet" theory of the JFK assassination that the panel had publicly endorsed.[5]

October 2017: The CIA is required by Congress to declassify thousands of pages of JFK assassination–related documents. (Howard Hunt's voluminous CIA files are among those slated for declassification.) What more will we learn about our thirty-fifth president's slaying when these long-secret papers are released? If they are declassified, will they be heavily censored? (Another potential hurdle: President Donald Trump has the power to prevent the release of the documents if he believes national security would be impaired.)

THE MAFIA'S PRESIDENT

ONE

The Mob in the Age of Nixon

Unbeknownst to most people even now, the election of 1968 placed the patron saint of the Mafia in the White House. Richard Nixon would not only go on to lead a criminal presidency, but he would be totally indebted to our nation's most murderous gang lords. Without massive contributions from his Syndicate sponsors, Republican Richard Nixon might not have edged out Democrat Hubert Humphrey.

How much Mafia money financed Nixon's 1968 bid? Estimates range from $400,000 to $2 million—much of it under the table and unreported. (Official post-election reports put Nixon's total spending at $25 million in 1968 dollars; Humphrey's at $5 million.)

The Mafia has been one of the most widely known, feared, and influential criminal groups for much of American history. La Cosa Nostra, meaning "this thing of ours," was the American offshoot of the Italian Mafia and became the main target of the FBI by the latter half of the twentieth century. La Cosa Nostra was powerful and prosperous, to say the least, as the various families combined brought in billions of dollars a year.[1]

While moneymaking is its main goal, the Mafia has always had a flair for political corruption, from which the FBI was not immune. In 2002, it came to light that FBI director J. Edgar Hoover, from 1965 on, sanctioned the hiring of Mafia-connected criminals as informants while protecting them from prosecution, even in cases of murder. This was all in the name of bringing down the Mafia, as Hoover was perhaps overcompensating for ignoring its existence for so long. Yet it mostly resulted in murderers escaping prosecution and innocent men going to jail for their crimes.

Hoover's crusade against the Mafia was weak at best, but Richard Nixon treated the organization as if it were the fourth branch of government. While Hoover might have succumbed to the power of the Mafia, Nixon courted and pampered the crime machine. Throughout the 1950s and 1960s, the Mafia developed its political tastes. It is now known that the CIA involved the Mafia in failed attempts to assassinate the late Cuban leader Fidel Castro during his early years in power. Vice President Nixon initiated and supervised the Castro assassination plots. In addition, historians now suspect that key Mafia-connected players were involved in the assassination of President Kennedy in 1963. The mere existence of Mafia-plot conspiracy theories surrounding JFK's murder—whether accurate or not—points to the amount of actual and perceived power of organized crime at the time.

As Nixon accumulated political value during his vice presidency in the 1950s, Americans were becoming more aware of the Mafia's overwhelming influence. Senate Resolution 202 funded the Committee on Organized Crime in Interstate Commerce—known to the public as the Kefauver Committee. The panel's chairman was Estes Kefauver, a Tennessee Democrat. Starting in

1951 and lasting over one year, the Kefauver Committee traveled to at least 14 major U.S. cities to conduct interviews with hundreds of witnesses about organized crime.[2]

In March 1951, the Kefauver Committee televised some of its hearings, and a record 30 million Americans tuned in to watch. The live coverage ensured that the committee's investigations on the Mafia became common knowledge among Americans. The committee interviewed important Mafia men, like Frank Costello, a notorious New York Mob boss. To the public, Costello epitomized the American gangster, so to see the U.S. government go after him was quite significant in the history of U.S.-Mafia relations.

While the legislative outcomes of the Kefauver Committee were mostly cursory, the cultural effects were easily seen. Americans became much more concerned about the shady connections between their elected representatives and organized crime; the hearings illustrated just how many officials had helped or even profited from Mafia activities.

The Kefauver Committee's final report in 1951 stressed that the Syndicate had greatly transformed itself since Prohibition:

Where smaller local crime groups once specialized in boot-legging, bookmaking, prostitution or drug dealing, [today's] groups are multipurpose in character, engaging in any racket where there is money to be made. The Mafia . . . has an important part in binding together into a loose association the . . . major criminal . . . gangs and individual hoodlums throughout the country.[3]

Chillingly, the committee concluded that Mafia domination was based fundamentally on "muscle" and "murder. [It] . . . will ruthlessly eliminate anyone who stands in the way of its success."[4]

As Nixon was preparing for his first run for the presidency in 1960, a Senate committee called the Select Committee on Improper Activities in Labor and Management—in short, the McClellan Committee—examined Mafia-union connections from 1957 through the early 1960s. Somewhat ironically, Nixon's political rivals, John F. Kennedy and his brother Robert (Bobby), the committee's chief counsel, did much of the questioning.

Bobby was especially relentless in grilling mobsters and union bosses as the brothers exposed sinister ties between the Mafia and certain American labor organizations. As *Boston Globe* reporters Bryan Bender and Neil Swidey observed: "[Bobby's] chief nemesis during these hearings was Jimmy Hoffa, the squat bull-faced leader of the Teamsters union. Bobby accused Hoffa of funneling millions in worker pension funds into a money-laundering scheme with Mob leaders. That alliance bought the Teamster leader muscle to silence his enemies and scare corporate leaders into submission."[5]

The McClellan hearings are also often referred to as the Valachi hearings. Joseph Valachi was a low-ranking member of the Genovese crime family of New York, and he became the first Mafia member to testify for the U.S. government.

Valachi's often-sensational six days of televised revelations proved addictive entertainment for the American public. The mobster's most memorable moment in the witness chair was his discussion of La Cosa Nostra's initiation ceremony:

Then they called us [new recruits] one at a time . . . there was a gun and a knife on the table . . . I repeated some words they told me . . . He [Salvatore Maranzano] went on to explain that they lived by the gun and by the knife and you die by the gun and the knife . . . that is what the rules were, of Cosa Nostra . . . then he gave me a piece of paper, and I was to burn it . . . that is the way I burn if I expose this organization.[6]

When he was through testifying, Valachi was granted special privileges and continued special protection within the prison system. He also had a $100,000 gangland price on his head. Attorney General Robert Kennedy praised the Valachi hearings and said they would give him added ammunition in his crusade to dismantle the Mob.[7]

Mainly through the efforts of Bobby Kennedy, Jimmy Hoffa was eventually locked up for jury tampering and fraud. But that didn't keep President Richard Nixon from granting clemency to the notorious union boss in 1971—due to a massive Teamsters-Mob payoff in exchange for Hoffa's freedom.

While both the Kefauver and McClellan Committees were instrumental in defining the organized crime problem in the United States, they did little to weaken the Mafia's power and influence. The Senate committees made their wary conclusions surrounding the Mafia, but that didn't prevent La Cosa Nostra's favorite politician from seizing the White House.

An FBI agent investigating widespread Teamsters-Mafia deals told Jack Nelson and Bill Hazlett of the *Los Angeles Times* in 1973, "This whole thing of the Teamsters and the Mob and the White House is one of the scariest things I've ever seen."[8]

When Richard Nixon became president, organized crime was raking in at least $70 billion a year. And the $1 billion Teamsters Central States Pension Fund was considered the prime source of working capital for the Mob. The *Oakland Tribune* said the fund was the "bankroll for some of America's most sinister underworld figures."

Nixon's longtime favors-for-money partnership with the Mafia hit its zenith during his presidency, and the godfathers ascended to their greatest era of power and profits.

TWO

The Nixon-Mafia Relationship

At the height of the Nixon-Mafia relationship, the blood-drenched Mob "enjoyed unprecedented prosperity and capital acquisition, drawing an annual income of $100 billion and gaining control of 50,000 U.S. firms. Especially significant was its major penetration of banking and finance, resulting in a rash of U.S. bank failures . . . and the estimated loss of $50 billion in stolen U.S. securities by 1973."[1]

Mob bosses had venerated Nixon for decades. He had been on the take from organized crime since his first run for Congress. His earliest campaign manager and political adviser was Murray Chotiner, a chubby lawyer who specialized in representing hoods—and who enjoyed dressing like them too. His wardrobe featured monogrammed white-on-white dress shirts with garish cuff links, and silk ties with jeweled stickpins.

Chotiner befriended a "Who's Who" of American mobsters—including the top boss in Los Angeles, Mickey Cohen. In 1946, thanks to Chotiner, Nixon held a hush-hush meeting with Cohen behind a screened-in booth at Goodfellow's Fisherman's Grotto in L.A. Cohen later said that Nixon "was just starting to get his foot in the door, and Orange County, where he was from, was important to my bookmaking program."[2]

In the cigar-chomping, wheeling-and-dealing Chotiner, Nixon had also found a below-the-belt political fighter—what Nixon White House aide Len Garment later called "his Machiavelli, a hardheaded exponent of the campaign philosophy that politics is war."

For over two decades before he became president, Nixon engaged in criminal dealings with some of the most notorious Mafia-connected men of the time, namely the aforementioned Cohen, mob finance man Meyer Lansky, Teamsters Union leader Jimmy Hoffa, and even godfathers Carlos Marcello, Santos Traffi-cante, and Sam Giancana. Nixon's closest pal, Bebe Rebozo, was linked at the hip with top Mob figures. So it was no surprise that Nixon kept Chotiner as a secret adviser once he ascended to the White House.

Richard Nixon's close relationship with Murray Chotiner was always beneficial. In 1946, Nixon undertook his first politi-cal campaign, running as the anti-Communist candidate when he won a seat for the twelfth district in the California House of Representatives. This was in large part thanks to Chotiner, who was able to convince Mickey Cohen to contribute $5,000 to Nixon.

Then in 1950, again due to Chotiner, Cohen raised $75,000 at a Los Angeles event for Nixon, which would help the politi-cian defeat Democratic representative Helen Gahagan Douglas in the race for the U.S. Senate. Later recounting the event, Cohen said that "everyone from around here that was on the pad natu-rally had to go . . . it was all gamblers from Vegas, all gambling money. There wasn't a legitimate person in the room." According to Cohen, Nixon was present to address the shady crowd when Cohen announced that the exits would be closed until the full amount was raised. The quota was quickly met with major stacks of cash—and Mickey's cronies allowed the exit doors to be reopened.

Also in 1950, the generous gangster rented and personally supervised a campaign headquarters for Nixon in the Pacific Finance building at Eighth and Olive Streets in L.A. To quote Cohen: "We posted Nixon signs and literature, and I paid for the headquarters for three or four weeks in that building. During the period when I ran this Nixon headquarters, I contacted most of the gambling fraternity in Los Angeles County to tell them what their share of the contributions to the Nixon campaign would be."

Though, to be fair, Nixon's Senate victory over Douglas can also be blamed on Nixon's own nefarious tactics, as he painted Douglas as "pink right down to her underwear," implying that she was a Communist sympathizer.

Yet, amid all of this support, Cohen apparently had little respect for Nixon. Just before the 1968 presidential election, the then-imprisoned Mob boss sent journalist Jack Anderson a signed letter stating that Nixon was directly connected to the Mafia. Unfortunately, according to Anderson biographer Mark Feldstein, when that column was published, it was "largely dismissed . . . and lost amid the end-of-the-campaign hoopla." In a subsequent letter to Anderson, after Nixon's election to the presidency, Cohen voiced his hope that there was a new Nixon:

In my wildest dreams [never] could I ever have visualized or imagined 17 or 18 years ago that the likes of Richard Nixon

could possibly become the President of the United States. . . .
Let's hope that he isn't the same guy that I knew—a rough
hustler [when he was] a goddamn small-time ward politician.
Let's hope this guy's thinking has changed, and let's hope it's
for the betterment of our country.

This is a sobering letter about the character of a president,
considering it's from a man who controlled the Mafia's drug and
gambling operations in California and who was subsequently
arrested over 30 times—once for murder.[3] Cohen also admitted
that "the proper persons from back east," meaning Frank Costello
and Meyer Lansky, were the ones who pressured him to support
Nixon.

Why would Meyer Lansky become a big fan of Richard Nixon?
Senate crime investigator Walter Sheridan offered this opinion:
"If you were Meyer, who would you invest your money in? Some
politician named Clams Linguini? Or a nice Protestant boy from
Whittier, California?"

In the 1950 race for the Senate, Nixon didn't confine his at-
tacks on Helen Gahagan Douglas to his speeches. He put out
an array of campaign pamphlets, the most famous of which—
printed on pink paper—became known as the "Pink Sheet." It
compared Nixon's votes (and those of left-wing Congressman
Vito Marcantonio) on foreign affairs with those of Representative Douglas to prove that she was "soft on Communism." And
to capture the latent anti-Semitic vote, a whispering campaign
harped on the fact that her husband, actor Melvyn Douglas, was
Jewish.[4]

Though not a member of La Cosa Nostra, Lansky, Jewish
himself, was the Mafia's financial genius. Known as the "Little
Man" because he was barely five feet tall, Lansky developed

Cuba for the Mob during the dictatorship of Fulgencio Batista, when Havana was known as the "Latin Las Vegas." Under its towering palms, gambling and prostitution, as well as the illicit drug trade, netted the U.S. Syndicate at least $100 million a year—even after generous payoffs to Batista.

Meyer Lansky had a rare reputation of being an honest gambler. In his opinion, it was unnecessary to fix any casino tables in order to make money. As a result, in the mid-1950s, Batista gave Lansky unofficial discretion over the gambling scene in Havana. Lansky took his newfound power to heart and ordered the casino operators in Havana to "clean up, or get out." In return for the position, Lansky reportedly paid the Cuban dictator large sums of money quite frequently. Lansky associate Joseph Varon once said, "I know every time Meyer went to Cuba he would bring a briefcase with at least $100,000 [for Batista]. So Batista welcomed him with open arms, and the two men really developed such affection for each other. Batista really loved him. I guess I'd love him too if he gave me $100,000 every time I saw him."[5]

Lansky did have his problems with the law elsewhere: to escape U.S. tax evasion charges, he fled to Israel in 1970. But in 1972, Israel sent him back to the United States. And, according to Lansky biographer Hank Messick, Meyer purposely timed his return to assist the re-election of his longtime secret partner in crime, President Richard Nixon:

So the wandering Jew of 1972 turned his back on the graves of his grandparents and flew across four continents to arrive in the land of the goyim some forty minutes before the polls opened on Election Day. And, eerily, the landslide he predicted so confidently [on his arrival in the States] came to pass and headlines proclaimed FOUR MORE YEARS.[6]

After all, Lansky's devotion to Nixon—and vice versa—went way back: they'd become friends in Havana in the 1940s, where the mob boss gave Nixon free hotel accommodations. Meyer was also the first major criminal figure to recognize Nixon's crookedness and to start green-lighting tainted underworld cash in quid pro quo deals with the rookie California politician in 1946, and continued to do so in future Nixon campaigns.

In 1974, Lansky was acquitted of the tax charges and went on to lead a quiet, rather middle-class retirement (for a Mob boss the FBI believed had squirreled away a fortune) in Miami Beach. A many-pack-a-day smoker, Meyer Lansky died of lung cancer at the age of 80 in 1983.

But in his life, the Little Man saw to it that his friends were generous to Fulgencio Batista too. In February 1955, Vice President Richard Nixon traveled to Havana to embrace Batista at his lavish private palace, praise "the competence and stability" of his regime, award him a medal of honor, and compare him with Abraham Lincoln. He even hailed Batista's Cuba as a land that "shares with us the same democratic ideals of peace, freedom and the dignity of man."

When he returned to Washington, the vice president reported to the Cabinet that Batista was "a very remarkable man ... older and wiser ... desirous of doing a good job for Cuba rather than Batista ... concerned about social progress. ..." And Nixon reported that Batista had vowed to "deal with the Commies."[7]

What Nixon omitted were myriad Batista-Lansky underworld connections, rampant government corruption under Batista—and the extreme poverty of most Cubans. The American vice president also ignored Batista's suspension of constitutional guarantees, his dissolution of the country's political parties, and his use of the police and army to murder political opponents. Nixon, even more unforgivably, conveniently ignored reports of up to 20,000 Cuban deaths at the hands of Batista's thugs.

Under Batista, Cuba was the decadent playground of the American moneyed elite. Havana was its Sin City paradise—where you could gamble at luxurious casinos; play the horses or the lottery; frolic with premier prostitutes; and enjoy the best rum, cocaine, heroin, and marijuana in the Western Hemisphere. Should you have been in the mood, you could also have obtained a ringside seat for "an exhibition of sexual bestiality that would have shocked Caligula."[8]

Cuba was convenient for America's high rollers, only a one-hour flight from Florida. There were 80 tourist flights a week from Miami to Havana—at a cost of $40, round trip.

Three Syndicate gamblers from Cleveland—including Nixon buddy Bebe Rebozo's friend Morris "Moe" Dalitz—were part owners of Lansky's glittering Hotel Nacional in Havana. In fact, during the Batista regime, as recalled by Mafia hit man Angelo "Gyp" DeCarlo, "The Mob had a piece of every joint down there. There wasn't one joint they didn't have a piece of."[9]

Another Rebozo associate, Tampa godfather Santos Trafficante, was the undisputed gambling king of Havana. Trafficante owned substantial interests in the San Souci—a nightclub and casino where fellow gangster Johnny Roselli had a management role.[10]

Nixon and Rebozo's relationship developed over the gambling tables in Cuba. Nixon preferred to stay at Meyer Lansky's glittering Hotel Nacional, where he occupied the Presidential Suite, compliments of the owner. During one trip to Cuba in the early 1950s, Rebozo covered up to $50,000 of Nixon's gambling losses, quickly solidifying their friendship.[11] In 1997, Lansky henchman Jimmy "Blue Eyes" Alo, then a "sprightly" 94 years of age, recalled for a Nixon biographer that he had handled cash for Nixon at the Hotel Nacional. Alo was also the hotel official who signed off on Nixon's complimentary stays there. Blue Eyes said Nixon and Lansky met in Havana in the 1950s.[12]

For some time, Rebozo had been involved with Lansky in illegal gambling rackets in southern Florida. In more recent years, former crime investigator Jack Clarke disclosed those operations, adding that Rebozo was pointed out to him, back then, as "one of Lansky's people. . . . When I checked the name with the Miami police, they said he was an entrepreneur and a gambler and that he was very close to Meyer."[13]

Information uncovered in recently released FBI files shows that, in 1959, a reliable informant reported that Rebozo had shares in shady business interests in Batista's Cuba. He "fronted for the Italian money" and was also influential at the Presidential Palace. Then the informant dropped a bombshell: "Vice President Nixon is also in on investments in Cuba" and that, like all involved, he "benefited financially." The informant also passed along to the FBI that "when Vice President Nixon visits Miami, Florida, he stays at the home of Bebe Rebozo." There is no record that this information ever left agency files.[14]

THREE

Dick and Bebe

Richard Nixon was a man almost entirely consumed by his own ego and personal ambitions, a trait that would lead to the end of his presidency. Considering this, it is unsurprising that he rarely connected with people in open or emotional ways. Bebe Rebozo seemed to be the exception. Despite the attention from his long-term wife, Pat, Nixon's closest and most honest relationship was with Rebozo.

Bebe's obituary in the *New York Times* after his death in 1998 describes his and Nixon's friendship as existing without judgment. While everyone deserves a loyal confidante to help air their general neuroses, Nixon notoriously surrounded himself with enablers and ego boosters, and Bebe was rarely immune. The lack of judgment one may have when making friends might ordinarily serve as a positive trait, but presidents and powerful people are held to a higher standard. Or rather, they should be.

The same obituary chronicles Bebe's misfortune surrounding

the suspicion he was under following the Watergate scandal. It is difficult, however, to feel sympathy for a man who used his influence in the world of the Mafia to help his friend corrupt the office of the presidency even further.

After his dear friend's forced resignation, Bebe himself took personal affront to the *Washington Post*'s coverage of his own possible pre-Watergate crimes. In 1978, Rebozo sued the newspaper for libel for reporting that, in 1968, Rebozo had trafficked in IBM stock that was stolen from E. F. Hutton by Mafia hoods— including Jake "the Mace" Maislich and Joseph Anthony Lamattina. The suit was settled ten years later without any payment to Rebozo.[1]

Despite Nixon's flaws surrounding his ego and his tendency to lash out at those around him, Bebe stood by the man until the end of their lives. In fact, Nixon passed away in 1994, giving Bebe four whole years to trash the man or reveal some of his secrets, but he did not. Apparently Bebe was able to see something in the ex-president that others were not privy to. In 1990, Rebozo was quoted as saying that Nixon was "everything they say he's not" adding that "he's a very sensitive man, very thoughtful and, of course, very brilliant, with a memory like an elephant."[2]

No one can deny that Nixon had a superior intelligence. It is really a shame that he became so shrouded in his own ego that he developed a prideful ignorance that produced so many blind spots throughout his political career. Still, Bebe seemed to be able to look past that, or maybe Nixon "let his hair down," so to speak, when in the company of his close friend. In 1950, during one of their first Key Biscayne outings together, Bebe claims that Nixon severely disliked the fishing. According to Rebozo, Nixon "couldn't bear to kill anything" and subsequently didn't have a good time.[3]

While Bebe had no real reason to fabricate this part of the story, Nixon doesn't strike the average history lover as being abject to killing. This was the same man who ordered the relentless bombing of Cambodia during the Vietnam War, which he consistently lied about afterward. But apparently the man couldn't bear to see a fish take its last breath. It's likely that if Nixon had been more apt to act on his more thoughtful nature, free of ego, that he shared with Bebe, he would have been a better man and leader for it.

EARLY DAYS

Perhaps a look into the early years of Dick and Bebe's rare friendship will help to illuminate the oddities of it.

Nixon and Rebozo first met, by one credible account, in Florida in 1947. Richard Danner, a Miami native with close ties to Rebozo and Florida Mafia boss Santos Trafficante, made the introductions. Danner was the city manager of Miami when the Mafia controlled it, and Nixon and Danner were already tight. In 1952, the two secretly visited Havana and gambled at a Syndicate-run casino. Danner later credited Nixon for using his influence with the Mob to land him a cushy job at a Las Vegas casino.[4] During Nixon's presidency, Danner was a top aide and the payoff man for bribes to Nixon from Las Vegas casino–owning, Mafia-linked billionaire and generous Nixon financial angel Howard Hughes.

Bebe Rebozo was charming, well-dressed, and desperate to

gain the favor of anyone with power or an elevated social status.
After graduating from high school, the American-born Cuban
quickly rose from airline steward to wealthy Florida banker and
land speculator. Once a small-time crook—who, as a youth, had
sometimes trafficked in stolen appliances—Rebozo was eventually looked up to by the nation's top gangsters. Bebe had ad-
vanced to the pinnacle of his own influence and power as both a
friend of powerful racketeers and "First Friend" of the President
of the United States.

Nixon and Rebozo hit it off almost immediately after their
initial meeting, and they became even closer as Nixon climbed
the ladder of power and prominence in Washington. Their mu-
tual friend, Senator George Smathers of Florida, once said, "I
don't want to say that Bebe's level of liking Nixon increased
as Nixon's [political] position increased, but it had a lot to do
with it."[5]

Indeed, the two men were nearly inseparable throughout
Nixon's political career. Rebozo was there throughout Nixon's
political career to lend moral as well as financial support to what
one acquaintance called his "Little Jesus." From the time of
Nixon's vice presidency in 1950 to his election to the presidency
in 1968, Bebe was there to comfort him following the defeats, as
well as congratulate him during times of triumph. In 1962, when
Nixon lost the California governor's race, Bebe held Nixon's
hand to console him. Then, in 1968, when Nixon finally achieved
his goal of being elected president, he and Bebe spent a vacation
drinking and sunbathing in Key Biscayne. During Nixon's White
House years, rough estimates show that Rebozo was at Nixon's
side one out of every ten days. The president also made 50 trips
to Key Biscayne—most of them without family members—to be
with Bebe.

In DC, Bebe came in and out of the Executive Mansion as he desired—without even the hassle of being logged in by the Secret Service. Though he had no official government job, Rebozo had his own private office with a telephone and a designated bedroom always at his disposal at 1600 Pennsylvania Avenue. During his frequent flights aboard Air Force One, Rebozo wore a blue military flight jacket bearing the presidential seal and his embroidered name.

At Key Biscayne, Rebozo's home was right next door to the president's. It was equipped with free worldwide White House telephone service. The same held true at Rebozo's private villa on the grounds of the Western White House in San Clemente, California.

MORE THAN FRIENDS?

By the time he ascended to the presidency, Nixon and his First Friend were so inseparable that there were even several sightings of them holding hands. Nixon aide Alexander Haig often mocked the president in front of Henry Kissinger and other White House staffers with a limp-wrist gesture—insinuating Nixon and Rebozo were homosexual lovers. Kissinger told friends how weird it was to work in the Nixon White House because of its "slightly . . . homosexual atmosphere,"[6] and according to published reports he privately termed Secretary of State William Rogers a "fag" who had some strange hold over Nixon and who kept a "hot young stud in a Georgetown townhouse."[7]

In fact, like the man he adored, Bebe had little use for women. He was reportedly very active in Miami's homosexual scene, often hosting male-only barbeques and houseboat cruises at his

Key Biscayne home. On a newly released tape, Nixon chides Rebozo for having so few women friends that he wasn't able to give Nixon any female reactions to a speech he made the night before. But then "Beeb," as Dick called his buddy, remembered how one woman did get through to him. Yet, before Bebe could report on what she had said, the president interjected that "she must have got your number in a toilet stall." This sent both men into huge fits of laughter more appropriate to teenage boys.

It was the type of laughter that was usually heard when the pair played "King of the Pool" in Key Biscayne. One White House aide described one such outing as quite bizarre:

It was late at night. The two men had been drinking. Nixon mounted a rubber raft in the pool while Rebozo tried to turn it over. Then, laughing and shouting, they'd change places and Nixon would try to upset Rebozo.[8]

Adding to the spectacle of this teenage frivolity was that Nixon, as we only recently learned, never went into a pool without a bathing cap. His barber had told the president that chlorine in pool water would ruin his dye-job.

Despite rampant rumors of an intimate Nixon-Rebozo relationship, in 2015 Nixon aide Alexander Butterfield disclosed that Nixon creeped out two White House women staffers with awkward seduction attempts. In one of the incidents, Butterfield says Nixon—in front of him and others aboard Marine One— patted the bare legs of a 42-year-old miniskirted secretary sitting next to him. The president patted away for about ten minutes while he made small talk with the woman. Butterfield describes the leg patting as like a grandfather might do to a four-year-old girl. He says that during Nixon's patting, the woman "stiffened up like you can't believe." As for the president, Butterfield concludes, "I just thought, 'the poor, pitiful son of a bitch.'" Bebe Rebozo was among those on the presidential chopper who witnessed this incredible scene.[9]

During the Watergate investigation, Richard Danner turned over a batch of curiously intimate, homoerotic letters he had exchanged with Rebozo. Nixon withdrew all his prepresidential correspondence with Bebe from his official papers, so the exact nature of their relationship remains unclear. As President Lyndon Johnson's press secretary George Reedy correctly concluded, Nixon's tightknit friendship with Rebozo "was the most important mystery in Nixon's life."[10]

The main problem with Nixon's sexual leanings—be they toward men or women or both—is that they expose this self-advertised family man and loyal husband as a high-grade hypocrite. For many politicians of that era, the exposure of an extramarital affair was a career ender.

MONEY AND CORRUPTION

One of Nixon's indisputable ties to the Mafia is in the form of real estate and other monetary holdings. Nixon frequented casinos owned by mobsters, deposited money in banks owned by crime bosses, and even sometimes took payoffs from the Mob for political favors (like in the case of Jimmy Hoffa). It's fair to say that at points during Nixon's political career, it seemed as if he was a puppet of the Mob whose strings were in the form of the dollars he made. This includes direct payoffs, but it also involves radically sweet deals for the corrupt president on land deals and even sometimes relief of debts at Mob-owned casinos. One such land deal involved an island off the coast of South Florida, in which Nixon acquired shares for a criminally cheap price.

William Vanderbilt once owned Fisher Island, a 213-acre spit of land off the southern end of Miami Beach where he built an elaborate mansion in the 1920s. But Vanderbilt had little time to spend on Fisher, and the mansion and all of its buildings and cabanas for servants and guests fell into disrepair. Still, by the 1960s, the property—which had gone through a succession of owners—had great potential. There was an expectation that a bridge would eventually link Fisher Island with the mainland.

By 1968, 90 percent of Fisher stock was held by Bebe Rebozo, Richard Nixon, and a group of bankers and businessmen associated with Senator George Smathers. An early investor in Fisher, Nixon owned nearly 186,000 shares that cost him one dollar each. In 1969, he sold his stock for two dollars a share.

Early in 1972, several nephews of Bebe Rebozo lived on the island, and reportedly enjoyed themselves with attractive gals they ferried back and forth from Miami to Fisher on the 50-foot yacht, *Enterprise*. According to investigative reporter Hank Messick, "the role of counselor or den mother to this rather far-out group fell to Manolo Sanchez, valet to the President of the United States. A refugee from Cuba, Sanchez and his wife, Fina, were introduced to Nixon by Bebe, and remained close to the Rebozo family. On the president's frequent visits to Key Biscayne, Manolo renewed his friendship with the nephews, and on one occasion bailed one of them out of jail."

Once a quarter acre plot of marijuana was reportedly discovered on Fisher Island, and in June 1973, according to the *Miami Herald*, "the twenty-five-year-old nephew of President Nixon's confidant, C. G. (Bebe) Rebozo, was sentenced to a year in jail for possession of narcotics." Specifically, Mike Rebozo was nabbed with "almost a half-pound of cocaine."

Bebe also purchased land in Florida with Robert Fincher, a reputed front for Meyer Lansky. An examination of Fincher's telephone calls revealed that he was in regular contact with Mafia godfathers Carlos Marcello and Santos Trafficante. Vincent Teresa, a high-ranking Mafioso, later admitted that he had used Rebozo's Key Biscayne bank to launder stolen money. (The bank was never charged with wrongdoing.)

Bebe's dealings with the Fisher Island property represent only a small portion of his propensity for criminal activity. Yet, it's important to remember: this was a man who was closest to the president of the United States, a man who had undue influence on the most powerful office in the world, all without holding any government title. The Fisher Island stories might seem trivial to some, but, taking them in stride with the other activities of Nixon and his First Friend, it becomes clear that the world was their playground.

During Nixon's presidency, Rebozo was such a frequent guest of his that Nixon's children, Trisha and Julie, would refer to him as "Uncle Bebe." For both Nixon's daughters and his wife, Pat, Uncle Bebe would often buy extravagant gifts, such as the $100,000 house he purchased and rented at a bargain rate to Julie and her husband, David Eisenhower, in a DC suburb.

Behind the scenes, Beeb was also "deeply involved" with expensive government-funded remodeling plans at both Key

Biscayne and San Clemente, according to Nixon aide John Ehrlichman:

> He flew to Los Angeles for meetings with the General Services Administration official in charge of the [San Clemente] project. Over the months, he so successfully co-opted the GSA project manager, that the GSA began carrying out Rebozo's instructions without question. If there was undue government expenditure, at either the San Clemente or the Key Biscayne house, Mr. Rebozo should be given full credit for his persuasive involvement.[11]

Rebozo was no penny-pincher when it came to upgrading Nixon's presidential habitats. In the summer of 1973, the General Accounting Office revealed that taxpayer-financed improvements to the president's California and Florida properties cost nearly $2 million, adding greatly to public outrage over other Watergate disclosures.[12]

At this time, a "White House source" leaked a pretty good story to me. (I can't identify him or her because he or she is still alive.) To help quiet the public uproar over the massive Rebozo-supervised home-improvement expenditures, the president was considering giving the San Clemente estate, at his death, to the American people for their future use as a convention center. Sure enough, the president soon announced his intention to offer such a grand gift as a public service. Not only did the announcement do nothing to quiet the clamor for Nixon's impeachment, years later Nixon sold the home he once promised to the American people and used the profit to move back east. Bebe Rebozo's organized crime connections were as solid as those that attached him to Nixon. For one, he had both legal and financial links with "Big Al" Polizzi, a Cleveland gangster and drug kingpin. Rebozo also built an elaborate shopping center in Miami that he let Big Al—a convicted black marketeer described by the Federal Bureau of Narcotics as "one of the most influential members of the underworld in the United States"—contract to whomever he wished.[13]

Nixon and Rebozo bought Florida lots in upscale Key Biscayne, getting bargain rates from Donald Berg, a Mafia-connected Rebozo business partner. The Secret Service eventually advised Nixon to stop associating with Berg. Nixon and his First Friend could no longer even dine at their favorite restaurant on Key Biscayne, the Berg-owned Jamaica Inn. The lender for one of Nixon's properties was Arthur Desser, who cavorted with both Meyer Lansky and mobbed-up Teamsters president Jimmy Hoffa.

In 1968, as previously noted, the FBI and other agencies investigated Rebozo and his Key Biscayne bank for selling stocks that had been stolen by the Mob from New York brokerage firm E. F. Hutton. The stock was worth $195,000. The mobsters involved in the theft were close associates of Bebe's buddy Meyer Lansky. Senate investigators wanted to grill Bebe about the deal and were preparing "to subpoena him and go to his bank. . . . He was keeping stock in there that was fraudulent, stolen," asserted William Gallinaro, a senior investigator for the Senate Subcommittee on Investigations. Gallinaro added, "When we started making inquiries about this, somebody tipped [Rebozo] off to watch himself. And the next thing we know, he's sold the stolen stock. That's a crime in itself, and he should have been arrested and gone to prison for that. Bebe Rebozo was a friendly banker when it came to the Mob."[14]

Rebozo avoided prison and never faced trial. Under ordinary circumstances, federal law requires a fine of up to $10,000 or a prison term up to ten years, or both, for anyone who knowingly takes part in such deals. Eventually, a civil case involving Rebozo and the sale of the stolen stock was dismissed by James King, a Florida judge appointed by President Nixon.[15]

Rebozo's mob-friendly bank was also a suspected pipeline for Syndicate money skimmed from an opulent gambling casino in the Bahamas. Operated by Nixon and Rebozo buddy James Crosby (who contributed $100,000 to Nixon for the 1968 primaries), the Paradise Island Casino was linked to top U.S. mobsters. Despite *Life* magazine's report that Crosby's casino would be run by "Lansky & Co.," Nixon showed up as the star attraction at its opening party, on January 7, 1968, where he was photographed with Crosby. At the 1968 Republican convention in Miami Beach, Nixon accepted the use of a luxurious yacht owned by Crosby's casino.[16]

By the 1960s, FBI agents keeping track of the Mafia had identified Bebe Rebozo as a "non-member associate of organized crime figures."[17] Former Mafia consigliere Bill Bonanno—the son of legendary New York godfather Joe Bonanno—asserts that Nixon "would never have gotten anywhere" without his old Mob allegiances. And he reports that, through Rebozo, Nixon "did business for years with people in [Florida Mafia boss Santos] Trafficante's Family, profiting from real estate deals, arranging for casino licensing, covert funding for anti-Castro activities, and so forth."[18]

During the final act of the Watergate scandal, Danner helped deliver a $100,000 under-the-table donation from Hughes to President Nixon through Rebozo.

Just before Nixon's 1974 resignation, former presidential aide Chuck Colson concluded "that Bebe used that one hundred grand for himself and for the President, his family and the girls. Hughes can blow the whistle on him . . ."[19]

Nixon aide Bob Haldeman later confessed there was "much more money [than the Hughes $100,000] in Bebe's 'tin box,' " as Rebozo's secret fund was known in circles close to the president. Nixon's chief of staff said a "much larger cash kitty" was kept in Bebe's safety-deposit box at his Key Biscayne bank, declaring that "Rebozo, in effect, maintained a private fund for Nixon to use as he wished."[20]

As president, Nixon also reportedly received payoffs from Hughes totaling $200,000 for the purpose of stopping atomic testing in Nevada. The bribes were "masked" by Rebozo, according to organized crime expert Alan Block.[21]

THE COSMOS BANK

Bebe Rebozo's "tin box" apparently was not big enough to hold all of Richard Nixon's ill-gotten U.S. treasury notes from the Mafia and other nefarious entities and individuals.

In one of the least-known major political claims in modern U.S. history, three reliable sources say Nixon stashed an incredible bundle in a now-defunct Swiss bank named Cosmos. The bank had offices in Zurich, New York, and Nassau. Former Cosmos partner Huntington Hartford said that Nixon made deposits totaling $35,883,070 between October 21, 1971, and June 11, 1972. Hartford made the stunning claim in an interview with Mafia expert Dan Moldea. An heir to the A&P supermarket chain fortune, Hartford once owned Paradise Island in the Bahamas, where Nixon and Rebozo frequently frolicked. Cosmos went out of business in 1974 due to bank failure.

Nixon, Rebozo, and Huntington Hartford were longtime friends. In a 1962 visit to the Bahamas, Dick and Bebe were honored guests at Huntington's Nassau estate.[22] Mob expert Don Bauder says Cosmos was a Mafia-friendly institution and that Hartford's hope to build a Mob-free casino on Paradise Island was dashed by one of Nixon's original Syndicate sponsors, Meyer Lansky:

> Researchers have found that Cosmos was deeply involved with mobbed-up casino operations in the Bahamas and so was Nixon, often with his friend Bebe Rebozo. After Fidel Castro drove the Mafia out of Cuba, mob moneybags Meyer Lansky looked to the Bahamas for a casino haven. Huntington Hartford, heir to a grocery fortune, set up a casino in the Bahamas and initially wanted it free of mob influence. But that was not to be, and Hartford eventually sold most of his holdings.[23]

Nixon biographer Anthony Summers reports that documents seized by the Internal Revenue Service say Nixon's deposits in Cosmos were made under the heading "N&R."[24] Summers says IRS investigator Norman Caspar confirms the Nixon deposits— but Caspar puts the total far higher than even Hartford's gaudy figure: an awesome $42,845,345.[25]

Cosmos had been a heavy investor in the Paradise Island Bridge, which transported gamblers to the Lansky-linked Bahamian casino run by Nixon and Rebozo associate James Crosby.

Robert Morgenthau, the former organized crime–fighting district attorney of New York County, had interviewed Cosmos officials. He concluded that they were holding a big investment in the bridge for Richard Nixon. "Could I prove it? No. Am I sure of it? Yes," Morgenthau told Anthony Summers.[26]

Even if he didn't secretly own part of a lucrative bridge in the Bahamas, suspicion that Nixon had possibly deposited an immense stash in a secret Swiss bank account at least makes one of the Watergate-beleaguered president's most famous statements much easier to understand. When aide John Dean told him in 1973 that it might take $1 million in cold cash to keep the Watergate burglars silent, Dean also warned Nixon that only Mafia experts knew how to raise that kind of untraceable dough. To Dean's surprise, the president responded nonchalantly: "Maybe it takes a gang to get that." Then, solidly endorsing the criminal scheme, Nixon enthusiastically added: "We could get that! On the money, if you need the money you could get that. You could get a million dollars. You could get it in cash. I know where it could be gotten."

If he didn't want to tap into any of his reported Swiss millions to provide blackmail to the Watergate burglars, perhaps Nixon had some of his many Mob contacts in mind. One possible option could have been the Little Man, Meyer Lansky, who was now raking in big bucks in the gambling business in the Bahamas.

In the 1970s, the Bahamas had become a world drug-smuggling center, a haven for tax evaders, and a magnet for gamblers in casinos owned and run by the U.S. Syndicate. The IRS smelled something particularly fishy about the aforementioned Bahamian company called Resorts International (not to be confused with a present-day company with a similar name), according to IRS expert Alan Block:

> [The agency's] interest was peaked [*sic*] because Resorts appeared to have suspicious connections to the Lansky syndicate, plus a financial package put together by scads of "funny-money" types, some clearly connected to organized crime. Moreover, the head of Resorts International was a close friend of President Richard M. Nixon and Charles "Bebe" Rebozo, his most intimate associate.

Richard Nixon was the main attraction when Resorts president James Crosby opened his casino on Paradise Island in 1968. Just two years earlier, an internal Justice Department memo had warned that "the atmosphere [on the island] seems ripe for a Lansky skim."

Many years later, Crosby was turned down when he sought a gambling license in New Jersey. State gaming enforcers cited Crosby's "links with disreputable persons and organizations" (including Meyer Lansky), especially those on Paradise Island. In later years, Crosby was finally approved for a casino license in Atlantic City.[27]

James Crosby contributed $100,000 of his own money and helped raise an additional $1 million for Richard Nixon's 1968 presidential bid. Those efforts probably had something to do with the fact that, in 1969, Crosby (and other dubious Nixon pals Richard Danner, Bebe Rebozo, and Robert Abplanalp) dined at a White House state dinner for Prince Philip, the Duke of Edinburgh.[28] Crosby died in 1986 at the age of 58.

The Senate Watergate Committee did not fully investigate what became known as the Bahamian Connection. But the possible link with Meyer Lansky did set off alarms inside the committee. As UPI's Jane Denison reported on January 18, 1974, that while "not on the public record as a target of the Watergate committee's probe, the name of powerful crime syndicate leader Meyer Lansky has figured prominently in past investigations of corruption and criminal activities in the Bahamas."

FOUR

Mobsters in Cuba

Santos Trafficante Jr., based in Tampa, was one of the most powerful Mafia godfathers in the country—and he was brutally vicious to his enemies. Known as the "Silent Don" because he was a keen adherent of the Mob's vow of silence, he wore thick glasses and dressed more like a bank president than a hood.

Yet Santos never hesitated to order hits on fellow mobsters who tried to encroach on his territory—or who had committed, in his deep green eyes, any other unpardonable sin. Among those Mafiosi reportedly bumped off on Trafficante's orders were Brooklyn boss Albert "the Mad Hatter" Anastasia; Chicago godfather Sam "Momo" Giancana; and Giancana lieutenant John "Handsome Johnny" Roselli. Trafficante also played a leading role in secret U.S. murder plots against Cuban leader Fidel Castro, instigated in 1959 by Vice President Richard Nixon.

By then, Trafficante had learned the intricacies of a full panoply of Mafia crimes—from common to lethal—from his dad, Santos Trafficante Sr. The senior Trafficante came to Tampa from

Sicily in 1904. In Tampa, he built his crime family—which would operate there for the next 50 years. In 1954, a year after surviving a shotgun attempt on his life, Santos Jr. succeeded Santos Sr.[1]

Over the ensuing years, political buff Trafficante became a big Richard Nixon fan, according to the godfather's lawyer, Frank Ragano: "[Santos] viewed Nixon as a realistic conservative politician who was not a zealot and who would not be hard on him and his Mob friends."[2]

With headquarters in both Tampa and Miami, Trafficante controlled Florida's illegal drug and gambling operations. His largest criminal enterprise in the state was the "bolita lottery," a Cuban numbers game. A Meyer Lansky protégé, Trafficante could also be frequently found in Havana, where he was Lansky's top enforcer in the Syndicate's gambling casinos during Fulgencio Batista's dictatorship.

Also known as "El Hombre," Batista ruled Cuba for years through a series of puppets, and then as president by election in 1940. He met Nixon in 1955. Under Batista, corruption ran rampant. While the Cuban economy took a nosedive, the president had deposited bucketloads of funny money in foreign banks. He left the country in 1958—taking with him a fortune estimated at $300 million. Most of those funds came from Batista's favorite partner in crime, Meyer Lansky, head of the U.S. Mafia in Havana. Batista lived the rest of his life in ritzy, sunny locales in Florida, Spain, and Portugal.

During Batista's reign, a Santos Trafficante lieutenant named Norman "Roughhouse" Rothman ran the swanky San Souci casino for the Syndicate. Senator Richard Nixon and a wealthy California friend, Dana Smith, gambled there in 1952, just before Nixon was nominated for vice president. By several accounts, Smith lost a bundle—$4,200 to be exact. Though he gave a check to Rothman to cover his losses, Smith—claiming he'd been cheated—put a stop on the check as soon as he returned to the United States. In Washington, Smith's Cuba gambling partner also sprang into action.

Senator Richard Nixon wrote a letter to the State Department seeking intervention on Smith's behalf by the U.S. Embassy in Havana. By one account, mobbed-up Nixon pal Richard Danner—who knew Rothman very well—was a third member of that particular Nixon Havana gambling entourage.[3] A separate report adds Nixon's almost constant companion, Bebe Rebozo, into the mix on this particular junket.[4]

By yet another account, that of Norman Rothman himself, it was Nixon—not Smith—who had lost all those thousands at the San Souci. In a major favor for Nixon, Rothman lied and covered up for the Mob's favorite politician, though he later confessed to it. He admitted falsely telling a reporter that Nixon was not even with Smith at the casino that night. Rothman said he had further protected the senator by refusing to testify in a lawsuit brought against Smith. In response to those acts of Mafia goodwill, Rothman said Nixon sent him a verbal thank-you through another member of Congress.[5]

Later, as vice president, Nixon summoned the loyal gangster who had shielded him from a potential Havana gambling scandal into service for a hush-hush government assignment. Always scheming, Nixon wanted to take advantage of Norman Rothman's old Batista-era contacts in Cuba.

So in 1960, at Nixon's direction, Trafficante and several other Mafia heavyweights signed up as co-conspirators in secret Nixon-led Mafia-CIA plots to assassinate Fidel Castro. And among the key players in implementing the plots were Norman Rothman, former Nixon dirty trickster (and Hughes and Mafia associate) Robert Maheu, and CIA agents (and future Nixon dirty tricksters) Frank Sturgis and E. Howard Hunt. All of the Castro murder plots, of course, were miserable failures: the long-time ruler of Cuba died a natural death in his homeland in 2016.

For his part in the 1960 plots, though, the fearless Rothman was able to sneak back into Cuba—where he unsuccessfully tried to enlist several of Castro's bodyguards to carry out the assassination. The mobster was also a middleman with the CIA in the Nixon-supervised efforts to kill the Communist leader. Investigative reporter Gus Russo quotes a former CIA officer as saying, "Rothman was in touch with several CIA agents. They had many meetings concerning assassination plots against Castro."[6]

At the same time, Roughhouse Rothman was now funneling money from Santos and other ousted Havana casino owners into a paramilitary anti-Castro organization in Miami. Called the International Anti-Communist Brigade, it was headed by none other than future Watergate felon Frank Sturgis.[7]

In May 1973, Santos Trafficante demonstrated the closeness of his special longtime bond with President Richard Nixon—and the unique inside information he had on the Watergate scandal—when he privately disclosed to a friendly Washington law firm that the break-in at Democratic headquarters was "ordered by Nixon personally." The Mafia godfather said Nixon was "terrified" that the Democrats might have evidence of his prior role as organizer of the effort to assassinate Fidel Castro. (Nixon never even told the Warren Commission of those plots, or of his prior relationship with—of all people—Jack Ruby, the killer of alleged JFK assassin Lee Harvey Oswald.)

Trafficante additionally claimed that Nixon had dispatched the CIA's chief of security, Sheffield Edwards, to Florida in late July 1960 to assure Trafficante that the vice president was indeed the organizer of the Castro murder plans. The Florida Mob boss made these revelations to investigators for prominent DC attorney F. Lee Bailey—who once represented Trafficante, and who was then defending Watergate burglar James McCord.

The godfather's disclosures about Nixon's role in the Watergate scandal, and in earlier efforts to kill Castro, were not made public until recently. One of Bailey's investigators, Daniel Sheehan, revealed them in his memoirs, and in college lecture halls where he taught as a professor. Sheehan says Trafficante reported that Nixon used a secure "scrambler" phone to get Howard Hughes on board in the Castro murder scheme—adding that Hughes then chose his own right-hand man, Robert Maheu, to help coordinate the effort.

Just how did Santos Trafficante have so much intel from Richard Nixon's secret world? Sheehan says the godfather got most of his inside information from two of his former lieutenants—Nixon Watergate burglars Frank Sturgis and Bernard Barker.[8]

The lawyers at the Trafficante-friendly DC law firm who conducted the Watergate-era interview with the Mafia don kept his disclosures to themselves for decades. And Nixon's vice presidential sponsorship of the plots against Castro's life was not confirmed until well after Nixon's death in 1994.

Here it is important to step back and put forth the full extent of Nixon's connections with corrupt, Mafia-controlled, drug-ridden Cuba. By the 1950s—with Meyer Lansky and Santos Trafficante in charge, and with dictator Fulgencio Batista cooperating and profiting—Cuba had become the hub of heroin distribution in the Western Hemisphere. And Havana's casinos had become "way-stations" for the transfer of large shipments of the drug from Europe to the United States.

A Mob-run Cuban airline operating out of military airports brought in huge supplies of cocaine from Colombia and other coca-growing countries. The coke, destined for Trafficante's smoothly run drug distribution network, originated from a laboratory in Medellin, Colombia.[9]

While taking his visiting lawyer, Frank Ragano, on a tour of Havana's sizzling nightlife, Trafficante showed Ragano how some of Cuba's high-rolling casino-goers could drink huge quantities of booze yet still have the energy to cha-cha and gamble the night—and sometimes the next day—away:

[At the San Souci, Trafficante] led me to the men's rest room and unlocked a door at the back of the room to reveal a wall filled with safety deposit boxes. Inside the boxes the rich Cubans kept their private stashes of cocaine, effective as pep pills when they were nightclubbing.[10]

Ragano acknowledged that Trafficante's display of the casino's clandestine coke vaults "lent fuel to rumors that had dogged [Trafficante] at home and in Cuba that he and his family were drug dealers, but I never saw any other evidence that Santo was involved in narcotics."[11]

Other Mafia experts, however, have found convincing evidence that Santos was actually one of the world's top drug dealers. In pre-Castro Cuba, Trafficante was "personally responsible for drug channels and trafficking which brought in hundreds of millions of dollars," according to Mafia authority, Enrique Cirule. "Heroin was trafficked through Buenos Aires and brought up through Cuba into the United States." Cocaine was also a viable commodity in the Cuban drug trade. Cirule backs up other reports that a "powerful laboratory in Medellin produced 'powder' destined for Santos Trafficante."[12]

After Batista was overthrown and the U.S. Syndicate was tossed out of Cuba, Trafficante worked through Resorts International—a Nixon/Rebozo-connected firm—on how best to shift the Mafia's gambling and drug operations to the Bahamas. Journalist Penny Lernoux says Meyer Lansky joined with Trafficante as a key behind-the-scenes partner in Resorts. As Penny Lernoux in *In Banks We Trust* (New York: Anchor Press Doubleday, 1986), page 82, points out:

> [Resorts] was linked to a squadron of notorious people, from Eddie Cellini, brother of a top Lansky lieutenant, to Robert Vesco, Howard Hughes, Bebe Rebozo and Richard Nixon. Lanksy's contact there was Louis Chesler, a real estate developer in South Florida. Chesler's partner in Resorts was Wallace Groves. Chesler had close ties with Trafficante's buddy Mike Coppola.

Meyer Lansky's fixer in the Bahamas, Chesler contributed cash to Nixon's 1960 presidential campaign and even traveled around the United States with the Republican candidate that fall.[13]

After his 1962 defeat in the governor's race in California, Nixon moved back east and joined a New York law firm. But he kept up his close affiliation with major mobsters. He bought land on Key Biscayne, Florida, from an old friend, Donald Berg—a Meyer Lansky associate. The land had been owned by various fronts for organized crime and former Cuban dictator Batista for more than 20 years.

One lender on Nixon's properties was Arthur Desser—a front man for Jimmy Hoffa and a Lansky factotum.[14] Nixon got a real sweetheart of a deal: he was able to buy two lots for $50,000—at a time when each lot was valued at $75,000.[15]

Nixon and Rebozo also had Key Biscayne real estate dealings with the assistance of Keyes Realty, an underworld-linked business. Future Watergate burglars Eugenio Martinez and Bernard Barker (a Santos Trafficante associate) were top officials at Keyes.

The willingness of Nixon and Rebozo to do business with Mob-linked individuals and businesses didn't stop there. In the sixties, both men "were in on the negotiations for the [Paradise Island] casino license," according to former FBI agent Frank Smith. A later IRS investigation linked casino gambling in the Bahamas "to organized crime and international traffic in cocaine and marijuana, and Resorts International was a focus of the investigations," says IRS expert John Andrew.[16]

A beautiful Caribbean island nation close to both Cuba and Florida, the Bahamas offered American mobsters displaced by Fidel Castro fresh opportunities for gambling, drug trafficking, and offshore banking. When Castro closed Cuba to U.S. tourists in 1961, the Bahamas developed into a major destination not only for mobsters and wealthy gamblers but also for tourists who loved its pleasant climate, clear waters, scenic landscapes, and white sandy beaches.

The country's white rule ended in the mid-sixties, and independence from Britain came in 1973. But those developments did nothing to curb the influence of Lansky and Company, says organized crime expert Alan Block:

The black government, in power since 1966, was eager to claim its rights to illicit profits that were greatly heightened with the rise of cocaine trafficking during the 1970s, which made the Bahamas a world drug smuggling center.[17]

In 1967, top Mob figures were being investigated by the Royal Commission of Inquiry of the Bahamas. Max Courtney, a longtime bookie for Lansky, "shocked the panel when he unveiled a litany of persons connected with widespread illegal operations on their island—including the former vice president of the United States, Richard M. Nixon," according to Mafia expert Jeff Gerth.[18] This is confirmed by another authority on the Mob, Michael Newton, who writes that Courtney "told the panel he had been invited into the Bahamas because his list of clients included wealthy gamblers 'from the ex-Vice President [Richard Nixon] on down.'"[19]

By 1968, when Nixon ran for president again, Resorts and the Paradise Island casino were both being run by James Crosby. Nixon attended the gala opening of the casino that year. And, before long, Nixon had his own man, James Golden, in a key position at Resorts. Golden, a soft-spoken muscular redhead, had been one of Nixon's vice presidential Secret Service agents.[20]

Allegations surfaced in 1972 that funds from the Paradise Island casino were being secretly delivered to Nixon and Rebozo by a Crosby casino employee, Seymour "Sy" Alter. A Lansky lieutenant, Alter had known Nixon and Rebozo since 1962, and he ran the Bahamian bridge that Nixon and Rebozo are reported to have partly owned.

Described by organized crime expert Alan Block as "coarse, vulgar and gruff," Alter was suspected of hiding a major portion of the money collected from Paradise Island bridge tolls and secretly depositing them in Rebozo's bank for Nixon's benefit:

It was Alter's connection to the bridge which convinced some investigators that Nixon was being paid off with the bridge receipts. They knew Alter was quite friendly with Rebozo, and that he had accounts at Rebozo's Key Biscayne bank. Suspicion was immeasurably increased when they learned Alter actually hand-delivered some cash deposits to Rebozo outside normal banking hours.[21]

In a 1977 interview with *Barron's* magazine, Alter put the bridge's annual income at $1 million. A decade later, former attorney general John Mitchell told an interviewer that the only offshore holdings Nixon had were "whatever he received for his interest in the bridge . . . Nixon had the bridge."[22]

Nixon aide John Ehrlichman later recalled "a lot of back-and-forth" in the Oval Office about helping out James Crosby— with Rebozo acting as a go-between in dealings the president had with the chairman of mobbed-up Resorts International. Crosby was also the builder of the Paradise Island Bridge.[23]

During Nixon's presidency, thanks to the U.S. Mob and corrupt Bahamian officials, the Bahamas became a major transshipment point for cocaine and marijuana between South America and the United States. In 1972, police in the Bahamas displayed evidence of this when they seized 1,500 pounds of pot valued at $1 million.[24]

Santos Trafficante didn't limit his interest in getting back into drug trafficking to Crosby's Bahamian operations. In 1968, the year Nixon was elected president, Santos made a trip to Southeast Asia where—with a little help from the CIA—he reportedly made invaluable new drug contacts. CIA agent Ted Shackley introduced Santos to two key political figures in Saigon who could protect his future heroin supply lines: through "President Nguyen Van Thieu and former Vice President Nguyen Cao Ky, Trafficante arranged to funnel the Asian heroin into this country."[25]

While he was in Saigon, and again through Shackley, Trafficante met with Vang Pat, who had a monopoly over the heroin trade in Laos. According to Mob expert Robert Kirk Connell, Trafficante and Vang Pat established "smuggling routes and operations, including a major route from South East Asia to the United States."[26]

As a New York lawyer in the sixties, Nixon represented Pepsico; and, as president, his diplomatic efforts made Pepsi the only U.S. soft drink available in the Soviet Union. Under the guise of helping his parent company, Nixon was another visitor to Indochina during the run-up to the 1968 election. Reporters Alan Weberman and Michael Canfield say that, while there, Nixon "helped establish a Pepsi-Cola factory in Laos—with the help of AID [Agency for International Development] that never produced a single bottle of Pepsi. Instead it became one of the largest heroin factories in Southeast Asia."[27]

In one of his first and most enduring presidential actions, Richard Nixon declared an all-out "War on Drugs." Since then, upward of $1 trillion has been wasted and millions of nonviolent people imprisoned—and the "war" has had absolutely no effect on reducing illegal drug consumption. Yet it did keep prices sky high for Nixon's buddies—Mafia profiteers.

In 2016, it was finally disclosed by an insider that Nixon's War on Drugs was actually a scheme against his biggest domestic enemies. It was then that a startlingly frank 1994 interview with top Nixon adviser John Ehrlichman was finally published.

Ehrlichman told author Dan Baum: "The Nixon campaign in 1968 and the Nixon White House after that, had two enemies:

the anti-war left and black people. You understand what I'm saying? We knew we couldn't make it illegal to be against the war or blacks, but by getting the public to associate hippies with marijuana and blacks with heroin, and then criminalizing both heavily, we could disrupt those communities. We could arrest their leaders, raid their homes, break up their meetings, and vilify them night after night on the evening news. Did we know we were lying about the drugs? Of course we did."[28]

The escapades of Nixon and his Mob-affiliated friends did not go unnoticed by American law enforcement. In fact, a bombshell of a top-secret report from J. Edgar Hoover's number-one informant on Cuban affairs landed on the FBI boss's desk on January 9, 1959. The informant—who went by the name of Catherine Taaffe—declared that the American vice president, a U.S. senator from Florida, a U.S. ambassador, and a shady Florida banker who represented the Mafia in Cuba were among those Americans involved in numerous suspicious schemes in Cuba. Bebe Rebozo was identified by Hoover's snitch as the fixer who "fronted for the Italian money and was also influential at the Presidential Palace and in business ventures between [corrupt U.S.] Ambassador [Earl] Smith and former President [Fulgencio] Batista." Hoover was incredulous—not so much about Rebozo, who had long been listed in FBI files as an associate of key gangsters, but Hoover could hardly believe that Vice President Richard Nixon, Senator George Smathers, and Ambassador Smith were connected to the criminal side of the island's mineral mining, cement, and sugar businesses.

The next day, Hoover got an even scarier report from another top FBI informant, John Booth, one of Florida's top Republicans. Booth said he had "ascertained that Vice President Nixon is also in on investments in Cuba and that all individuals involved have benefited financially." Booth also asserted that "when Vice President Nixon visits Florida he stays at the home of Bebe Rebozo." Hoover's first reaction was to scrawl at the bottom of the document, "We certainly can't sit on this information." When Ambassador Smith resigned on January 10, however, Hoover had a change of heart (and probably put the incriminating material in his bulging blackmail file). He added to the bottom of the note: "Now that Ambassador Smith has resigned, this seems to be resolved." These exchanges were not released until 2008.[29]

FIVE

Nixon's Mafia Web

WILLIAM PAWLEY

One of Richard Nixon's Mob-connected secrets surfaced only in recent years—and it's a doozy: a "Top Secret" CIA report accuses Vice President Nixon of shaping U.S. foreign policy to benefit a wealthy campaign contributor, a right-wing zealot who championed the assassination of the late Cuban leader Fidel Castro.

This CIA document—completed in 1983—is known as "Official History of the Bay of Pigs Operation, Volume III: Evolution of CIA's Anti-Castro Policies, 1951–January 1961." (The CIA declassified only Volume III of the five-volume history in 1998. It was discovered in the National Archives by Villanova professor David Barrett in 2005 and first posted on his university's website. This volume is now posted on the website of the National Security Archive, which is suing the CIA for the release of the other volumes.)

Of course, it would not be the first nor the last time that Nixon—one of the stickiest-fingered politicians in modern times—would be caught doling out favors to mobbed-up fat-cats.

Yet this declassified document exposes something even seamier than Nixon's run-of-the-mill pay-for-play illegalities. Seamier, for example, than soliciting congressional campaign funds from L.A.'s top gangster; or keeping a secret senatorial slush fund rounded up by rich businessmen; or widespread pres-idential financial corruption—including the sale of ambassador-ships; soliciting bribes from billionaires; or a go-easy attitude toward the ultra-generous Mafia godfathers and their thuggish Teamster allies.

These fresh revelations involve war and peace, life and death. They lie buried among 295 pages of a CIA critique of the failed 1961 invasion of Cuba by CIA-trained Cuban exiles. Written by a CIA historian, this document provides rich new details on Richard Nixon's central role in plotting the invasion of a foreign country, Cuba, and the attempted assassination of its leader, the late Fidel Castro. It faults Nixon for taking risky anti-Castro actions, in large part, to satisfy a well-connected Castro-loathing U.S. plutocrat with CIA and Mafia ties: William Pawley of Miami.

Pawley's Mafia contacts included Johnny Roselli and John Martino. And he had been instrumental in establishing Air America—a CIA front that would later become infamous for smuggling drugs from Southeast Asia's Golden Triangle.[1] Au-thor Douglas Valentine notes that the Miami of Pawley's years was not only "the preferred habitat of America's mobsters" but that it was also "packed with dozens of CIA front companies, thousands of CIA informers and assets, and several drug smuggling terror teams financed by wacky privateers like William Pawley . . ."[2]

Historian David Kaiser notes that Pawley worked closely with the CIA "on building anti-Castro organizations both inside and outside of Cuba. He was, in effect, an informal [CIA] case officer." As such, it is almost certain that Pawley was aware of the recommendation, in early January 1960, by CIA heavyweight J. C. King for Castro's "elimination."[3]

On January 9, 1960, Pawley and Nixon had a long discussion over lunch about the Cuba problem. Pawley gave Nixon an expensive wristwatch, and Nixon arranged for President Eisenhower to enjoy a weekend of hunting at Pawley's Virginia farm, according to Kaiser. The author theorizes, "Pawley may actually have sold President Eisenhower on the assassination of Castro."

Several days after the February 15, 1960, Ike-Pawley meeting, Pawley called one of his CIA contacts to report that the head of the Republican Party in Dade County, Florida, in author Kaiser's words, "had promised 12 Cuban exiles either $20 million or $200 million on behalf of Vice President Nixon to finance the overthrow of Castro. The story was never confirmed."

On March 2, 1960, the vice president received a CIA briefing on Cuba, according to the declassified CIA history. One item mentioned was a CIA "drug, which if placed in Castro's food, would make him behave in such an irrational manner that a public appearance could have very damaging results to him."

At this same briefing, according to Nixon biographer Anthony Summers, Nixon was told about getting "goon squads" into Cuba. Summers observes that the dictionary definition of a "goon" is a man "hired to . . . eliminate opponents."

On April 3, 1960, according to the CIA history, Pawley told CIA director Allen Dulles "that if the CIA is interested in quickly removing Fidel Castro such could be arranged through (deleted). He said that (deleted) has two men of his confidence who are with Fidel frequently, and they would be prepared to eliminate Castro for a price."

The CIA history also recounts a July 1, 1960, telephone call from Nixon aide General Robert Cushman to Jake Esterline, a top CIA official. The general revealed that Nixon had "commissioned" Cushman to "keep Mr. William Pawley happy," and to see that he is regularly briefed by the CIA on Cuba-related events. In recounting this conversation, Esterline reported, "Cushman said he realized that this is much against our [CIA's] desire . . . but the fact remains that he (Pawley) is a 'big fat political cat' and, as such, the Vice President cannot completely ignore him."

Cushman knew Pawley had become a painful pebble in the CIA's shoe. For one thing, Pawley wanted Juan Antonio Rubio Padilla to be the leader of the Cuban "government in exile," while the agency's nominee was Antonio Varona. For another, Pawley—like his hero, Nixon—thought the State Department was infiltrated with left-leaning diplomats who couldn't be trusted with national security secrets. Nixon carried his hatred of the department into his presidency, where he once privately declared he did not want foreign policy run by those "striped-pants faggots in Foggy Bottom." In addition, both Nixon and Pawley were suspicious about the possible leftward leanings of some Cuban exile leaders.

The CIA's Esterline assured Cushman he "understood" the Pawley "problem" and would make sure Nixon had the appropriate briefing materials to show Pawley "after first clearing the paper with the appropriate agency officials and within the security regulations that applied to Mr. Pawley."

The CIA history concludes that "some of the Vice President's interest [in plans for the ouster of Castro] particularly in his insistence in placating William Pawley, especially in giving undue attention to Pawley's concerns that the agency-sponsored Cuban exile organization was being taken over by the pro-Communist groups—was politically motivated . . ."

Nixon acted in a politically motivated way on a critical national security issue? That's a pretty strong criticism for a CIA historian to make about a vice president. But it does seem credible.

After all, Nixon's Miami sugar daddy had a vested interest when it came to American policy toward Cuba. Bill Pawley was a CIA- and FBI- and Mob-connected rabid right-winger whose sugar refineries, bus company, airline, and other investments in Cuba had been seized by Castro.

Pawley was a former U.S. diplomat and a strident champion of Latin American dictators—most especially of Cuba's Fulgencio Batista. As the biggest Washington pal in Pawley's hip pocket, Nixon took his cue from Pawley in ingratiating himself with Batista.

As vice president, Nixon made a 1955 trip to Havana to exchange toasts with the Cuban strongman. He embraced Batista at the general's lavish palace, praised "the competence and stability" of his regime, awarded the despot a Medal of Honor, and compared him with Abraham Lincoln.

The deep-pocketed Pawley was also a pal of President Dwight Eisenhower, CIA boss Allen Dulles, and FBI chief J. Edgar Hoover.

So when Pawley proposed, Nixon listened. And one of Pawley's crucial Cuba proposals—an obsession, really—was killing Fidel Castro, according to former Senate investigator Gaeton Fonzi in *The Last Investigation*: "(Pawley) had been involved in the CIA's [1954] overthrow of the Arbenz government in Guatemala and he had backed more than one Castro assassination attempt. Pawley once told a Miami reporter: 'Find me one man, just one man who can go it alone and get Castro. I'll pay anything, almost anything.'"

Pawley's main sponsor, Nixon, was described by Philip Bonsal, the U.S. ambassador to Cuba, as "the father" of the anti-Castro operation. In *Live by the Sword*, Gus Russo also reports that President Eisenhower's national security adviser, Colonel Philip Corso, declared: "Nixon was a hard-liner. He wanted (Castro) hit hard . . . when he was Vice President. He was a rough customer."

Pawley's assistance to the agency in Guatemala brought him together with CIA agents E. Howard Hunt, David Phillips, Tracey Barnes, and J. C. King. (In 1971, President Nixon would appoint the trusted Hunt as his number-one White House spy. Hunt and former FBI agent G. Gordon Liddy went on, of course, to supervise the ill-fated Watergate burglary.) But, by 1960, Pawley was becoming a royal pain to certain other CIA officials. The agency, in its declassified Bay of Pigs history, concluded that the vice president's financial backer and special Cuba adviser was espousing "personal and rigid" views "that are inimical to the best interest of the United States." And the document quotes CIA director Allen Dulles himself as calling the Cuban exiles supported by Pawley "unreconstructed reactionaries."

In 1960, when Vice President Nixon headed top-secret Cuba operations, the CIA was given the green light to enlist the Mafia for the assassination of Castro. The Nixon plan was eventually known as the "Bay of Pigs," the name of the Cuban beach where the greatly outnumbered exile forces eventually landed and were overpowered by Castro's troops.

While dreamed up by Nixon, the invasion was not carried out

until April 1961—early on President John F. Kennedy's watch. While taking full responsibility for the military disaster, the new president was seething deep inside that the CIA had misled him about the invasion's chances of success. He was also disappointed that "Track Two" of the plan—Castro's murder—had failed.

After the Bay of Pigs debacle, JFK fired the top two men at the CIA—Allen Dulles and Richard Bissell—and privately pledged to splinter the agency "into a thousand pieces and scatter them to the wind." He placed his brother Robert, the attorney general, in full charge of all anti-Castro operations—including plots to murder the elusive bearded Communist.

How did the ill-conceived Bay of Pigs plan come to be? As Ike's go-to guy on Cuba, Nixon worked closely with the CIA. And he was familiar with CIA agent E. Howard Hunt's efforts on behalf of the clandestine U.S. policy to overthrow Castro.

Hunt was the agency's political officer for the Bay of Pigs, coordinating the Cuban exile invaders. A short, distinguished-looking spy with jug ears, he was known as "Eduardo" among his Cuban exile acolytes, some of whom he recruited for the CIA. Hunt was an early advocate of the assassination of Castro as a key part of the overall invasion plan.

The veteran agent was close friends with the top three leaders of the CIA—Allen Dulles, Richard Bissell, and (future director) Richard Helms. (Hunt called Helms his "good friend and idol.") Hunt secretly worked on "dirty tricks" for Nixon for many years. Researchers Robert Groden and Harrison Edward Livingstone say Hunt "helped run operations for Nixon against Aristotle Onassis in the late 1950s . . ." The billionaire shipping magnate held a monopoly on shipping Saudi Arabian oil—a monopoly the Eisenhower-Nixon administration wanted to break.

Robert Maheu was also part of Nixon's anti-Onassis plots. An ex-FBI agent and CIA go-between with the Mafia, Maheu later recalled that Nixon gave him a license to kill the Greek tycoon: "After a meeting with Maheu about Onassis, Vice President Nixon shook Maheu's hand and whispered, 'And just remember, if it turns out we have to kill the bastard don't do it on American soil,'" according to the 1986 Onassis biography *Nemesis* by Peter Evans.

Maheu went on to set up meetings between Mafia biggies and the CIA that resulted in numerous plots to murder Castro. The first were hatched on Nixon's watch. One involved Mafia figures Sam Giancana, Santos Trafficante, and Johnny Roselli, who still had contacts in Havana from pre-Castro days. Poison pills were to be sent to Havana and delivered to a contact inside a restaurant frequented by Castro. But no one knows if the pills ever arrived.

In a 1997 interview with journalist Anthony Summers, President John Kennedy's press secretary, Pierre Salinger, said he was assured by Maheu that Nixon authorized Castro's murder. In his book *The Arrogance of Power*, Summers wrote that "(Maheu) told me (in 1968) about his meetings with the Mafia. He said he had been in contact with the CIA, and that the CIA had been in touch with Nixon, who had asked them to go forward with that project. . . . It was Nixon who had him (Maheu) do a deal with the Mafia in Florida to kill Castro."

The godfathers were more than happy to oblige, for Castro had expropriated their vast hotel, prostitution, narcotics, and gambling empire in Havana. In fact, according to numerous sources, the Syndicate's financial brains, Meyer Lansky, had already offered a reward of $1 million for Castro's murder.

Is a combo assassination plot and invasion worth that price?

There's no evidence that the following payments are directly tied to the Castro murder plots. But Pawley contributed $100,000 to Nixon's losing 1960 presidential bid. And Nixon scored an even bigger payout from the Mob. According to Lamar Waldron in *Ultimate Sacrifice*, as the 1960 election approached, a reliable government informant witnessed a meeting in New Orleans between Mafia godfather Carlos Marcello and Teamsters boss Jimmy Hoffa: "The purpose of the meeting was a suitcase filled with $500,000 in cash destined for Nixon—only half of a promised $1,000,000 contribution organized by the two." Mob expert Dan Moldea, in *The Hoffa Wars*, confirms this payoff and the other details.

When John Kennedy moved into the White House, Nixon and Pawley were out of the government's secret anti-Castro loop. Several months later, they were reduced to mere distraught bystanders when their Bay of Pigs plan flopped so miserably. Nixon declared it was "near-criminal" of President Kennedy not to have given the invaders adequate air cover.

Kennedy's election and the Bay of Pigs debacle apparently did little to deter either Nixon or Pawley from meddling in Cuban affairs.

CIA pilot Tosh Plumlee later told the FBI that, in the spring of 1963, he had participated in an ineffective raid against Cuba that seemed to have been organized by Nixon and Pawley. In a freshly released FBI document, Plumlee said others involved included Mafia murderers Johnny Roselli and John Martino. Plumlee said planning for the raid took place at a meeting on Bimini Island among Pawley, Nixon, and Nixon sidekick (and major Mafia contact) Bebe Rebozo.

Pawley—who had served as President Harry Truman's ambassador to both Peru and Brazil—was not through waging his private war on what he now viewed as the biggest menace to democracy in the hemisphere: Fidel Castro.

In June 1963, Pawley's sixty-five-foot yacht, *Flying Tiger II*, set sail for Cuba from Biscayne Bay near Miami. The yacht anchored about ten miles off the coast of Oriente Province. A raiding party of some one-dozen exile commandos set out for land in a speedboat, but was never heard from again. Pawley believed the overcrowded boat sank before reaching shore.[4]

The Pawley saga has an odd ending. On January 7, 1977, as a House committee sought to question him about the JFK assassination, the still handsome 80-year-old Pawley died in the bedroom of his Miami mansion of a self-inflicted bullet wound to the chest. Talbot says Pawley, who had been suffering from "nervous disorders," left a note to his wife, Edna: "The pain is worse than I can bear."

HOWARD HUGHES

Early in the 1968 presidential campaign, nutty billionaire Howard Hughes—a Mafia and CIA front who believed his largess could buy anyone—had his eye on a corrupt politician he'd previously bought. In a note to a trusted aide, Hughes outlined his scheme: "I am determined to elect a president of our choosing this year and one who will be deeply indebted, and who will recognize his indebtedness. Since I am willing to go beyond all limitations on this, I think we should be able to select a candidate and a party who knows the facts of political life. . . . If we select Nixon, then he, I know for sure knows the facts of life."[5] The Hughes aide—Robert Maheu, a former Nixon operative with key ties to both the Mafia and the CIA—then set about to seal the deal.

After several false starts, in the early years of the Nixon presidency, Hughes gave Nixon $100,000 in washed currency skimmed from the billionaire's Las Vegas gambling emporiums.

When Hughes's secret DC lobbyist Larry O'Brien became Democratic Party chairman, Nixon had O'Brien's telephone at the Watergate tapped to find out, perhaps, if Larry knew about the Hughes bribe—or, possibly, to find potential scandalous proof of O'Brien's hidden financial ties to Hughes. The capture by plainclothes DC cops of five of Nixon's burglars cowering under desks in O'Brien's offices in June 1972 led, two years later, to the disgraced chief executive's forced departure from the White House.

Howard Hughes was a major contributor to every Richard Nixon campaign since 1946. And he apparently made his first $100,000 secret payoff to Nixon in early 1956 to halt a plot by fellow Republican Harold Stassen to get President Eisenhower to dump Nixon as vice president. In December of the same year, the Vegas tycoon loaned $205,000 to Nixon's brother Donald to fund a failing "Nixonburger" restaurant chain. The loan was never repaid. And a source close to Hughes back then, *Time* magazine's Frank McCullough, tells me that Hughes admitted to him that the loan story was fiction—and that, in Hughes's words, "[The money] was for political purposes. It was a gift for [Dick], not his brother."[6]

Howard Hughes had once been a daring pilot, an aircraft inventor (the *Spruce Goose*), a handsome, starlet-dating Hollywood producer, and a business genius. He was also a rabid anticommunist who helped Vice President Nixon with CIA/Mafia plans to invade Cuba and oust Castro. Yet the billionaire's motives in this venture were not entirely patriotic. His mind was also on the gambling and other high-profit tourist businesses he intended to rush into once Castro was gone. According to a former Hughes aide, "Hughes had a lot of respect for the Mob, especially [Meyer] Lansky. My guess is that he hoped to form some sort of partnership with Lansky."[7]

All of that was not to be, of course, because the Bay of Pigs invasion was a catastrophe when it eventually launched during the Kennedy presidency.

By the time Richard Nixon won the presidency, Howard Hughes was holed up in the darkened penthouse of the Desert Inn in Las Vegas. Nixon's primary financial angel had become a 90-pound, narcotics-addled shut-in who refused to cut his hair, beard, fingernails, or toenails. Through a heavy fog of Valium and codeine, Hughes ran his business empire via memos and telephone calls to Bob Maheu, who said he never even met his boss:

> He finally told me that he did not want me to see him because of the way he had let himself deteriorate, the way in which he was living, the way he looked. He felt that if I ever in fact saw him, I would never be able to represent him.[8]

As a result of Hughes's 1968 scheme to have a debtor in the Oval Office, Maheu served as the tycoon's delivery boy for the first part of the $100,000 payoff. And Nixon's chief bagman, Bebe Rebozo, was on the other end of both parts of this two-installment trade of cold cash for future political favors. Contained in neatly wrapped bundles of hundred-dollar bills, the dough came from a Mob-run Hughes casino in Las Vegas. It was "siphoned like a sip of champagne from the Silver Slipper," according to a later account by columnist Jack Anderson.

Chief Senate Watergate Committee investigator Terry Lenzner later said that if the Hughes $100,000 "had gone to a legitimate political campaign, it would have been perfectly appropriate and okay. This, however, was a bribe, in effect, through Rebozo to the president."[9]

In fact, Hughes's $100,000 went through a maze of bank accounts; and $46,000 of it, Senate investigators found, was spent on a putting green, pool table, and fireplace for Nixon's Key Biscayne home.[10] Rebozo reportedly used $5,660 of the Hughes money to buy a pair of earrings for Richard to give Pat Nixon for her birthday.[11]

Now, Bebe was in big trouble. The IRS started to look carefully into his financial affairs, with a focus on "misappropriation of campaign contributions, acceptance of money in exchange for favors by the Justice Department, distribution of Watergate hush money, and alleged diversion of campaign funds to Nixon's brothers and personal secretary."

Rebozo barely escaped prosecution. One of the IRS investigators, Andy Baruffi, later revealed, "I was assigned to review the entire case file. We had Rebozo primarily on a straight up-and-down provable false statement charge. It was a dead-bang case. I believe a deal was made with the White House to kill the investigation."[12]

Rebozo was also President Nixon's ambassador to Hughes in an extraordinary field—one Bebe knew almost nothing about: atomic testing.

During the summer of his first year in office, the president ordered National Security Adviser Henry Kissinger to consult with Bebe on pacifying Hughes, who keenly feared coming government tests of nuclear weapons in Nevada. The testing site was only about 100 miles from Las Vegas, and each underground blast shook Hughes's hotel, making it sway back and forth—greatly angering the wealthy recluse in the penthouse.

Nixon's planned use of his national security adviser to placate his biggest Mafia-linked financial angel was no surprise to those few insiders who were aware of the tightness of the Nixon-Hughes connection. What they perhaps didn't know at the time, however, was that the president had received secret payoffs from Hughes totaling $200,000 for the explicit purpose of stopping the tests. These bribes were concealed by Rebozo, according to organized crime expert Alan Block.[13]

In recently released summaries of telephone calls on July 9, 1969, the president directed Kissinger to call Rebozo and report that "the President has commissioned" Kissinger to call on Hughes in August to give him the background on the tests. Nixon noted that Hughes would not likely accept such a face-to-face briefing because "Hughes never sees anyone." The president told his chief national security adviser that if that didn't stop Hughes from worrying, Nixon himself might have to write a letter to Hughes on the matter.

Kissinger then phoned Rebozo, asking him to get word to Hughes that when Kissinger got to the West Coast next month he "would be delighted" to come up to Vegas to brief Nixon's billionaire benefactor. Rebozo asked whether that might be too late to calm down Hughes. "No," Kissinger replied. "There are so many review provisions built into [nuclear weapons test procedures] that it would still be useful."

As Nixon predicted, a Kissinger-Hughes meeting on a nuclear test deal arranged by Rebozo would never take place. The unkempt mogul flatly refused to see anyone outside his own small circle of caregivers at any time.

Hughes's fears of additional atomic tests reached a rage in early 1970, when he phoned Maheu and ordered him to proceed directly to Key Biscayne "and there offer Bebe Rebozo one million dollars for Richard Nixon—if the president would stop the bomb test," according to Hughes biographer Michael Drosnin.[14]

Maheu and another top Hughes executive (and tight Nixon pal) Richard Danner proceeded to the Florida White House, where they held an eight-hour session with Rebozo. Maheu reported back to Hughes that Nixon "is prepared to meet with you at a moment's notice, preferably at some place like Camp David."[15]

But Hughes promptly vetoed the idea of a summit at the rustic, secluded presidential retreat to seal the deal on a possible $1 million bribe to Nixon.

On March 26, 1970, one of the biggest nuclear explosions occurred in the Nevada desert, with tremors rippling through Las Vegas and shaking up Howard Hughes so much that he started to seriously consider leaving Sin City.

Hughes abruptly left on Thanksgiving Eve 1970. "A wasting wraith on a gurney," historians Roger Morris and Sally Denton wrote, "he was removed from Las Vegas by James Golden, a former Nixon Secret Service agent ... and was whisked by private jet to Resorts International's Britannia Beach Hotel in the Bahamas."[16]

James Golden was by now a top official of Resorts, which owned several Bahamian casinos. The Mafia's financial genius and longtime Nixon fan Meyer Lansky had purported ties to Resorts through a Bahamian casino managed by Edward Cellini. (Lansky reportedly first met Nixon in Cuba in the fifties and met him again during a later visit by both men to Florida.[17]) Golden was also a key member of a Resorts subsidiary named Intertel—considered by one IRS account as "an organized crime enterprise of some type aimed at the Bahamas."[18]

Hughes's departure was accompanied by a bitter corporate struggle over what remained of his Las Vegas Empire. The biggest immediate loser was Maheu, who was evicted from his ritzy mansion and was fired from his $500,000-a-year job. Before long, Maheu was filing huge lawsuits against Hughes and blabbing about the corrupt Nixon-Hughes relationship—blabbing that would eventually help bring down the Nixon presidency.

Bob Maheu eventually spilled the beans on the $100,000 payoff from Hughes that Maheu helped deliver to Nixon through Rebozo.

At the same time, as noted earlier, President Nixon was hoping to find proof of Hughes's secret contract with Democratic Party chairman Larry O'Brien as Hughes's Washington lobbyist. The president might also have desired to find out whether the DNC chairman might know about the Hughes $100,000 payoff to Nixon. These factors could well have played a critical role in Nixon's risky decision to break into O'Brien's DNC office.

Charles Colson—a key presidential link to mobbed-up Teamsters chief Frank Fitzsimmons—once said, "I've always believed that the real motive behind the Watergate break-in was to get dirt on Larry O'Brien, who was drawing a retainer from Hughes. Beneath it all we'll find some day that the real motive was Hughes."[19]

As for Rebozo, it is hard to imagine that a man the FBI considered to be an associate of top Mafia figures had the run of the entire Nixon White House. This aspect of the Nixon-Rebozo relationship is brought home by a recently released telegram addressed to Bebe in care of the super-secret Situation Room. Officials there dutifully forwarded Bebe's telegram to the Western White House in San Clemente, where the president's First Friend had his own bungalow. The date of the telegram is not legible. But it is from Fred O. Dickenson—a two-time GOP candidate for governor and who was the state comptroller who had been investigated by federal prosecutors for receiving unreported campaign money from bankers—and notifies Rebozo that $200,000 is being deposited in Bebe's Key Biscayne bank. Beyond that, there's very little information about the mysterious telegram.[20]

Another telling indicator of Bebe's importance is found in a newly released April 29, 1971, memo from Steve Bull to Bob Haldeman asking that a White House driver and car pick up Rebozo, Bob Abplanalp, and a third Nixon friend, Hobart Lewis, at LAX and take them to San Clemente. Bull sought to reserve rooms for them at the San Clemente Inn, but said maybe they'd stay at the Western White House because it was a "stag weekend." In that case, Bebe would stay in "Bebe's Cabin," Bob in "Julie's House." And Hobart in the guest room at the Nixon residence. Haldeman responded that the trio should stay at the inn.

ADNAN KHASHOGGI

Adnan Khashoggi once led the world in personal riches. In the 1980s, when he was implicated in the Iran-Contra scandal, he was worth an estimated $4 billion. The Saudi-born arms trader had even surpassed Howard Hughes—whose wealth was put at $1.5 billion back then.[21]

Just how rich was Khashoggi? Rich enough to own ten homes,

a $70 million yacht (which he eventually sold to Donald Trump), three luxurious jetliners, and two helicopters. He was a devoted playboy and a poster child for conspicuous consumption. Khashoggi was also rich enough to afford one of the most expensive marital breakups in history. In 1982, Soraya Khashoggi accepted a lump-sum divorce payment of $874 million.[22]

Khashoggi made the bulk of his fortune as a broker for companies selling military hardware to Saudi Arabia's royal family.

The suave, glib (in Arabic and non-accented American English) Khashoggi said he first met Richard Nixon "in Paris in 1967 and we had dinner at the Rasputin Restaurant . . . [and later] in New York, he gave a cocktail party for me."[23]

That same year, Khashoggi made one of his planes available to the former vice president for a tour of the Middle East after the Six-Day War. In 1968, Khashoggi contributed $50,000 to the Nixon campaign, and after the election he met with the president-elect aboard Bebe Rebozo's houseboat in Florida.

Before Nixon's 1968 election, the Saudi billionaire is said to have deposited as much as $200 million at Rebozo's Key Biscayne bank. Khashoggi then reportedly withdrew all but $200,000 in the form of checks made out to "cash" and signed them over to the Howard Hughes–owned Sands Hotel in Vegas—where Khashoggi was an inveterate big-time loser at the hotel's casino.

This link is confirmed, and amplified, by Hughes biographers Donald Bartlett and James Steele:

Khashoggi, highest of the high rollers, often ran gambling debts into seven figures and, sometimes, when he lacked ready cash to cover his losses, he arranged for the money to be transferred from the Key Biscayne Bank of his friend Bebe Rebozo.[24]

How did the roly-poly (at five-foot-four, Khashoggi weighed 200 pounds) billionaire happen to choose Bebe's bank? He candidly told Watergate investigators he did so hoping to "curry favor with Rebozo" in order to ingratiate himself with the man who might become president. The global wheeler-dealer actually looked down on Rebozo, however—dismissing him as "not very smart and not nearly well-informed enough to serve as an effective spokesman."[25]

Khashoggi attended Nixon's 1969 inaugural. In 1972, he reportedly gave $1 million in secret cash to the president—allegedly in a briefcase he "mistakenly" left behind at Nixon's San Clemente estate. Nixon later artfully dodged the question of whether he received such funds. In a sworn affidavit in 1979, the former president said only: "I have absolutely no recollection of speaking with or meeting Adnan Khashoggi at either my home or office in San Clemente."[26]

But Pierre Salinger, who had been President Kennedy's press secretary, and who was a good friend of Khashoggi's, maintained that the arms dealer told him he had, indeed, hand-delivered that cash-filled valise for the president. In Salinger's words, "Adnan showed up in Washington and had a secret meeting with Nixon . . . and later on, he told me, he'd given a million dollars to help with the campaign . . ."[27]

In 1973, Khashoggi attended Nixon's second inaugural. He later bragged that he had flattered the president's daughters with $60,000 worth of jewelry.[28] His divorced wife, Soraya, claimed that she assisted in the delivery of the jewels.[29]

If President Nixon received these reputed gifts from the Saudi billionaire, he would have broken a U.S. law barring politicians from soliciting or accepting such contributions from a foreign citizen.

Adnan Khashoggi was seated near the Nixon family at the former president's 1994 funeral. Since then, Khashoggi lived a quiet and quite comfortable life in Monaco until his death in 2017.

RICHARD KLEINDIENST

Nixon attorney general Richard Kleindienst was offered a $100,000 bribe to quash several Mob indictments. In sworn testimony in November 1971, Kleindienst admitted to being offered the money (to be paid in the form of a contribution to Nixon's 1972 campaign) in exchange for stopping stock fraud prosecutions of several underworld figures—including members of the Genovese crime family in New York. The bribe was offered by an aide of Senator Hiram Fong, a Republican from Hawaii and a member of the Senate Judiciary Committee.

John Mitchell's successor as the nation's top law enforcement officer said he rejected the bribe. But the attorney general admitted to lawmakers that his refusal to take the money came only after he learned that federal agents were investigating the case— one full week after the bribe offer was made.

In March 1973, obeying Nixon's orders to go easy on the Mafia and their Teamsters allies, Kleindienst refused to renew a 20-day extension of FBI wiretaps that were beginning to expose Teamsters complicity in a Mafia kickback scam involving Teamsters health and welfare benefits.[30]

The scam, with a projected take of $1 billion a year, would have been divided among Mob and Teamsters bosses. Despite Kleindienst's assurances that the surveillance was unproductive, the *New York Times* said that the taps "had begun to penetrate connections between the Mafia and the Teamsters union." The newspaper cited the attorney general's refusal to continue the wiretaps as an example of "the perversion of justice that pose(d) as law and order" in the Nixon administration.[31]

Later in 1973, Kleindienst resigned, saying too many of his friends had been implicated in Watergate for him to remain. In 1974, he was convicted of failing to fully testify at a Senate hearing into a separate case. But a judge later suspended Kleindienst's fine and sentence.[32]

In 1983, Kleindienst was acquitted of lying before the State Bar of Arizona in the case of a Kleindienst client who had been convicted of an insurance swindle.

A heavy smoker, Kleindienst died of lung cancer at the age of 76 in 2000.[33]

FRANK SINATRA

John Kennedy banished Frank Sinatra from Camelot when the singer's Mafia ties clashed with the new president's crackdown on organized crime. But those well-documented ties didn't keep President Richard Nixon from later wooing the popular crooner away from the Democratic Party.

The courtship actually started when Nixon's unsavory vice president Spiro Agnew first got together with Sinatra during Thanksgiving in 1970. They enjoyed each other's company so much that Agnew became a regular houseguest at Frank's Palm Springs, California, estate, and he made 18 visits in the months that followed.

The two men played golf together, dined out, talked through the night in Frank's den, and on one occasion watched the porn movie *Deep Throat* together. Frank's guest quarters, once remodeled for John F. Kennedy, were eventually renamed "Agnew House."[34]

The president himself evinced a keen interest in Sinatra's possible endorsement during a September 13, 1971, Oval Office meeting with top aide Bob Haldeman. Just to make certain he was pursuing someone who could be seduced, Nixon ordered Haldeman to look into Sinatra's possible ties to Democratic presidential hopeful Senator Edmund Muskie: "[The IRS is] after, you know, every one of our people. Goddamnit, they were after me.... Somebody told me that Muskie used Frank Sinatra's plane in California. Did you hear that? Maybe we should investigate that."

Haldeman was hot on the case the very next day. In a September 14 memo, he sought a secret White House probe to discover "whether this is true. If so, check with the Vice President's office and find out how this jibes with the reports that Sinatra wants to support the President.... As you probably know, we've received reports from a number of directions that Sinatra was on our side. His supplying a plane to Muskie would not seem to be evidence of that." Sent to several key assistants and stamped "Administratively Confidential," the Haldeman memo was declassified in 2010.

In another newly released confidential memo dated September 16, 1971, Haldeman aide Gordon Strachan cites the Sinatra-Muskie probe's main findings: Muskie had indeed used a plane jointly owned by Sinatra and Danny Schwartz, a San Francisco

Democrat and supporter of Hubert Humphrey. Schwartz okayed Muskie's use of the plane. But most importantly, Strachan reported, "The Vice President's Office [Roy Goodearle] reports that 'Sinatra is still with us.'"

Strachan's investigation also determined that aide Chuck Colson was pressing "very hard to have Sinatra introduced to the President quietly." And Strachan happily concludes that "Sinatra is still with us and could be brought into full endorsement if he met the President, if this were deemed appropriate."

On October 25, 1971, Chuck Colson sent out a "Confidential/ Eyes Only" memo to Haldeman. Also released in 2010, it recommends an informal "one-on-one" White House meeting, over drinks, between the president and the mobbed-up singer. Colson suggests that if such a session were held—and a number of other steps were taken—"we are relatively certain to have completed our seduction of Frank Sinatra."

In the memo, Colson concluded that a personal relationship between the president and Sinatra could yield major benefits because Sinatra "has a great deal of control over what we understand to be massive financial resources." Was Colson hinting at Sinatra's clout with Mafia biggies? (The Colson memo does not contain a single cautionary word about the singer's longtime ties to these mobsters.)

When a House committee sought to question Sinatra about those ties in 1972, Agnew unsuccessfully tried to delay the service of a subpoena. When Sinatra did testify, he was surly and defiant. President Nixon personally phoned Sinatra to congratulate him for stonewalling the panel.

Washington Post society columnist Maxine Cheshire was on Frank Sinatra's enemies list. A main reason: she had publicly raised with Sinatra his well-known Mob connections.

In late 1972, at an event in DC, Cheshire asked Frank: "Mr. Sinatra, do you think your alleged association with the Mafia will prove to be the same embarrassment to Vice President Agnew as it was to the Kennedy administration?" He answered: "No, I don't worry about things like that."

On January 19, 1973, at a preinaugural party hosted at the Fairfax Hotel by Louise Gore, the GOP national committee member from Maryland, Frankie Boy shouted down Cheshire—assaulting her with obscene language and gestures. Sinatra's rage boiled over when he spotted her at the function: "Get away from me, you scum. Go home and take a bath. You're nothing but a two-dollar cunt. You know what that means, don't you? You've been laying down for two dollars all your life." He thrust two dollar bills into her plastic cup of ginger ale and said, "Here's two dollars, baby. That's what you're used to."[35]

"Maxine Cheshire was so stunned and insulted, she burst into tears," according to Sinatra biographer Randy Taraborrelli.[36] Sinatra's hideous meltdown made big headlines of the sort that did not reflect well on him as the head of "Entertainers for Nixon."

But Nixon and Rebozo had Sinatra's back—and then some—on the singer's infamous anti-Cheshire inaugural eve rant. On July 9, 1973, the two men discussed Cheshire's recent reportorial efforts to nail down certain facts about government expenditures at Nixon's Florida retreat. In doing so, they harkened back to memories of Sinatra's verbal attack on the journalist:

REBOZO: I think [Sinatra] was too kind. [Laughter]
NIXON: Oh, yeah.
REBOZO: He was too kind.
NIXON: Two bits, not two dollars.[37]

Sinatra's "thick FBI package" included tight links to major Mafia figures like Johnny Roselli. Indeed, "Ol' Blue Eyes" even sponsored Roselli for membership in the exclusive Friar's Club of Beverley Hills. Roselli was tossed out, however, after he was indicted for fixing key gambling operations there.

"Handsome Johnny," it turns out, may have known Dallas mobster Jack Ruby since 1933, when both frequented the Santa Anita racetrack in Los Angeles.[38] The CIA gave Roselli the rank of a colonel.

After President Kennedy was forced by FBI boss J. Edgar Hoover to stop associating with Sinatra, the singer hooked up with the longest-reigning strongman in the Mafia's arsenal of political power—Richard Nixon. (At one private event, Nixon was hailed by an Italian-American group's leader: "You are our Terrestrial god.") And more than one political commentator has observed that Nixon seemed to run the presidency like the godfathers ran their sleazy and deadly enterprises. Just to make sure the Mob had the president's ear, Frank Sinatra hung around with Nixon and Agnew so much that he even acquired a Secret Service code name: "Napoleon."

Sam Giancana, the dapper don of Chicago, was so tight with Sinatra that he always wore a star sapphire pinky ring—a prized gift from the Mafia's favorite entertainer. In turn, Sinatra had such great affection for Giancana, he ended every personal performance by belting out a tribute to Sam, "My Kind of Town (Chicago Is)."

By 1960, Giancana had been arrested some 70 times and had reportedly ordered some 200 torture-murders of men who had done him wrong. Sinatra's friend, movie actor Peter Lawford (President Kennedy's brother-in-law), told Sinatra biographer Kitty Kelley that "when the word got out around [Hollywood] that Frank was a pal of Sam Giancana, nobody but nobody ever messed with Frank Sinatra. They were too scared. Concrete boots were no joke with [Giancana]. He was a killer."[39]

Frank Sinatra's Mob ties go back at least as far as Nixon's. In 1947, he was photographed with the notorious Lucky Luciano on a balcony of the Hotel Nacional in Havana. Luciano, who headed the world's largest illegal drug cartel, was in Havana for a convention of about a dozen American crime bosses, including Trafficante, Marcello, and the owner of the Nacional, Meyer Lansky. Sinatra used the occasion to give Luciano a gold cigarette case that was inscribed, "To my dear pal Lucky, from his friend, Frank Sinatra."

As president, Nixon lured Sinatra out of retirement so that he could sing at a White House state dinner for Italian prime minister Giulio Andreotti in April 1973. In introducing Sinatra, the president lavishly praised the singer—even comparing him to the Washington Monument, "the Top." Andreotti—who had alleged Mafia links in Italy—expressed his gratitude to Nixon for inviting Sinatra: "I am going to be able to listen to him singing here. This is something which will give much prestige to me with my children."

CARLOS MARCELLO

Carlos Marcello was one of the most powerful crime lords of the twentieth century. He rose to notability under the tutelage of another famous Louisiana mobster, Sam Carolla. Adept at many things, Marcello specialized initially in the trade of marijuana, a "new" drug to many Americans. He once sold 23 pounds of pot to an undercover agent and was sentenced to one year in prison and was told to pay a $75,000 fine.[40] The crafty criminal only ended up spending nine months in prison and managed to have the fine reduced to a paltry $400.

Marcello's skill set mirrors that of President Nixon's. Ruthless and ambitious, the pair created a lucrative and rewarding partnership. The first dealings between the two involved the CIA-Mafia plots to kill Fidel Castro. In addition, Marcello was one of Nixon's most generous financial supporters, albeit under the table. According to organized crime expert John Davis, Marcello admitted, after the fact, that he had been a primary operator in the plots to kill Castro. The CIA confirmed as much in 2007 in releasing long-secret documents known as "the Family Jewels."

Through his ties to Marcello, Nixon aligned himself with many other unsavory types. Marcello rather obviously had numerous ties to other vice lords. In 1961, when he was deported to Guatemala by the Kennedy administration, he returned on a small, private plane piloted by JFK assassination suspect David Ferrie. Ferrie knew Lee Harvey Oswald since at least 1955. He was accused by former New Orleans district attorney Jim Garrison and CIA operative Robert Morrow as being a prime planner of the assassination.

Marcello was also an associate of Jack Ruby, Oswald's murderer. According to the House assassinations report in 1979, Ruby had concrete connections to Marcello's top deputy in Dallas, Joseph Civello. But the connections to Ruby, and in turn the JFK assassination, are even deeper. The second most powerful Mafia man in Dallas, Joe Campisi, was so close to Marcello that he sent the family a gift of homemade sausage every

Christmas. Furthermore, Ruby and Campisi were close associates as well. The pair was seen dining together at Campisi's restaurant the night before President Kennedy was killed. Campisi even visited Ruby in jail, six days after he shot Oswald.

Assassination expert Anthony Summers concludes that it is highly likely that Marcello was involved in the killing of JFK. He asserts that "to say otherwise is to reject at least nineteen witnesses and informants as fabricators, and to reject the web of interconnections between the Marcello apparatus and Oswald and Ruby."

Carlos Marcello once told a fellow prisoner, "I had the little bastard [JFK] killed. He was a thorn in my shoe." Jack Van Laningham—a cellmate of the Mafia don—disclosed Marcello's confession in a 2009 TV interview on the Discovery Channel's *Did the Mob Kill JFK?* Van Laningham subsequently passed a polygraph test. He said Marcello explained that Oswald had visited him in New Orleans and that "he was my man. He did what the hell I told him to do."

As for Jack Ruby, Marcello told his cellmate that the Dallas strip club owner was under his thumb, deeply in debt, and owed the Mob boss "big." So Marcello, according to Van Laningham, ordered Ruby to erase the debt by rubbing out Oswald.

Van Laningham, who was at the Texarkana Federal Prison for bank robbery, ratted out Marcello for the FBI in a deal that sprung him from prison early. The FBI agent who supervised the informant says he has no reason to disbelieve Van Laningham's story.

Marcello biographer John H. Davis describes Nixon as "Carlos's favorite politician," and says the Louisiana godfather was "able to extend his reach into the White House" through Murray Chotiner and a number of other Nixon-loving mobsters.

Davis observes that the Mafia worked in mutually beneficial tandem with Richard Nixon early and often:

> If there ever was a candidate for the presidency whom the Mob wanted elected it was Richard Nixon. Since the earliest days of his political career in California, Nixon had seemed to walk hand-in-hand with the Mafia, functioning with the family bosses in an apparent symbiotic relationship that was to last right down to his resignation from the presidency in 1974, and perhaps even beyond.[41]

After entering the White House, Nixon moved to strengthen his ties to Marcello and used an old loyalist of his, Murray Chotiner, as a go-between. Chotiner was responsible for defending 221 mob figures in California. He also had concrete ties to other underworld figures such as Meyer Lansky and LA's top gangster, Mickey Cohen—further increasing Nixon's interests and investments in organized crime.

When the lawyer first sought aid from Marcello, the mobster was about to serve a two-year prison sentence for assaulting a federal official. Nixon, with the aid of his attorney general, managed to have the sentence reduced to six months and gave him a comfortable setting at the medical center for federal prisoners in Springfield, Missouri. When Marcello finished his sentence, he arrived on the scene just in time to help Nixon and Chotiner arrange for Jimmy Hoffa's release from prison.

SIX

Hoffa and Clemency

During Watergate, Martha Mitchell—the attorney general's unpredictable, hard-drinking wife—told UPI's Helen Thomas, "Nixon is involved with the Mafia. The Mafia was involved with his election." White House officials privately urged me and other reporters to treat any anti-Nixon comments by Martha as the ravings of a drunken crackpot. Several times, spokesman Ron Ziegler told me, not for attribution, that Martha was often in her cups, and that—when that was so—Helen would unethically coax her into saying outrageous things. I just laughed at that bizarre and untrue suggestion. In 1976, Nixon aide Charles Colson backed up Martha's claim, theorizing that the Mafia "owned Bebe Rebozo and got their hooks into Nixon early."[1] Time has proven Martha Mitchell and Charles Colson to be right.

If friendships enabled Nixon to craft links with the Mafia, so did hatred. Teamsters Union leader Jimmy Hoffa hated John and Robert Kennedy as much as Nixon did. Robert Kennedy had been trying to put Hoffa in jail since 1956, when RFK was the staff counsel for a Senate probe into the Mob's influence on the labor movement. In a 1960 book, Kennedy said, "No group better fits the prototype of the old Al Capone syndicate than Jimmy Hoffa and some of his Lieutenants."[2]

The Nixon-Hoffa relationship goes back to 1959—when Hoffa was the original fixer of Mafia-CIA plots to kill Cuban dictator Fidel Castro overseen by Vice President Richard Nixon. And when Jimmy campaigned for Nixon in 1960, the veep returned the favor by getting the Justice Department to hold up Hoffa's indictment for misuse of labor funds.[3] Nixon's action followed a September 26, 1960, contribution to his presidential campaign of a suitcase filled with $500,000 in cash. The money was from New Orleans godfather Carlos Marcello through Hoffa and the Teamsters.[4]

When Nixon moved back to California after being beaten by John Kennedy in the presidential race, he had another connection to the Teamsters president. In 1961, Texas tycoon Clint Murchison Sr. sold Nixon a lot in the exclusive Trousdale Estates development in Beverley Hills for $35,000. This was a gated community Murchison had financed through a $6.7 million Hoffa-approved loan from the Teamsters pension fund. Nixon profited very nicely from the deal—selling the lot two years later for $86,000. Investigative reporter Gus Russo finds this particular favor not all that surprising:

> In the 1960 election, the Teamsters not only endorsed Nixon, but Hoffa also personally coordinated a $1 million contribution to the Nixon campaign from the Teamsters and various mob bosses, including Louisiana's Carlos Marcello.[5]

On June 16, 1969, President Richard Nixon read a *Wall Street Journal* story reporting on the anti–Jimmy Hoffa stance then being taken by former Teamsters official Edward Partin. Nixon scribbled an action memo to his attorney general: "Mitchell: Go after him." Nixon accompanied his command by noting that Partin "was something of a hero to men who worked for Robert Kennedy."[6]

A major milestone in the Nixon-Hoffa relationship had occurred on December 13, 1959, when the Teamsters chief met with Nixon representative Oakley Hunter—a former California congressman—in Hunter's suite at the posh new Americana Hotel in Miami Beach. Both men took off their suit jackets to show they were not recording the conversation, such was the secrecy of the meeting. A few days later, in a detailed memo to Vice President Nixon on his meeting with Hoffa, Hunter reported that Hoffa complained about not getting a fair shake from the federal government. "He feels he is being made a scapegoat and a whipping boy," revealed Hunter. "He said he is cleaning up his union as best and as rapidly as possible, that this kind of thing cannot be done overnight." In return for relief from the feds by a potential future Nixon administration, the Teamsters boss promised that, during the 1960 campaign, union officers in key cities could openly endorse Nixon and help him get elected.[7]

But that was far from the extent of Hoffa's assistance to Nixon. In speeches, Hoffa strongly urged the 1.6 million Teamsters members to help defeat Senator John Kennedy. And when the fall of 1960 rolled around, the union boss was able to secretly arrange the delivery of $1 million in laundered Mafia cash to Nixon's campaign coffers. Former Hoffa aide and later government informant Ed Partin said that half the contribution came from New Orleans godfather Carlos Marcello. He told

Mob expert Dan Moldea, "I was right there . . . Marcello had a suitcase filled with $500,000 cash which was going to Nixon. . . . [Another half million dollars] was coming from mob boys in New Jersey and Florida."

A New Orleans meeting between Hoffa and Marcello on September 26, 1960, had paved the way for the uncommonly huge bribe intended to sway a potential Nixon administration to be kind to Jimmy Hoffa and his mobbed-up associates.[8] As an even more immediate payoff for Hoffa, mere weeks after the million changed hands, Nixon managed to delay a Florida land fraud indictment against the Teamsters chief.[9]

Nixon would go on to lose the election that Hoffa worked so hard to buy and, as a result of Attorney General Robert Kennedy's investigation into Hoffa's jury tampering and unsavory financial practices with the Teamsters, Hoffa would be sent to prison. Hoffa had drained around $2 million from the union's pension funds, but the Nixon-Hoffa relationship was far from over. Hoffa was able to pressure Nixon into granting him clemency by threatening Frank Fitzsimmons, the new leader of the Teamsters. And in 1971, as president, Nixon gave clemency to Hoffa, relieving him from eight more years in prison.

Breaking from clemency custom, Nixon did not consult the judge who had sentenced Hoffa. Nor did he pay any attention to the U.S. Parole Board, which had unanimously voted thrice in two years to reject Hoffa's appeals for release at least in part because they had been warned by the Justice Department that Hoffa was Mob-connected.

Before the finalization of his pardon, Hoffa was granted a four-day compassionate leave from prison to be with his wife, Jo, who had suffered a heart attack in San Francisco. During his leave, Jimmy summoned Fitzsimmons to his suite in the

Fairmont on Nob Hill. Also present were Frank Ragano, Hoffa's lawyer (who also represented godfathers Carlos Marcello and Santos Trafficante), and Allen Dorfman, the Teamsters' main financial link to the Mafia. Hoffa, according to Ragano, "was poking a finger in Fitz's chest and yelling that Fitz had double-crossed him by not getting him released within two years." Ragano recounted a chilling threat that Hoffa then issued to his Teamsters successor: "Jo is very sick and needs me. I'm going to give you until Christmas to get me out of prison. If I'm not out by Christmas Day, you won't be around to celebrate New Year's."

Ragano further recalled, "Now it was clear why I had been summoned from across the country for this confrontation. Jimmy wanted Fitz to believe that I was the surrogate for [Trafficante and Marcello] and that they represented the brute force he could command to kill or maim Fitz."[10] The message was indeed very clear. And Hoffa was out of prison before Christmas Day 1971.

But it was not until November 1, 1971, as Bob Haldeman noted in his diary, that a plan to free Hoffa was nearing completion:

> Mitchell raised the point that the time has probably come for the P [the president] to exercise executive clemency. He suggests burying this in the Christmas list in a batch of 250 or so. The P was trying to get at the point of how you position it. The question is what our political benefit is, and what is in the balance. The line the P would use is that [Hoffa's] met the normal requirements for release and there should not be discrimination against him because he's a labor leader.[11]

Indeed, on that same date, the Oval Office recording system overhears Nixon and Mitchell begin to tentatively outline the deal:

NIXON: Well, you've got a parole problem?

MITCHELL: It's known as executive clemency, unfortunately.

NIXON: You mean the pardon problem?

MITCHELL: Well, it's not a complete pardon, but there is an executive clemency aspect of it, where you would reduce the sentence enough so that he could get out of the clink. The pardon would be considered at a later date which probably would be better to hold over his head, to see what commitments he'll undertake and how he'll act in the matter.

NIXON: Executive clemency has the same problems.

MITCHELL: Fitzsimmons, of course, has been pushing this thing for years and years.

NIXON: He wants executive clemency.

MITCHELL: He wants Hoffa out of there. And he has had substantial troubles with his union because he isn't out of there, for whatever reason, or whatever conversations or commitments.

NIXON: Executive clemency. The Attorney General? Or who does it? The pardon board or, ah.

Watergate authority James Warren says such taped White House conversations—released long after Nixon's death—shine new light on significant aspects of the deal that ended Hoffa's incarceration:

For starters, the tapes prove that former Atty. Gen. John Mitchell lied to Watergate prosecutors in denying any political considerations in the Hoffa action. In addition, they bolster long-held, never-proven conspiracy theories about a deal between Nixon and Frank Fitzsimmons, Hoffa's successor, who wanted to make sure that his mentor would not be able to get his old job back.[12]

Mitchell, who did jail time for perjury and other Watergate offenses, also lied in an October 15, 1973, affidavit to aid Hoffa's legal efforts to lift the pardon restrictions. In the deposition, Mitchell swears that "neither I, as Attorney General of the United States, nor, to my knowledge, any other official of the Department of Justice during my tenure as Attorney General initiated or suggested the inclusion of restrictions in the presidential commutation of James. R. Hoffa." He also swore that "to my knowledge" Nixon had nothing to do with the restrictions they had so painstakingly placed on Hoffa's freedom.[13]

A newly released tape of a clemency-eve phone call between the president and Colson demonstrates just how badly Fitzsimmons (perhaps partly driven by Hoffa's death threat against him) wanted Hoffa out by Christmas. But the hard-bargaining union boss was also demanding a stipulation that would keep a freed Jimmy from challenging him:

COLSON: First of all, Fitz wants to get Hoffa out because that's the only way that he can keep control of the pro-Hoffa forces within the Teamsters.
NIXON: All right.
COLSON: He is shot down eventually if Hoffa doesn't get out.

NIXON: Right.

COLSON: If Hoffa gets out with no strings attached, he, Fitzsimmons will undoubtedly at some point be in a power struggle and may lose.

NIXON: Right.

COLSON: So he wants him out, but he wants him out with strings. There are two kinds of strings. The one kind and the best would be the parole board which puts obvious conditions upon the parole.

NIXON: Well that's apparently not what we're talking about, though.

COLSON: The second—well.

NIXON: I understand. I understand, isn't that true? They can't, he this, what we're—What Mitchell is talking about is putting it on the Christmas list.

COLSON: Right, that's—To me, that bridge shouldn't even be crossed until Mitchell is satisfied that he can't get him through the parole board process. In other words, there is new evidence, and if Mitchell thought the parole board could do it, then that would be the route I would try. Uh, if Mitchell says he doesn't think the parole board can do it, then you've got another set of circumstances. The strings then would be uh, other things which they have on Hoffa that if he were out, would be charges that would be brought against him if he tried to get back into the Teamster movement.

NIXON: Yeah.

COLSON: Fitzsimmons is very happy with us at the moment that we are trying to work this out in a way that accommodates him. I can, I can make him happy either way. In other words, if you decide not to go, I can make him happy on the grounds that we're protecting him. If you decide to go, I can him make him happy on the grounds that we have other strings on Hoffa. Other than those which the parole board would in the normal course of things would have. Now from the heat from your standpoint, obviously the parole board is preferable.[14]

This key criminal conversation—replete with juicy gangland-style verbiage—ends with Nixon promising to call Mitchell once more to get a full and final green light for the deal. Nixon and Mitchell finally agreed to grant Hoffa clemency on December 8, 1971.[15]

That same day, the president conveyed the happy news to Colson—and directed him to tell Fitz that, as a result of the deal, Mitchell looked forward to doing "everything" Fitz's heart desired. Nixon told Colson that "[Fitz] is to tell Mitchell everything he wants, and that Mitchell will do it. How's that sound?" Colson responded, "Oh, that's perfect . . . I think that will pay enormous dividends."

Neither conspirator in this corrupt arrangement paid any mind to the fact that it is against the law for a president to benefit in any way from a pardon. And Nixon pardoned Hoffa knowing Fitz would reciprocate with cash-filled luggage. Among those "enormous dividends" Colson foresaw were bound to be stacks of crisp Mob-skimmed C-notes secretly delivered to Nixon's coffers or to Bebe Rebozo's "tin box." Teamster biggie Frank Sheeran said he later learned that another $500,000— from Tony Provenzano on behalf of Fitz—was paid to ensure that Hoffa could not run for union office until 1980.

On the eve of Nixon's get-out-of-jail-free card for Hoffa, the president also put in a perfunctory call to J. Edgar Hoover, the nation's top cop, with whom he had obviously failed to consult on the advisability of letting Jimmy walk early. Nixon told Hoover that their common enemy—Robert Kennedy—had persecuted Hoffa (only Nixon's side of the conversation is heard on this newly released tape):

> I decided, after long deliberation, and John Mitchell recommended it—that we ought to let Jimmy out. Well, his wife is terribly sick, ya know, and the guy's been a model prisoner—so I thought, what the heck. . . . Bobby [Kennedy] was on a vendetta against the man.

Hoover apparently voiced no objection to Nixon's generous Christmas gift for Hoffa.

Former governor and future senator Paul Laxalt of Nevada, a longtime close associate of the previously mentioned Allen Dorfman, also had no objections. In fact, he petitioned for Hoffa's release. Laxalt received campaign contributions from Las Vegas gambling interests with alleged links to organized crime. In June 1983, the *Wall Street Journal* reported "an extensive review provides evidence of [Laxalt's] long and continuing associations with men alleged to have unsavory ties."[16] Laxalt was never accused of any personal wrongdoing.

When he was governor, Laxalt had bestowed the honor "special assistant to the governor" on Bebe Rebozo's associate Murray "Moe" Dalitz, who was, according to the retired head of the FBI's Las Vegas office, "a tool of organized crime."[17] Laxalt called the designation "purely PR conferring no authority whatsoever." Laxalt was also closely connected to the ubiquitous Allen Dorfman, who Mafia expert David Scheim says "presided over the drain of Teamster pension funds into Mob enterprises."[18]

In a chummy 1971 letter to "President Dick," Laxalt said

discussions with Dorfman led him to conclude that Bobby Kennedy had a "personal vendetta" against Hoffa, and that "Jim [Hoffa] is a victim of Kennedy's revenge." Describing Hoffa as a "political prisoner," the senator went on to ask Nixon to let him out of prison.[19] Veteran Mafia bigwig Bill Bonanno describes Nixon's clemency for Hoffa as "a gesture, if ever there was one, of the national power [the Mob] once enjoyed."[20]

There were some strings attached to Hoffa's early prison release, due mainly to the concerns of Fitzsimmons. Nixon required that Hoffa agree to never again manage the Teamsters Union. Apparently, New Jersey Teamster leader Anthony Provenzano, known as "Tony Pro," contributed $500,000 to Nixon's campaign in order to secure this requirement against Hoffa. "Tony Pro" was the acting head of the Provenzano family, which controlled the Teamsters New Jersey Local 560 for many years, according to a House panel in 1999.[21] The Provenzanos, who were linked to the Genovese crime family, used Local 560 to carry out a full range of criminal activities, including murder, extortion, loan sharking, kickbacks, hijacking, and gambling.[22]

Exactly how much did the Teamsters and the Mob funnel to Nixon to get Hoffa sprung from Lewisburg—$300,000 dollars? Or perhaps $500,000? Or possibly even $1 million? The exact figure isn't known, but the monetary connection is explicitly clear.

In 1977, a Phoenix newspaper obtained the diary of a Mafia hit man showing that Nixon received a $500,000 payoff. The diary of FBI informant Gerald Denono contains a January 5, 1973, entry that seems to refer to Fitzsimmons, underworld figures Allen Dorfman and Anthony Provenzano, as well to Charles Colson and the president himself. The *Arizona Republic* reported that entry as saying: "Fitz OK. Al Dorfman Chi OK.

Tony Pro Jersey OK ($500—to C.C. [equals] Nix OK)."[23] Other reports suggest a payoff of $300,000—not $500,000—was made to secure Hoffa's release. And several separate sources put the figure at $1 million.

Among those claiming a $1 million payoff was another Mob hit man, this one named Frank "The Irishman" Sheeran—only one of two non-Italians on U.S. attorney Rudy Giuliani's list of members of "the Commission of La Cosa Nostra." Sheeran said he personally delivered half of that amount, in an uncommonly heavy black suitcase, to Attorney General John Mitchell in the lobby of the Washington Hilton Hotel in May 1971.

In a deathbed confession, made public in 2004, Sheeran said that he and Mitchell chatted comfortably in lobby chairs for a bit before the $500,000 changed hands. He said Mitchell quipped "Nothing comes cheap" when he accepted the payoff money. The mobster added that, at that point he asked Mitchell, "Don't you want to go somewhere and count it?" Mitchell replied, "If I had to count it, they wouldn't have sent you." Sheeran was impressed: "He knew his business, that man."

President Nixon threatened to take Jimmy Hoffa's freedom away if he tried to rekindle his Teamsters career. In a newly transcribed February 23, 1973, Oval Office conversation with Richard Kleindienst, the president issued an unambiguous order to his new attorney general: "I want you to be sure when you get back to your office: Jimmy Hoffa announced that he was going to run for the Detroit Local. I want you to call Hoffa's lawyer or somebody to call his lawyer and tell him that if he does that I will—that you're going to revoke his parole." The president stressed, "You should let him know that he must revoke that, and if not, then his parole is being revoked and he's going to go back to jail, Goddamn it! I'm not going to allow that!"[24] But the attorney general was too savvy to follow Nixon's orders. Apparently not wanting to be personally linked to a threat against such a dangerous individual, Kleindienst talked the president out of this idea by the end of their conversation.

If he ever got word of the president's harsh intention, Jimmy Hoffa totally ignored it. On December 20, 1973, Jimmy even announced that he would fight to recapture the union's presidency in 1976. "There may be a contest. If there is, so what?" A defiant Hoffa predicted a victory over the Nixon-backed Frank Fitzsimmons.[25]

NIXON AND FITZSIMMONS

Midway through Nixon's first term, White House aide Chuck Colson signaled his intention to win re-election endorsements for his boss from Frank Fitzsimmons and other Mafia-affiliated union leaders. On September 14, 1970, Colson wrote a memo to Chief of Staff Bob Haldeman suggesting that the administration take a less punitive attitude toward certain union members with federal legal problems. As Mob expert James Neff later observed of this memo, "If [Colson's] activities had been known in detail by the Watergate Special Prosecutor, Colson's actions might have earned him additional charges of obstruction of Justice."[26]

After ushering Fitzsimmons into his spacious White House office on April 29, 1971, Colson politely listened to a litany of complaints about alleged government harassment of Teamsters officials. As a result, according to Neff, Colson—through White House counsel John Dean—asked the Justice Department to "go easy on some of the administration's most powerful labor union allies who were being charged with corruption."[27]

On June 21, 1971, Nixon himself moved to strengthen White House ties to Fitzsimmons—showing up at a meeting of top Teamsters officials at the Playboy Plaza Hotel in Miami Beach. After a 45-minute closed-door meeting, Nixon press secretary Ron Ziegler emerged to quote the president as telling the assembled union officials: "My door is always open to President Fitzsimmons, and that's the way it should be."[28]

Nixon's visit with the numerous criminals associated with Teamsters leaders got little attention in the news media. But at least one political commentator was outraged by it: *Chicago Sun-Times* columnist D. J. R. Bruckner pointed out that Nixon's audience included "an officer who admitted guilt in faking payments from companies in violation of federal labor laws and one under indictment accused of counterfeiting. Mr. Nixon's insensitivity to the public image he projects by chumming with that kind of company is not new. He had previously opened the White House door to a group of hard-hat union leaders, among whom a couple who had fallen afoul of federal law."[29] Such opinions did not prevent Nixon from keeping his promise to Fitz on the open-door policy. The Teamsters boss was eventually accorded numerous private audiences with the president—in the Oval Office, at the Southern and Western White Houses, and even aboard Air Force One.

A big payoff for Fitzsimmons came in Nixon's appointment of mobbed-up New York labor leader Peter Brennan to be Secretary of Labor. Nixon sent aide Charles Colson to interview Brennan for the job—and to emphasize just how kindly the department should treat the Teamsters chief. Historian Stanley Kutler reports that during the three-hour session, "Colson 'explained' the 'pre-eminent' role of Teamsters Union President Frank Fitzsimmons, implying that 'Fitz' was not to have any trouble."[30]

And that was exactly how things worked out. Nixon (sounding somewhat drunk in this telephone call) and Colson discussed administration-friendly labor leaders feted by Nixon at Blair House on December 12, 1972.

> NIXON: These labor guys. They're all in our corner. We've got them. Old Fitz [Frank Fitzsimmons], for example. I had lots of his people . . . and I mention him to everybody. Hell, they all know.
> COLSON: Yeah.
> NIXON: And Joe T. [Joe Trerotola, director of the eastern conference of Teamsters] and the rest. [Trerotola was "Tony Pro's" top henchman.]
> COLSON: Well.
> NIXON: We're going to have them forever.
> COLSON: Yes, they're great. Oh yeah, we are. No doubt about that. My God, that's one organization that I'm going to see that we control. Fitz and I have already started to clean out. We're going to get rid of [Harold] Gibbons [a top Teamster who was a Democrat].

Gibbons was a McGovern (and Hoffa) supporter who wound up on Nixon's infamous enemies list. Later, in this December 15, 1972, conversation with Colson, Nixon brought up a conversation he had at the labor event with Fitz:

> NIXON: [I asked Fitzsimmons] what happened to Gibbons. He said, "Fuck him, he wasn't with us."
> COLSON: [after big laugh] He's [Fitzsimmons's] dying for me to get in with him now. He wants me in as his counsel so

we can clean 'em all out . . . get rid of all the people we can't trust.[31]

Colson did eventually wind up working for Fitz as the union's $100,000-a-year legal representative.

Nixon, of course, already knew that Fitz was in his corner. This was made crystal clear in a May 5, 1971, Oval Office conversation Nixon had with aide Bob Haldeman. They were discussing the possibility of using some of Fitz's thugs to physically assault antiwar demonstrators. When the president observed that Fitz "had guys who'll go in and knock their heads off," Haldeman quickly agreed: "Sure. Murderers!"

HOFFA'S MURDER

Just before his death, in his biggest confession of all, Teamsters hit man Frank Sheeran said he murdered Jimmy Hoffa—with two pistol shots to the back of the head—on orders from Russell Buffalino, a Mafia biggie with close ties to Tony Provenzano.[32]

Provenzano was a short, stocky, handsome man with huge hands. He was listed by law enforcement agencies as a member of the Vito Genovese crime family, which a New Jersey State Police report described as "primary suspects in Hoffa's disappearance." *The Mafia Encyclopedia* is even more emphatic about Tony's involvement in Hoffa's death:

According to the FBI reconstruction of the Hoffa murder, Tony Pro called the so-called peace parlay with Hoffa and then ordered him killed. Provenzano denied even being in

Detroit at the time, and seemed to go out of his way to seal an airtight alibi.

Indeed, Tony Pro was seen by several people at his New Jersey home on the day Jimmy vanished.[33] But other reports indicate he was in the Detroit area when Hoffa was hit.

Provenzano's enemies were frequent subjects of threats, beatings—and in two cases, even murder. In 1961, a rival was beaten and garroted by Mob executioners led by the infamous ex-fighter Harold "Kayo" Konigsberg. In 1963, another Provenzano enemy was shot to death in Hoboken, New Jersey.[34]

A little more history: Back in 1971, the parole board had just refused Jimmy Hoffa's third request for an early release, and Fitz had just fired Hoffa's wife and son from their cushy Teamsters jobs. In revenge, Jimmy planned to write a book charging Fitz with "selling out to mobsters" and giving low- or no-interest loans from Teamsters pension funds to Mob-related businesses.[35]

One of Jimmy's pals in the pen, former Teamsters official Sam Berger, later explained that Hoffa had turned "vicious" and was "walking around like an animal . . ." Another Hoffa pal at Lewisburg, a huge and intimidating Mob hit man named Charlie Allen, served as Jimmy's bodyguard. It was in prison that Allen was recruited by Hoffa to kill Frank Fitzsimmons. Allen, who would go on to become a protected government witness, agreed to assist Hoffa in a plot to execute Fitz and allow Jimmy to retake control of the union.[36] However, in 1982, Allen sold out his former protectee and testified under oath to a Senate committee that Hoffa's plan called for him to ambush Fitzsimmons in the underground garage of Teamsters headquarters on Capitol Hill.

He was to spring out of hiding and shoot Fitz to death. "I was supposed to kill Frank Fitzsimmons," Allen told the lawmakers. "Yes sir, right here in Washington."[37]

The professional assassin swore that Mafia leaders got wind of this plot and had Jimmy bumped off before he could carry out Hoffa's own deadly edict. Allen quoted Tony Provenzano as later telling him, "Jimmy was killed, ground up into little pieces, shipped to Florida and dumped in a swamp." In his testimony, Allen seemed to infer that Hoffa also wanted Tony Pro murdered. Under oath, he admitted carrying out a multitude of dirty deeds for the Mob—including murder, drug dealing, extortion, hijacking, and assault.[38]

In a 1985 interview with the *Richmond Times Dispatch*, Allen flatly stated that Provenzano arranged for Hoffa's murder. He told the newspaper that Hoffa was shot with an electric stun gun, and that his body was then ground up at an iron works, stuffed into a steel drum, and transported to a swamp in the Florida Everglades for disposal.[39]

Among others who have speculated on just how Hoffa was killed, Hoffa biographer Dan Moldea has weighed in with a slightly different story:

> In the first act, Hoffa drives from his home and arrives at the restaurant expecting to meet two underworld figures. He's picked up by one, perhaps two close associates, driven to a private residence four minutes away from the restaurant where he is ambushed and killed. His body is then stuffed into a 55-gallon drum and taken to a location where it is placed in a compactor for junk cars and he is crushed and he is smelted. Hoffa's body will never be found."[40]

In another instance, Moldea quotes a source as telling him, "Hoffa is now a goddamn hub cap."[41] A captain in New York's Bonanno crime family, Bill Bonanno has his own version of how Hoffa was eliminated—but he agrees with most experts that Jimmy's remains are long gone:

> Hoffa was abducted and a devastating and exotic poison called curare was shoved down his throat. The poison perfectly feigns a heart attack and it was explained to me that it was untraceable. Afterward, if the body is not quickly attended to, decomposition rapidly follows. Hoffa's unrecognizable remains were left in the car that was used to abduct him. The car, in turn, was put in a compacting machine; Jimmy Hoffa, so the story goes, is part of someone's front fender today.

Of all the Hoffa theories, the main commonality is the gruesome form of post-death disposal. One popular theory about Jimmy Hoffa's disappearance is contained in a 1978 book by Hoffa biographer Steven Brill—who quotes an FBI memo as saying that three of Provenzano's associates had kidnapped Hoffa, put him in a garbage shredder and cremated the remains in an incinerator."[42] Then there is the recollection of Florida godfather Santos Trafficante, as relayed by Mob lawyer, Frank Ragano:

> In our final conversation Santo specified that Fitzsimmons was terrified that Jimmy had marked him for death. He said Fitzsimmons inspired Provenzano to carry out the hit on Jimmy. Fitzsimmons virtually confirmed the same scenario when I saw him in his office at the Marble Palace [Teamsters

headquarters in Washington] six months after Jimmy's disappearance. He called Jimmy an ungrateful double-dealer
who was "crazy and nutty" and had tried to kill his son.
Fitz admitted, in effect, that in self-defense he wanted Jimmy
eliminated.[43]

Not only was Fitzsimmons scheming against Hoffa, he was
also letting the Mob have its way with the Teamsters pension
fund. "Jimmy Hoffa could say no to the Mob on a loan," explained Ragano, "whereas Fitzsimmons did not have the courage or the nerve to do so. So they were a lot more comfortable
with Fitzsimmons. They didn't want Jimmy back."

And Chris Ragano, Frank's son, explained the Mob's reason
for murdering Jimmy: Hoffa was apparently planning to squeal
to the feds on his Mafia pals. "Jimmy was going to be a whistleblower. And he was really a man who was just obsessed with
telling all. He was an egomaniac."

Chris Ragano said his dad once told him why Hoffa's body
would never be found: that a rule among Sicilian gangsters required that the victim's family be hurt financially. The Hoffas
were not able to collect benefits until Jimmy was formally declared dead. That did not occur until 1982.[44]

A 1975 FBI report concluded Hoffa's disappearance was "directly connected with his attempts to regain power within the
Teamsters union, which would possibly have an effect on [Mafia]
control and manipulation of the Teamster Pension Fund."[45]

After Hoffa's disappearance, New Jersey State Police and FBI
agent Jim Sweeny tracked down Tony Provenzano at a diner in
Hasbrouck Heights, New Jersey. Tony Pro told Sweeny he had
"nothing to gain" from the disappearance and that Jimmy was
a close friend. "He's my type of man . . . aggressive and hard-

working."[46] But this was a lie. Hoffa and Tony Pro had become mortal enemies while they were at what was dubbed by the Mob as "Mafia Manor," Lewisburg Federal Penitentiary. In 1969, the bad blood boiled over when Hoffa made a smart-aleck remark to Tony. Provenzano "lunged at Hoffa, and the two went at it, hurling threats at one another that they were going to kill the other's family. Tensions only ramped up when the equally ferocious pair hit the streets again in the 1970's. A peace conference at a Miami hotel arranged by Frank Fitzsimmons and a chance run-in inside a lounge at JFK airport both turned physical and resulted in more threats, this time involving massacring each other's grandkids."[47]

Organized crime expert Lester Velie wrote of the airport clash: "Hoffa and Provenzano went at it with their fists, and Hoffa broke a bottle over Provenzano's head." Tony vowed to retaliate against Hoffa's grandchildren—adding, "I'll tear your heart out."[48]

Hoffa, Provenzano, and Fitzsimmons are merely numbers on a long list of murderous figures Richard Nixon courted, nurtured, and favored during his long political career. The true depth of his shadowy ties to the Mafia is only now becoming fully known and understood as historians, researchers, journalists, and others uncover fresh evidence of the corrupt tentacles that bound our criminally minded thirty-seventh president to a secret organization that used murder as a cornerstone of its huge illegal domain.

MOB FAVORS

Nixon's generosity toward top Mob and Teamsters officials was truly remarkable: To cite just a few more examples:

During Nixon's vice presidency, his good friend and the number-two man at the Justice Department, William Rogers, declined to prosecute Meyer Lansky for tax evasion. Nixon and Rogers had made frequent vacation trips together to the Bahamas and Key Biscayne, Florida.[49]

In 1956, Vice President Nixon fixed a deportation case against Marco "The Little Guy" Reginelli, a notorious Pennsylvania gangster and client of Nixon aide Murray Chotiner. "Chotiner quietly met with several Justice Department officials, including [close Nixon chum] William Rogers [President Nixon's first secretary of state], then an assistant attorney general, who helped reverse the deportation ruling and allowed Reginelli to remain in the country."[50]

As vice president, he reportedly took a bribe of $5,000 from mobbed-up Washington lobbyist/fixer Irv Davidson. The cash—from the dictator of the Dominican Republic, Anotonio Somoza—was, according to Davidson, handed by Davidson to Nixon, who said in response, "My fingers are sticky."[51]

From 1969 through 1973, more than half of the Justice Department's 1,600 indictments in organized crime cases were tossed out because of "improper procedures" followed by Attorney General John Mitchell in obtaining court-approved authorization for wiretaps.

Shortly before the midterm elections of 1970, Nixon issued this order to his attorney general: "Mitchell—no prosecutions whatever re Mafia or any Italians until after Nov."[52]

Under Mitchell, in 1970, a federal judge reduced the two-year prison term of Mafia godfather Carols Marcello to only six months at a medical facility.[53]

Shortly after his 1972 re-election, President Nixon gave

unconditional pardons to three men associated with a shady accounting firm. The men had been convicted of distributing false financial statements and mail fraud.

A few months after trouncing Senator George McGovern in 1972, Nixon secretly entertained Teamsters chief Frank Fitzsimmons in a private room at the White House. Attorney General Richard Kleindienst was summoned to the session "and ordered by Nixon to review all the Teamsters investigations at the Justice Department and to make certain that Fitzsimmons and his cronies weren't hurt by the probes."[54]

Nixon appointed Fitz to a prestigious seat on the Wage Board.

In April 1973, the *New York Times* disclosed that FBI wiretaps had uncovered a massive scheme to establish a national health plan for the Teamsters—with pension fund members and top mobsters playing crucial roles . . . and getting lucrative kickbacks. Yet Kleindienst rejected the FBI's plan to continue taps related to the scheme. The chief schemers included Fitzsimmons and Teamsters pension fund consultant Allen Dorfman.

During Nixon's administration, the Treasury Department declared a moratorium on $1.3 million in back taxes owed by former Teamsters president Dave Beck.

In December 1972, President Nixon pardoned Angelo "Gyp" DeCarlo, a Genovese crime family captain cited by the FBI as a "methodical gangland executioner."[55] FBI informants say DeCarlo's release was arranged by Mafioso Frank Sinatra and was followed by an "unrecorded contribution" of $100,000 in cash and another contribution of $50,000 forwarded by Sinatra to a Nixon campaign official.[56]

In May 1973, the *Oakland Tribune* reported that Nixon

aide Murray Chotiner had interceded in a federal probe of Teamsters involvement in a major Beverly Hills real estate scandal. As a result, the investigation ended with the indictment of only three men. One of the three—Leonard Bursten, a former director of the shady Miami National Bank and a close friend of Jimmy Hoffa—had his 15-year prison sentence reduced to probation.

In June 1973, ex-Nixon aide John Dean revealed to the Senate Watergate Committee that Cal Kovens—a leading Florida Teamsters official—had won an early release from federal prison in 1972 through the efforts of Nixon aide Charles Colson, Bebe Rebozo, and former Florida senator George Smathers. Shortly after his release, Kovens contributed $50,000 to Nixon's re-election effort.[57]

John Dean later disclosed that, during Watergate, when "I was first placed in the witness protection program, a Justice Department official told me that they were in fear for my life. They were afraid the president's friend Bebe Rebozo would arrange to have me encased in concrete and buried . . . off the Bahamas."[58] (Dean later told me he has no hard facts that Rebozo had either an inclination or ability to order Mafia hits.)

In the same vein, Pentagon Papers whistleblower Daniel Ellsberg now reveals that Watergate prosecutors told him that, in May 1972, "a dozen CIA assets from the Bay of Pigs, Cuban émigrés, were brought up from Miami with orders to 'incapacitate me totally. . . . These guys never use the word kill.' "[59]

As Nixon was contemplating his resignation in 1974, a special army investigative unit found "strong indications of a history of Nixon's connections with organized crime."

The president's suspicious chief of staff, Alexander Haig, had ordered the secret probe.[60]

As Nixon was about to leave office, a Justice Department official told investigative reporter Dan Moldea, "The whole goddamn thing is too frightening to think about. . . . We're talking about the President of the United States . . . a man who pardoned organized crime figures after millions were spent by the government putting them away."[61]

By contrast, the Kennedy administration's war on organized crime was highly effective: indictments against mobsters rose from zero to 683; and the number of defendants convicted went from zero to 619.[62]

After Nixon left office in August 1974 to avoid being impeached by Congress for the criminal activities he supervised and concealed in the Watergate scandal, he spent more than a year brooding in self-exile at his walled estate in San Clemente, California. The very first post-resignation invitation the disgraced ex-president accepted was from his Teamsters buddies. On October 9, 1975, he played golf at a California resort with President Frank Fitzsimmons and other top union officials. Among those who attended a postgame party for Nixon were Tony Provenzano, Allen Dorfman, and the union's executive secretary, Murray "Dusty" Miller.[63] Mob authority David Scheim would later opine, "Nixon's involvement with men of Provenzano's and Dorfman's background drives home an important axiom. The Mafia's millions are extracted by murder. And its bribes are bathed in blood."[64]

Tony Pro would later die in prison a convicted killer. The top Mob-Teamster financial coordinator, Dorfman, was later murdered gangland style. Dusty Miller was the man, records show, that Jack Ruby had telephoned several days before Ruby murdered Lee Harvey Oswald.

There is even compelling evidence that now suggests Nixon knew deep secrets about the Syndicate's suspected hit on his archrival, President John F. Kennedy. This is bolstered by numerous historical clues—and by fresh evidence from declassified government documents and tape recordings, which will be fully explored in the coming chapters.

SEVEN

The Most Violent Man in the Oval Office

The assassination of a despised political rival seems within the realm of possibility for Richard Nixon, the most violent man to occupy the Oval Office. That prospect increases dramatically now that we know Nixon was behind what one political commentator described as the most "wicked action in American history"—the sabotage of the 1968 Vietnam peace talks to help cement his anticipated win in that fall's election.[1] If candidate Nixon could commit what President Lyndon Johnson termed "treason," and then go on to allow an additional 20,000 American soldier deaths on his White House watch, it should not be a big stretch to imagine that he could also consider the killing of his most despised political enemy.

At the least, Nixon could well have had insider's knowledge of what really happened in the streets of Dallas on that dreadful day of November 22, 1963; information he kept from officials investigating the brutal Kennedy assassination—and information that likely would have given the American people closure in a time of great uncertainty. Did he know, for example, that Mafia bosses probably had a hand in Kennedy's killing—as a 1970s House investigation concluded? After all, Nixon and the Syndicate had been trading favors since his first run for office in 1946. A wink and a nod from Nixon to a Mafia boss who wanted to kill JFK anyway might have certified Washington's approval (even though Nixon was not a government official at the time) of the hit.

At an August 22, 1973, presidential press conference—at the height of the Watergate Summer—in defending his use of surveillance in national security matters, Nixon himself strongly hinted there was Mob involvement in the assassination:

> I shall also point out that when you ladies and gentlemen indicate your great interest in wiretaps, and I understand that, that the height of the wiretaps was when Robert Kennedy was Attorney General in 1963. I don't criticize it, however. He had over 250 in 1963, and of course, the average in the Eisenhower Administration and the Nixon Administration is about 110. But if he [RFK] had had 10 more and, as a result of wiretaps, had been able to discover the Oswald plan, it would have been worth it.

In an apparent effort to tar the Kennedy brothers by sickly suggesting Bobby may have been responsible for Jack's murder, Nixon was also indicating that there had been a conspiracy to kill JFK. For if there was indeed an "Oswald Plan" discussed on tapped phones, that would certainly suggest that more people than just Oswald were involved. As many Mob and government

officials knew back then—chief among them Richard Nixon—
Attorney General Bobby Kennedy's major wiretap targets were
Mafia bosses.

Furthermore, assassinations were a tactic of choice for Nixon,
as he considered or authorized an incredible number during his
years in high office. He gave thumbs-up to murder plots against
Cuban leader Fidel Castro (as well as left-leaning Cuban exile
leaders in the United States), Greek shipping tycoon Aristotle
Onassis, Panamanian presidents A. J. Ramon and Omar Torri-
jos, and Chilean president Salvador Allende.

Vice President Spiro Agnew said he feared President Nixon
might have him killed if he didn't resign the office over corruption charges. An obstinate South Vietnamese president Nguyen
Van Thieu was shaken to the core by a diplomatic letter from
Nixon containing a not-so-subtle threat on Thieu's life. In addition, President Nixon vigorously rejected attempts to cut back
on funds for "Operation Phoenix," in which small U.S.-led assassination teams killed up to 40,000 Vietnamese civilians. "We've
got to have more of this! Assassinations! Killings! That's what
they're [the other side's] doing," Nixon ranted.[2]

Nixon's violent tendencies did not end with his love of assassinations. In addition, his love of violence was not always so
obvious; often it festered in his personality and his actions in
more insidious and deceitful ways. It was only divulged in recent
years that Nixon sabotaged the trials of American soldiers involved in the My Lai massacre so that none would be convicted
of war crimes. At My Lai, some 500 unarmed South Vietnamese
civilians, including women (who were first raped) and children,
were slaughtered by out-of-control U.S. troops.

Even more damning, Nixon appears to have often threatened his political rivals, both in government and in the media.

Pentagon Papers whistleblower Daniel Ellsberg recently revealed that Watergate prosecutors warned him about plans by a group of thugs from Miami to "eliminate" him in DC.

Now, a personal anecdote: On the Sunday morning following the early Saturday morning Watergate burglary, my good friend Tom Girard, a press officer for the Committee to Re-elect the President and a trustworthy young man who knew right from wrong, gave me a great tip. A distraught Tom revealed that James McCord, Committee for the Reelection of the President's (CREEP) security director, was among the five Nixon burglars arrested on the morning of June 17, 1972 (much too late for Saturday's papers).

Tom was in DC while I was in Key Biscayne covering the president. Girard's phone call to me came at 8 a.m., just after he had read the early Sunday edition of the *Washington Post*, which contained mug shots of the five Watergate arrestees. But Tom said that the guy ID'd in the paper as "Edward Martin" was, in reality, James McCord.

Tom feared for his life too and swore me to lifelong secrecy, which I honored. He died about ten years ago. His leak, plus a little checking, enabled me to quickly air a 45-second radio spot linking the Nixon campaign to the burglary. It was the first (and only) time I ever beat Bob Woodward and Carl Bernstein on a big Watergate story, but at least my luck in knowing Tom gave me my forty-five seconds of fame, and UPI Audio beat the competition by hours. As a result of the original story, we were also the first to broadcast CREEP chairman John Mitchell's official denial of such a link.

Threats against Tom Girard were not the only ones delivered to journalists due to the Watergate scandal. Woodward and Bernstein were alerted by their secret FBI source Mark Felt (aka "Deep Throat") that their lives (and that of their *Washington Post* editor, Ben Bradlee) were in danger. Understandably, there were also threats against whistleblower McCord and his family.[2]

During Watergate, Nixon is strongly suspected of ordering the killing of American journalist Jack Anderson. Nixon operative E. Howard Hunt certainly had that impression, according to Anderson biographer Mark Feldstein:

> [H]unt told me . . . he believed that [Nixon aide Charles] Colson was acting at the behest of the president himself. . . . I find it very difficult to believe that Colson and the other aides were acting without the implicit support of President Nixon. It defies logic to imagine that they would cook this up, the assassination of a journalist as prominent as Jack Anderson, unless they had the signal from above to do it.[3]

Colson always denied knowing anything about the plot— which was canceled at the last moment. Nixon aide G. Gordon Liddy admits that, if directed to do so, he was ready to carry out Anderson's assassination by slitting the journalist's throat and making his death look like an ordinary DC street crime. Liddy said he was even prepared to murder his Watergate cohort E. Howard Hunt—should such an order come—when both were serving Watergate sentences in the same prison.

All this evidence begs the question: did President Nixon also know something about the Mafia hit on ex-Teamsters boss Jimmy Hoffa? During the Carter administration, a Detroit Grand Jury investigating the Hoffa case sought the ex-president's testimony—and that of Hoffa's successor, Frank Fitzsimmons, only to have the idea rejected by the Justice Department. One excuse made was that Fitz was acting as an informer for the FBI.

A thorough analysis of all the newest information about both Nixon and the JFK assassination raises serious questions about Nixon's many connections to the most infamous crime of the twentieth century.

EIGHT

The JFK Assassination and the Warren Commission

At about 12:30 p.m., Central Standard Time, on November 22, 1963, in Dallas's downtown Dealey Plaza, a large and Kennedy-friendly crowd lined the street, cheering and waving excitedly at the approaching presidential motorcade. Riding in the third car—an oversized Lincoln with the Plexiglas "bubble" top removed—were President John F. Kennedy and his wife Jackie, along with Texas governor John Connally and his wife Nellie.

Almost everyone alive knows what happened next. The president of the United States was assassinated. But today, nearly 55 years after that fact, the details on specifically how John F. Kennedy was killed, and by whom, are still open to question.

According to the report of the Warren Commission, released in September 1964 after a full year investigation, one single shooter—Lee Harvey Oswald—shot Kennedy to death and wounded Governor Connally by firing three bullets from the sixth floor of the Texas School Book Depository.

The most significant documentary record of President

Kennedy's assassination, however, is the famous 8mm home movie taken that day by Dallas dress manufacturer Abraham Zapruder. It seems to show Kennedy reeling from shots fired from more than one location. The film's apparent crossfire causes one to conclude that there were several gunmen—and a conspiracy. The number of shots, reportedly heard by witnesses, ranges from two to more than eight.[1]

The most important eyewitness to the assassination was Governor John Connally. Questioned by Arlen Specter, a future U.S. senator from Pennsylvania, Connally's testimony to the Warren Commission solidly supports the Zapruder film:

MR. SPECTER: "In your view, which bullet caused the injury to your chest, Governor Connally?"

GOVERNOR CONNALLY: "The second one."

MR. SPECTER: "And what is your reason for that conclusion, sir?"

GOVERNOR CONNALLY: "Well, in my judgment, it just couldn't conceivably have been the first one because I heard the sound of the shot . . . and after I heard that shot, I had the time to turn to my right, and start to turn to my left before I felt anything. It is not conceivable to me that I could have been hit by the first bullet."[2]

Governor Connally's vivid account of those horrific moments never changed. And they fit a more-than-three-bullet scenario. Connally firmly believed different bullets struck him and President Kennedy.

In a later interview for a TV program, Connally recalled hearing a rifle shot over his right shoulder "because that's where the sound came from." He said he saw "nothing out of the ordinary" when he looked that way and was in the process of turning to look over his left shoulder "when I felt a blow in the middle of my back as if someone had hit me with a double-fist . . . it bent me over and I immediately saw I was covered with blood and I knew I'd been hit, and I said, 'Oh my God, they're going to kill us all.' " Connally then heard another shot and said, "I knew that the President had been fatally hit, because I heard Mrs. Kennedy then, I heard her say, 'My God, I've got his brains in my hands.' "[3]

Connally's insistence that he was struck by a separate bullet from the one that first struck President Kennedy clearly contradicts the Warren Commission's lone-killer conclusion that a single bullet hit both men. The commission asserts that Oswald shot Kennedy to death and wounded Connally by firing three bullets from a sniper's nest in his Dealey Plaza workplace with an old Italian-made mail-order rifle.

The cheap, prone-to-malfunction Mannlicher-Carcano was found on the sixth floor of the book depository building and was originally identified as a 7.65mm German Mauser. Before the Italian rifle could be test-fired by military investigators, some repairs had to be made: The telescopic sight had been rebuilt and then remounted for a left-handed shooter (Oswald was right-handed), and other deficiencies corrected. The weapon, then nearly twenty years old, had a terrible reputation. The October 1964 issue of *Mechanix Illustrated* described it as "crudely made, poorly designed, dangerous and inaccurate."

The commission said the first shot struck the president in the base of his neck and exited from his throat. This very same bullet, it said, proceeded to hit Connally in the back—shattering his fifth rib. The bullet then emerged from the governor's chest, passed through his right wrist—breaking several bones—and finally came to rest in his left thigh. This is known as the "magic bullet"—because it inflicted so many wounds, broke so many bones, and even took an implausible sharp turn in the air, and yet still wound up in nearly perfect condition on a stretcher at Parkland Memorial Hospital.

The Warren Commission uncovered "no credible evidence that any shots were fired from the Triple Underpass [near the grassy knoll] ahead of the motorcade, or from any other location." This determination was intended to support the scenario that Oswald could have fired the purported number of shots within an allotted time frame—and that one of the bullets fired that fateful day hit both men. Despite this public assertion, assassination expert Anthony Summers, in his book *Not in Your Lifetime*, emphasizes that most of the commission's seven members had private doubts about the theory:

> John McCloy had difficulty accepting it. Congressman Hale Boggs had "strong doubts." Senator John Sherman Cooper was, he told me [Summers] in 1978, "unconvinced." On a recently released tape, held at the Lyndon B. Johnson Library, [Senator Richard] Russell is heard telling President Johnson, "I don't believe it." And Johnson responds, "I don't either."

And it now turns out that the commission's chief public supporter of the solitary shooter scenario—Republican congressman Gerald Ford—also harbored serious skepticism about the single-bullet theory. As noted, Pulitzer Prize–winning reporter Pat Sloyan is the unimpeachable source for this news. He covered the Warren Commission for UPI and had his own "Deep Throat" on the panel—Jerry Ford, who regularly fed him key details of the commission's top-secret deliberations.

Ford's doubt was supported by Boggs, Russell, and Cooper, enough to vote down the single-bullet theory if it came to that. Ford's leak (to Sloyan about the possibility of a dissenting opinion) might have been designed to rally other commission members against the single-bullet theory. In any event, Warren settled for language of uncertainty. "Persuasive evidence from the experts" was cited along with an acknowledgment of a "difference of opinion" as to the journey of (the single bullet) through two men, 15 layers of clothing, seven layers of skin, and 15 inches of tissue.

Ford confided to Sloyan that Warren was outraged by Pat's story about the potential for a less-than-unanimous verdict. Ford said Warren took Sloyan's story from his briefcase and brandished it before the six other commission members at a closed-door session. Ford said the chairman then demanded, "Who is doing this?" The reporter later asked Ford what he did when Warren shouted his angry question: "I just lit my pipe and looked around the room," the congressman replied.[4]

Many other Warren Commission conclusions do not match some of the evidence it collected. As Facts on File points out, "Of the 266 known witnesses to the assassination, the commission questioned 126. Of these, 51 thought the shots came from the direction of the grassy knoll, 32 said that they came from the Texas School Book Depository. Thirty-eight did not offer an opinion, but most of these witnesses were not asked. The remaining five thought the shots came from more than one location."[5]

Those who thought the shots came from the grassy knoll seem to be supported by NBC cameraman Dave Weigman's herky-jerky 16mm film of the assassination scene. With his camera rolling, Weigman jumped out of the seventh car in the JFK motorcade and ran up to the knoll. Experts who made a frame-by-frame examination of his film say it clearly shows puffs of smoke coming from bushes at the top of the knoll.

Dallas County deputy constable Seymour Weitzman also ran toward the top of the knoll—where he found a man carrying Secret Service identification. Weitzman later identified this man as Bernard Barker, a veteran CIA agent who, in 1972, would lead the four-man contingent of Watergate burglars from the Miami area. Barker was as a close associate of Florida Mafia godfather Santos Trafficante—and of Mob-connected Key Biscayne banker Bebe Rebozo, Richard Nixon's longtime bosom buddy. Bernard Barker's day job was as a real estate agent on Key Biscayne. He was a close friend and neighbor of fellow CIA agent Eugenio Martinez, the Watergate burglar.. Martinez's real estate firm had extensive dealings with Rebozo, and he had brokered Nixon's purchase of a home on Key Biscayne. Along with JFK assassination suspects E. Howard Hunt, Frank Sturgis, and David Ferrie, Barker had helped plan the unsuccessful 1961 CIA-sponsored invasion of Cuba, a mission fathered, as we have seen, by Vice President Nixon.

Barker would have had no difficulty obtaining Secret Service credentials; CIA operatives have a way of coming up with badges and other items to suit their various goals (as a Nixon White House spy, Howard Hunt once wore a CIA-provided speech alteration device and a red wig to a secret encounter), and this lends weight to the statement of Seymour Weitzman, who placed him at the scene. In fact, all the Watergate burglars carried fraudulent IDs. It was not generally known in 1972, but Barker had been fired from the CIA in 1966 because of his Mafia connections.

Barker was not the only future Watergate conspirator to reportedly show up in Dallas on November 22, 1963. Under oath in a 1985 trial, CIA operative Marita Lorenz placed CIA agents

Hunt and Sturgis at the assassination scene. Of course, Richard Nixon himself was also in Dallas that fateful day. With the placement of all of these figures in Dallas on the day Kennedy was shot, it becomes more difficult to believe it could all be a coincidence. In fact, it points in strong circumstantial ways toward a conspiracy.

In the years following the Warren Commission Report, its findings have been repeatedly questioned. In 1979, the House Select Committee on Assassinations suggested that at least two gunmen were involved, and that the probable conspirators were Mafia-connected. In 1998, a presidential review board found nothing in secret JFK assassination records to bolster the single-bullet theory. In fact, as the Assassination Records Review Board went out of business, it complained that records of the postmortem examination of President Kennedy's body were incomplete. Information contained could have cleared up mysteries about Kennedy's head wound, or wounds, and helped determine whether he was shot from the front or, as the Warren Commission claims, the rear.

In its final report, the review board said, "There have been shortcomings that have led many to question not only the completeness of the autopsy records of President Kennedy, but the lack of a prompt and complete analysis of the records by the Warren Commission." While it collected and released millions of pages of previously secret government records, the board also expressed worry that "critical records may have been withheld" from its scrutiny. The panel stressed that it was not able to secure "all that was out there."[6] (The law requires that all currently withheld documents be declassified and made public in October 2017—as long as the president at that time concurs.)

The ARRB determined that unnecessary government secrecy

about the assassination "eroded confidence in the truthfulness of federal agencies in general and damaged their credibility." At the same time, board member Anna Nelson responded to claims that national security necessitated the secrecy: "Releasing documents of 35 years ago has caused no diminution of our intelligence ability, our foreign policy or anything else. The sky has not fallen."[7]

In 2005, appearing at a scholarly symposium, assassination expert Dr. Jack Gordon went over doctors' statements from the hospital in Dallas where President Kennedy was taken after the shooting. Gordon produced quotes from nine doctors who gave the same description of a huge softball size hole in the occipital-parietal region of Kennedy's skull, and one nurse who said, "in layman's terms, 'One large hole, back of his head.' " This contradicts the official story that the back of the head was completely intact.

With all of these contradictions emerging—both during the Warren Commission hearings and in the aftermath of its final report—one has to wonder how the Warren Commission managed to arrive at the conclusions it did. A critical eleventh-hour edit certainly helped. The commission's first draft report said, "A bullet had entered [President Kennedy's] back at a point slightly below the shoulder to the right of the spine." Had that stood, the trajectory would have made it impossible for the bullet that struck Kennedy to come out his neck, and then somehow critically wound Connally.

As we have seen, documents released decades later, however, show that Warren Commission member Gerald Ford changed the panel's description of the wound and placed it higher in Kennedy's body. Crucially, Ford wanted the wording altered to: "A bullet had entered the back of his neck slightly to the right of the spine." The final compromise version said: "A bullet had entered the base of the back of his neck slightly to the right of the spine." (In actuality, the back wound was a full six inches below the collar—not anywhere near the back of the neck, or even the base of the back of the neck.)

When the alteration was brought to Ford's attention in 1997, he said it "had nothing to do with [thwarting] a conspiracy theory" and was made "only in an attempt to be more precise." But assassination researcher Robert Morningstar called the change "the most significant lie in the whole Warren Commission report." He pointed out that if the bullet had hit Kennedy in the back, it could not have gone on to strike Connally the way the commission said it did. Morningstar contended that the effect of Ford's editing suggested that a bullet hit the president in the neck— "raising the wound two or three inches. Without that alteration, they could never have hoodwinked the public as to the true number of assassins."[8]

Ford's edit supports the single-bullet theory by making a specific point that the bullet entered Kennedy's body "at the back of his neck" rather than in his uppermost back, as the commission staff originally wrote. Harold Weisberg, a longtime critic of the Warren Commission's work, said, "What Ford is doing is trying to make the single bullet theory more tenable." (And, as we now know, Ford did it despite having grave misgivings about the single-bullet theory.)

Even with the changes Ford made, however, Cyril Wecht, president of the American Academy of Forensic Sciences, finds the magic-bullet theory totally unacceptable:

The angles at which these two men were hit do not permit a straight-line trajectory (or near straight line trajectory) of commission exhibit 339 (the so-called magic bullet) to be established. Indeed, quite the opposite is true. In order to accept the single-bullet theory, it is necessary to have the bullet move at different vertical and horizontal angles, a path of flight that has never been experienced or suggested for any bullet known to mankind.[9]

Throughout most of his long life, Gerald Ford—at least publicly—stuck solidly by the single-bullet theory and the Warren Report's finding that Oswald was President Kennedy's sole assassin. In the December of his life, however, Ford radically changed his tune. He acknowledged in a little-noticed foreword to a new edition of the Warren Report, published in 2007, that the CIA's decision not to tell the commission about the plots to kill Castro "did interfere marginally with our investigation." Then the former president unloaded a bombshell: because the commission's investigation "put certain classified and potentially embarrassing operations in danger of being exposed," the CIA's "reaction was to hide or destroy some information, which can easily be misinterpreted as collusion in JFK's assassination."[10]

Death-car passenger Nellie Connally, the Texas governor's wife, rediscovered her assassination diary in 1993. When *Newsweek* published it in 1998, the magazine said the diary "reaffirms the Connallys' verdict that the Warren Commission was wrong in concluding that a single bullet passed through JFK's neck and Connally's chest." Noting the commission's finding that one bullet missed the car, the magazine added: "Some conspiracy theorists argue that if three [author's note: the commission said only two bullets hit the two men] bullets hit their targets, and an additional bullet missed, then there must have been a second gunman: nobody could have fired so many rounds so quickly."[11]

House investigators concluded in 1979 that President Kennedy's murder was "probably . . . the result of a conspiracy," and that there was a strong possibility of a shot from the grassy knoll—meaning that two gunmen must have fired at the president within split seconds of each other.[12] While a special panel of the National Academy of Sciences later disputed the committee's finding, in 2001, a peer-reviewed article in *Science and Justice* determined there was a 96.3 percent chance a shot was fired from the grassy knoll to the right of the president's limousine.[13] The author of the new analysis, JFK assassination researcher D. B. Thomas, believes this was the shot that killed the president.

G. Robert Blakey, former chief counsel of the House probe, called the new study "an honest, careful scientific examination of everything we did, with all the appropriate statistical checks." And he said it "increased the degree of confidence that the shot from the grassy knoll was real, not static [contained on a police dictabelt of the sounds in Dealey Plaza that day]."[14] In 1979, Blakey's committee described the FBI's probe of the assassination as "seriously flawed" and "insufficient to have uncovered a conspiracy."

The House panel's own investigation showed that the probable plot to kill the president likely involved the Mafia and certain anti-Castro groups. Later, Blakey flatly concluded that organized crime bosses orchestrated the JFK assassination. He identified the key conspirators as Mob godfathers Carlos Marcello, Santos Trafficante, and Sam Giancana—as well as Teamsters Union president (and known Nixon associate) Jimmy Hoffa. Early in this century, Blakey was astonished to learn that the official who served as his committee's chief CIA go-between compromised its work. That particular spook, George Joannides (a.k.a. Walter Newby), violated the CIA's pledge that no operational officer from the time of the JFK assassination would work with House investigators.

Yet newly declassified documents show that, in 1963, Joannides was involved with a CIA-funded Cuban exile group known as the DRE, which had various interactions with Lee Harvey Oswald—Kennedy's alleged assassin. This disclosure was so upsetting to Blakey that, in 2003, he blasted his own committee's finding that there was no CIA relationship with Oswald. He also bellowed, "I now no longer believe anything the Agency told the committee any further than I can obtain substantial corroboration for it from outside the Agency for its veracity."

In addition, Blakey publicly accused the spy agency of failing to cooperate with the Warren Commission's 1964 investigation into Kennedy's slaying:

We now know that the Agency withheld from the Warren Commission the CIA-Mafia plots to kill [Cuban leader Fidel] Castro. Had the commission known of the plots, it would have followed a different path in its investigation. The Agency unilaterally deprived the commission of a chance to obtain the full truth, which will now never be known.

Significantly, the Warren Commission's conclusion that the agencies of the government cooperated with it is, in retrospect, not the truth. We also can be sure that the agency set up a process that could only have been designed to frustrate the ability of the committee in 1976–79 to obtain any information that might adversely affect the agency.

Many have told me that the culture of the agency is one of prevarication and dissimulation and that you cannot trust it or its people. Period. End of story. I am now in that camp.

George Joannides died in 1990, without ever having been quizzed about his knowledge of Oswald's contacts with the CIA-dependent DRE he supervised.

Washington journalist Jefferson Morley has a pending lawsuit against the CIA seeking the release of its records about Joannides. But the CIA maintains their release would harm "national security." In his latest legal filing, Morley explains why the agency's Joannides files are so important:

> Joannides's duties (in 1963), according to my declaration and declassified CIA records, included guiding and monitoring an anti-Castro student exile group which was harshly critical of JFK's Cuba policy.
>
> The group made headlines within hours of JFK's murder by denouncing accused assassin Lee Harvey Oswald as a Castro supporter. The Warren Commission was not told of Joannides's involvement with the group.
>
> Fifteen years later, Joannides served as the agency's liaison to the congressional committee re-investigating JFK's assassination. Congress was not told of Joannides's actions in 1963.

Morley is not the only JFK assassination researcher who has called on the CIA to come clean on Joannides. A group of two-dozen experts of differing opinions about JFK's murder has urged the CIA to stop its "stonewalling" on the Joannides files. This group described the spy agency's position as "spurious and untenable."

In a 2005 letter published by the *New York Times Review of Books*, these experts maintained that "[the CIA's] continuing non-compliance with the JFK Records Act does no service to the public. It defies the will of Congress. It obscures the public record on a subject of enduring national interest. It encourages conspiracy mongering. And it undermines public confidence in the intelligence community at a time when collective security requires the opposite."

The group—which includes Blakey, filmmaker Oliver Stone, and Vincent Bugliosi—added: "We insist the CIA observe the spirit of the 1992 JFK Assassination Records Act by immediately releasing all relevant records on the activities of George Joannides and any records at all that include his name or are related in any way to the assassination story—as prescribed by the JFK Records Act. The law and common sense require it." In fact, the Chairman of the Assassination Records Review Board, federal judge John Tunheim, bluntly opines that the Joannides case now "shows that the CIA wasn't interested in the truth about the assassination."

John McAdams, a seasoned expert on the JFK assassination, says George Joannides is an important new character in this decades-old saga. He says fresh proof shows Joannides was an agent of the Special Affairs Staff in Miami in 1963. McAdams adds, "The bulk of the available evidence indicates that Joannides in late 1963 was running a psychological warfare operation designed to link Lee Harvey Oswald to the Castro government without disclosing the CIA's hand."

It's important to ask: What motivation did Congressman Gerald Ford have for altering critical assassination data? For starters, he had strong personal ties to two staunch advocates of the lone assassin theory, one being Richard Nixon, the man responsible for Ford's placement on the Warren Commission. In the assassination's aftermath, when President Lyndon Johnson asked Nixon, as the titular head of the Republican Party, to pick a party representative for a seat on the Warren Commission, the future president chose Ford. It didn't hurt that Nixon chose a man who would do his bidding; Ford did not need much arm-twisting to encourage and support the lone-gunman assassination theory—an explanation that would keep hidden Nixon's close ties to the Mafia, Bebe Rebozo, Howard Hunt, Howard Hughes, and Jimmy Hoffa, as well as top Mob and CIA killers. This would certainly help take the heat off Nixon's pals.

Ford's other connection with a vested interest in the Warren Commission findings was FBI director J. Edgar Hoover, who had proclaimed Oswald was the lone killer long before the panel had even been appointed. Late on the afternoon of November 22, 1963, Richard Nixon phoned the FBI boss, getting directly through to Hoover with no trouble. Though Nixon's word on anything is suspect, he later remembered asking Hoover: "What happened? Was it one of the right-wing nuts?" Nixon said Hoover responded, "No, it was a Communist."[15]

While Oswald would not be formally charged with murdering President Kennedy until early the next morning, Hoover issued an internal memo that same afternoon stating that Dallas police "very probably" had Kennedy's killer in custody. In the memo, Hoover described Oswald as being "in the category of a nut and the extremist pro-Castro crowd . . . an extreme radical of the left."[16] In retrospect, Hoover may have wanted Oswald deemed the sole killer to protect himself. Some JFK assassination experts are convinced Hoover knew about the plot in advance and helped cover it up. In his 1992 book *Act of Treason*, researcher Mark North contends that—as the result of covert FBI surveillance programs against the Mafia—Hoover learned of the sordid plot in September 1962. North claims that Hoover found out that "the Marcello family . . . had, in order to prevent its own destruction [through prosecutorial pressure resulting from the administration's war on organized crime], put out a contract on the life of John F. Kennedy . . . Hoover did not inform his superiors within the Justice Department, or warn the Secret Service . . . [Hoover] did this because JFK had made it known that he intended . . . to retire the director . . ."

Former CIA operative Robert Morrow agreed that Hoover had learned in advance of both the contract on JFK and the ensuing plot to assassinate him. In a 1992 book, Morrow said the contract "called for the assassination of the president prior to November 4, 1964 [author's note: the date of the next presidential election], and was clearly the directive of New Orleans crime boss Carlos Marcello."

In a tantalizing but undocumented footnote, Morrow said: "It was from his good friend Hoover that Richard Nixon learned of the pending assassination."

Nixon's acolyte, Congressman Gerald Ford, was so close to Hoover that he served as the FBI director's informant while he was on the Warren Commission. This is confirmed by an internal FBI memo of December 12, 1963. Written to Hoover by his deputy Cartha DeLoach, it says, "Ford indicated he would keep me thoroughly advised as to the activities of the commission. He stated that would have to be done on a confidential basis, however, he thought it had to be done."[17] Hoover biographer Curt Gentry concurs that Ford was Hoover's inside man on the commission. In fact, in his 1991 book *J. Edgar Hoover*, Gentry notes that the Hoover-Ford connection went back a number of years. Discussing the FBI's "favored politicians," the author said these people "were warned who their opponents would be, what background they had, and what skeletons might be hidden in their closets. In some cases, they were even elected with the FBI's help. Impressed with a young congressional hopeful in Michigan, the bureau in 1946 arranged support for Gerald Ford, who then expressed his thanks in his maiden speech in the House by asking for a pay raise for J. Edgar Hoover."

If Ford was leaking to Hoover, he was likely sharing the commission's deliberations with his patron, Richard Nixon, as well. Or perhaps he did not need to, because Nixon was even closer to Hoover than Ford was. As president, Nixon was caught boasting by one of his hidden microphones that he had seen Hoover socially "at least a hundred times. He and I were very close friends . . . [expletive deleted]—Hoover was my crony. He was closer to me than [Lyndon] Johnson actually, although Johnson used him more."[18] The Nixon-Hoover relationship began in the mid-1940s, during Nixon's early years in Congress. William Sullivan, a former top Hoover aide, recalled spending "many days preparing material based on research taken from FBI files that I knew was going straight from Hoover to Congressman Nixon, material which Nixon used in speeches, articles and investigations."[19]

Both Nixon and Gerald Ford rushed to endorse the Warren Commission's finding that Oswald was solely to blame for Kennedy's murder. In a piece for *Reader's Digest* in November 1964, Nixon asserted: "On April 19, 1959, I met for the first and only time the man who was to be the major foreign policy issue of the 1960 presidential campaign; who was destined to be a hero in the warped mind of Lee Harvey Oswald, President Kennedy's assassin; and who in 1964 is still a major campaign issue. The man, of course, was Fidel Castro."

In the October 2, 1964, issue of *Life*, Congressman Ford also portrayed Oswald as the lone assassin. He stressed a theme similar to Nixon's—that the "sorely disturbed" Oswald's "faith in

Communism and the writings of Karl Marx" made him "look to Cuba as the place where . . . his shadowy philosophical theories might possibly come to fruit." Nixon and Hoover's man on the commission declared, "[T]here is not a scintilla of credible evidence" to suggest a conspiracy to kill JFK:

> The evidence is clear and overwhelming: Lee Harvey Oswald did it. There is no evidence of a second man, of other shots, of other guns. There is no evidence to suggest that Oswald went to work at the Depository for the long-range purpose of killing the President, that Jack Ruby knew Oswald before he killed him, or that either of them knew Officer Tippit.[20]

Why did these two future presidents think it was necessary to declare their belief in Oswald's guilt just before publication of the commission's report? Were they acting in league with their friends at the CIA and the FBI to give advance backing to what they knew would be the report's lone-killer conclusion? In later years, both Nixon and Ford made statements that seemed to be at odds with their initial conclusions that Lee Harvey Oswald was alone responsible for President Kennedy's murder.

Another critical moment in the assassination saga—also underreported—occurred when former president Gerald Ford, on his deathbed, stated that the CIA kept critical assassination secrets from the public. As touched on earlier, in 2005, Ford said the commission's probe put some secret CIA operation in danger of being exposed, so the agency hid or destroyed some information. Ford's claim of an ostensibly inadvertent CIA cover-up is accompanied by a fresh concession by him: that there "conceivably" could have been a conspiracy to kill Kennedy—but that "no verified evidence to date shows a link to, or any direct involvement by any government agency, federal employees or subversive groups."[21]

Now there's a very carefully worded statement for you. Particularly the use of qualifiers "verified," "to date," and "direct." The former president also conveniently omitted Mafia leaders from his comments. At the time, Ford's words were verified to your author by Ford family spokeswoman Penny Circle—who had arranged the publication of Ford's final assassination statement. Ford died late in 2006 at the age of 93.

FBI director J. Edgar Hoover also helped promote the Warren commission's lone-shooter conclusion. And he did so two days before the commission was even formed. He personally ordered a leak to United Press International that resulted in a national wire story that began: "WASHINGTON—An exhaustive FBI report now nearly ready for the White House will indicate that Lee Harvey Oswald was the lone and unaided assassin of President Kennedy, government sources said today."[22]

NINE

Nixon and Ford

The Nixon-Ford relationship proved useful to both men in later years as well. When Nixon was president, Ford served as his top congressional agent in a failed effort to impeach liberal Supreme Court justice William O. Douglas. At Nixon's direction, Ford later succeeded in stopping the first congressional Watergate probe. And in the summer of 1973, as the heavy pressures of Watergate forced President Nixon to start thinking aloud about an eventual resignation, he might very well have realized that if he someday needed a pardon from his successor to keep him out of a federal penitentiary, he would do better with his friend, Gerald Ford, serving as his vice president than he would with Spiro Agnew. As a result, Nixon paved the way for his man Jerry Ford's likely ascension to the presidency by secretly greasing the skids for Spiro Agnew—who later contended that White House pressure for his resignation included what Agnew took as a death threat.

Back in 1968, presidential candidate Nixon had praised

Agnew—his surprise pick for a running mate (reputedly as a Nixon payoff to the generals who ran Greece)—for his "tremendous brain power, great courage and unprejudiced legal mind. He has vigor and imagination and, above all, he acts." Privately, however, Nixon thought Agnew was a political bungler. In fact, in the view of Nixon's national security adviser Henry Kissinger, Nixon, "always sensitive to being overshadowed," may well have twice picked Agnew to be his vice president for that very reason. Kissinger disclosed that the president had a rather dark take on the real reason he chose the little-known Maryland governor: "[Nixon] never considered Agnew up to succeeding him. He once said, only partly facetiously, that Agnew was his insurance policy against assassination."[1]

Shortly after the Nixon-Agnew ticket won re-election in 1972, Nixon told top aides Bob Haldeman and John Ehrlichman that Agnew wanted the 1976 GOP nomination, "but we will not help him." Ehrlichman quotes Nixon as saying, "By any criteria he falls short. Energy? He doesn't work hard. He likes to play golf. Leadership? (Nixon laughs) Consistency? He's all over the place. He's not really a conservative, you know." When Haldeman suggests that what Agnew might need is the president's "benign neglect," the president declares: "Yes, that should be our strategy."[2]

That strategy changed radically on June 27, 1973. That's when Attorney General Elliot Richardson told White House Chief of Staff Alexander Haig that Agnew was under investigation for tax evasion, bribery, and extortion. While Nixon henceforth posed in public as taking a hands-off policy toward his vice president's legal problems, he was actually a big behind-the-scenes advocate of Agnew's resignation. And he made sure two of his top aides—Haig and lawyer Fred Buzhardt—were involved in the negotiations over Agnew's fate. In a book about Agnew, reporters Jules Witcover and Richard Cohen quote an aide to Richardson as saying the White House negotiators "wanted the guy out of there. They wanted resignation without anything. They just wanted him out."[3]

On October 10, 1973, Agnew resigned in disgrace in order to stay out of jail. He pleaded no contest to cheating on his income taxes. Haig is said to have later bragged that "arranging that cop-out was one of the greatest feats of bureaucratic skill in the history of the art."[4]

In his book *Go Quietly . . . Or Else*, Agnew stated that in early October Haig had made a threat "that made me fear for my life." He said the threat came at a meeting between Haig and the vice president's military aide, General Mike Dunn. According to a Dunn memo about the meeting, Haig said that if Agnew admitted guilt on the tax charge, "there would be no economic worry for debts and defense . . . no further trouble with the Federal government and no jail sentence."[5]

The Dunn memo also quotes Haig as warning that "anything may be in the offing" once an indictment is handed down. "It can and will get nasty and dirty. Don't think that the game cannot be played from [the White House] . . . The President has a lot of power—and don't forget that." Agnew said Haig's words "sent a chill through my body. I interpreted it as an innuendo that anything could happen to me; I might have a convenient 'accident.'" He said he had been close enough to the presidency to know the "tremendous power" it could exert:

I knew that men in the White House, professing to speak for the president, could order the CIA to carry out missions that were very unhealthy for people who considered enemies.

Since the revelations have come out about the CIA's attempts to assassinate Fidel Castro and other foreign leaders, I realize even more than before that I might have been in great danger. . . . This directive was aimed at me like a gun at my head. That is the only way I can describe it. I was told, "Go quietly or else."

Agnew pointed out that, if a decision were made to "eliminate him—through an automobile accident, a fake suicide, or whatever—the order would not have been traced back to the White House any more than the 'get Castro' orders were ever traced to their source." The vice president decided to go quietly.

About one year after Nixon's own resignation, Agnew got a telephone call from the former president. But he refused to take it. Agnew later explained that Nixon had snubbed him up until then, and he thought Nixon's call "was a little late."[6]

In a bizarre postscript, Agnew—much to the dismay of the Nixon family—inexplicably showed up, uninvited, at Nixon's 1994 funeral in Yorba Linda, California.

Congressman Gerald Ford was rewarded for his many years of service to Nixon by being picked to replace the disgraced Agnew as vice president. And then later, as president, Ford returned the favor when he gave Nixon a pardon that kept Nixon well-heeled and out of jail for all of his long post-resignation life.

The 1974 pardon shows Nixon at his secretive, behind-the-scenes, manipulative best. And it is certainly instructive in demonstrating just how much influence he exerted over Ford.

There's no question that Ford paid an enormous political price for his action. The highly unpopular pardon helped make his presidency a national joke. After nearly losing the 1976 Republican presidential nomination to Ronald Reagan, Ford stumbled onto a general election defeat at the hands of Jimmy Carter, who promised—in sharp contrast to Nixon's behavior—never to lie to the American people. But how much courage did it really take for Ford to bail out his biggest political benefactor, especially when Nixon resorted to heavy-handed pressure—including a reported blackmail threat? The idea for the pardon—even its possible wording—originated with Nixon, not Ford; and the president broached the subject to his hand-picked vice president even before he quit the White House.

A little pardon history should make that, as Nixon used to say, "perfectly clear": Eager to avoid the risk of winding up in jail, on August 1, 1974, Nixon dispatched his chief of staff, Alexander Haig, to the veep's office.[7] Ford was told Nixon would probably step down soon, and was asked whether he was ready to assume the presidency. Haig then raised questions about whether Nixon should pardon himself before resigning, whether others should be pardoned at the same time—or whether Nixon should be given a pardon by Ford if he resigned. Ford has allowed that Haig specifically suggested, "Nixon could agree to leave in return for an agreement that the new president, Gerald Ford, would pardon him."[8] Ford aide Robert Hartmann reported that, after discussing the matter with his wife, the vice president made a post-midnight phone call to Haig, saying, "They should do whatever they decided to do; it was alright with me."[9] Ford insists Haig initiated the call, and he claims he told the presidential aide, "We can't get involved in the White House decision-making."[10]

In *Shadow*, star Watergate reporter Bob Woodward reveals Haig also used the August 1 meeting to deliver to Ford two sheets of yellow legal paper that had been prepared by Nixon Watergate lawyer Fred Buzhardt. "The first sheet contained a handwritten summary of a president's legal authority to pardon. The second was a draft pardon form that only needed Ford's signature and Nixon's name to make it legal."[11]

Over the years, several top Nixon aides have weighed in on the Haig-Ford discussions. Bryce Harlow found it "inconceivable" that Haig was not, indeed, carrying out a mission for Nixon. Charles Colson concluded that Haig had "negotiated" with Ford over the pardon.[12] John Ehrlichman said, "I'd bet that Jerry Ford promised to pardon Richard Nixon, and that the promise was made before Nixon's resignation."[13] Nixon aide Alexander Butterfield declared that Ford would gladly do such a favor for his political angel: "Nixon had Ford totally under his thumb. He was a tool of the Nixon administration—like a puppy dog. They used him when they had to—wind him up and he'd go 'Arf, Arf.' "[14] Hartmann is convinced that Haig reported to Nixon on his pre-resignation talks with Ford, and that "Nixon believed he had a deal." And investigative reporters Clark Mollenhoff[15] and Seymour Hersh[16] have made compelling cases that Nixon and Ford secretly reached an agreement before Nixon stepped down on August 9, 1974.

Hersh even claims that, on September 7, an angry Nixon telephoned his successor threatening to disclose their arrangement unless Ford issued a speedy pardon. Nixon's message was blunt, according to those few White House aides who knew of the private call: if Ford did not grant him a full pardon, he, Nixon, would go public and claim that Ford had promised the pardon in exchange for the presidency, because Ford was so eager to get it. During this same period, Ford got a memo from Nixon counsel Len Garment saying the ex-president's mental and physical condition could not withstand the continued threat of criminal prosecution. The memo implied that, unless he was pardoned,

Nixon might kill himself. The memo was accompanied by a draft pardon statement for the new president.[17]

On September 8, only one month after Nixon had resigned in disgrace, Ford jolted the nation by pardoning his predecessor, thereby writing his own political obituary. Yet he proved his worth to Nixon, granting him preemptive clemency for all presidential crimes he might have committed. Ford also agreed to a Nixon-inspired deal giving the former president ultimate control over all his White House papers and tapes. And the new president asked Congress to give Nixon $800,000 in transitional expenses.

An outraged Congress could do nothing about the pardon. But it did move quickly to block the Ford-Nixon tape accord, and it slashed Ford's request for the transition funds to $200,000.

The pardon got Nixon off the hook on a host of criminal activities he led and/or covered up. Watergate crimes alone ranged from burglary to campaign sabotage, espionage, and illegal fundraising. They extended to efforts to exploit, subvert, or pervert the Justice and State Departments, the CIA, the IRS, the FBI, and the Secret Service. They also included a wide variety of other assaults on the U.S. Constitution, and on many of the rules of democratic fair play.

And then there is the pièce de résistance—the final irony. In 2001, the John F. Kennedy Library Foundation bestowed its "Profile in Courage" award on Gerald Ford for pardoning his corrupt predecessor—and the greatest Kennedy-hater the world has ever known. The foundation said Ford met the annual award's test of being "an elected official who followed his conscience despite the political cost."

In his final public words, former president Gerald R. Ford said the CIA destroyed or kept from investigators critical secrets connected to the 1963 assassination of President John F. Kennedy. The stunning admission by a key member of the Warren Commission is contained in the foreword to a new edition of the commission's report. Ford died in late 2006 at the age of 93.

Shortly after the book was published, Ford family spokeswoman Penny Circle confirmed to this author that the late president approved every word in the foreword, and even autographed 3,000 copies of the book. A joint venture between Ford and publisher Tim Miller of Nashville, the book is titled, *A Presidential Legacy and the Warren Commission*. Circle said she acted as an intermediary between the two men, who never met.

FBI memos released in recent years show that Gerald Ford served as FBI director J. Edgar Hoover's informant on the commission. Hoover, of course, had proclaimed Oswald the lone killer long before the panel had even been appointed. Was it at Hoover's behest that Ford made a crucial change in the Warren Commission's final report—a change that made the Oswald-did-it, single-shooter theory easier to believe? Ford, we now know, revised the description of the bullet wound in President Kennedy's back and placed it higher to make the "magic-bullet" theory more plausible, enabling the commission to conclude that Oswald was the lone gunman.

In a press release promoting the "final word" of President Ford, the book's publisher, Tim Miller, goes even further than the ex-president:

> There was a conspiracy to kill John F. Kennedy. There is no doubt that President Gerald Ford knew more about the JFK death. There is no doubt President Clinton knows more. Has

he or any other U.S. president since November 22, 1963 ever
swore under oath that they know no more?

But Penny Circle, the Ford spokeswoman, thinks Miller has gone
way overboard in some of his promotional comments:

> Miller's press release stating that he worked closely with Pres-
> ident Ford and edited as they went along is preposterous.
> Also, his statement that he believes "Ford and others knew
> more about the assassination" is nuts . . .

It seems Circle has adequate reason to contend with some
of Miller's questionable statements. On his website (which he says
gets an amazing 600,000 "hits" a year), Miller gives rave reviews to his own Ford-foreworded book: *Time* is ecstatic, saying, "Should become one of the best-thumbed books since the
Bible," while *Newsweek* raves, "The pages crackle with the
electricity of human feeling." When called on this, Miller explains he got the blurbs from 1964 issues of these magazines.
They were apparently clipped from reviews of the original Warren
Report.

When he made a prepublication appearance on G. Gordon
Liddy's radio show, Miller said of Ford, "I am privileged to have
known him." Yet, both he and Circle acknowledge the two men
never set eyes on each other. (Miller offered Liddy's listeners
$200 off the highest-priced version of the book in honor of the
disgraced Watergate burglary leader.)

Both Miller and Circle did not say exactly how Ford managed
to "write" his final words. Nor do they say just how this project
came about. Some might question why Ford would entrust such
an important piece of history to a stranger. Reliable sources say

Miller paid Ford a substantial sum for his final words on the assassination, and for his signatures on all those books.

But just how did an end-stage senior manage to autograph 3,000 copies of Miller's edition of the Warren Report?

Jerry Ford's good friend Tom De Frank met with the thirty-eighth president a number of times near the end of Ford's life. Ford had suffered a stroke in 2000, and he told De Frank in 2002 that he hadn't seen him for a long time—when they had, indeed, recently spent 90 minutes together at Ford's Rancho Mirage, California, home. According to De Frank, the former president had "dramatically exhibited a clear sign of slippage [in memory]."

Ford experienced frequent fainting spells in 2004—as byproducts of his stroke.

That same year, De Frank observed that Ford "looked awful . . . one of the Ford alumni remarked he appeared positively cadaverous." In January 2005, Ford tripped on a carpet and slammed headfirst into a door. He was out of commission for weeks.

In 2005, De Frank found that Ford's "stamina was waning, his speech halting, his ability to read diminishing. He could function normally for a half hour or so, then had to rest." In February 2006, De Frank reports that Ford "labored" with the inscription on an autograph. "It may have been the last autograph he ever signed."

So the question remains: How did this feeble senior citizen write his take on the Warren Commission and sign 3,000 copies of the book?

Others may someday solve that mystery of just how Ford's final words came to be written, but let's look at the bigger question here: Just how far did Ford stray from his once solid commitment to the anti-conspiracy, lone-killer position? A long way, it seems.

De Frank says Ford never had any doubts about the Warren Commission's conclusions. In a 1992 interview, the ex-president told the reporter, "I signed the report. I've never changed my opinion. I feel as strongly today, Tom, on the two basic fundamental issues. Number one, Lee Harvey Oswald was the assassin. Number two, the commission found no evidence of conspiracy, foreign or domestic."

In 2003, according to De Frank, Ford told historian Douglas Brinkley, "I am a total devoted person to the [commission's] conclusions. But 75 percent of the people don't believe the Warren Commission anymore. It just makes me sad and unhappy." De Frank was a longtime White House correspondent for *Newsweek* magazine and then ran the Washington bureau of the New York *Daily News* for many years.[18]

Ford's big change of mind has gone mostly unnoticed among JFK assassination researchers, but at least a couple of experts have weighed in on the subject.

Veteran Washington investigative reporter Dan Moldea—an authority on the Mafia's ties to the JFK murder—declares, "Had the Warren Commission known about the CIA-Mafia plots to kill Castro, a new avenue of investigation would have been created. CIA Director Allen Dulles, a commission member who had intimate knowledge of these plots, chose to engage in a cover-up, which doomed this investigation from the outset. The Mafia murdered an American President and got away with it."[19]

Debra Conway runs JFK Lancer, a leading pro-conspiracy assassination research group and website. Her take on Ford's final words: "If he admits to having doubts about the honesty of the CIA—and that he knows they withheld and destroyed evidence that may have affected their investigation—it takes the worth out of his previous statements . . ." Conway also provides an astute guess as to what might have been on Ford's mind when he made his deathbed confession: "It sort of takes the Warren Commission off the hook, if [the commission] can claim plausible deniability due to the CIA."[20]

TEN

Nixon and J. Edgar Hoover

Like Richard Nixon, J. Edgar Hoover was in the hip pocket of America's godfathers. For this simple reason, the FBI director put the Mafia on a low level of his crime-fighting priorities. That is until 1961, when John and Robert Kennedy put potent muscle behind the government's drive against organized crime—and Hoover reluctantly began paying more than just lip service to battling the Mob.

During Kennedy's administration, his brother and attorney general, Robert Kennedy, became a menace to the Mafia—and his take-no-prisoners tactics trickled down not only to Hoover but also to top local and state cops, district attorneys, and judges. Of course, this angered the dons of La Cosa Nostra—who had played a key role in John Kennedy's ascent to the White House. Organized crime felt betrayed by the Kennedys and their extreme change in behavior in regards to the mob.

Because he was a major bootlegger during Prohibition,

Kennedy family patriarch Joseph Kennedy rubbed elbows, and shared handsome illegal profits, with some of the nation's most notorious mobsters. Old Joe turned to some of these same men in 1960, when his son, Senator John Kennedy, faced Vice President Richard Nixon for the presidency. There was evidence of massive voter fraud by mobsters in Illinois and Texas. Those states threw the election to JFK.

Due to these favors, the Mafia was now looking for major quid pro quo, or at least leniency, from the Kennedys. But, under Bobby, by 1964 the Justice Department had increased Cosa Nostra convictions by 700 percent over 1960.[1] The crusading attorney general had federal agents arrest New Orleans godfather Carlos Marcello and physically deport him to Guatemala. And RFK initiated the process that landed mobbed-up Teamsters boss Jimmy Hoffa in a prison cell. As historian Anthony Summers notes, "If top Mafia bosses felt double-crossed, their law—the law of the Mob—might demand vengeance."[2] Thus did angry Mafia chieftains and Hoffa conclude that one or both of the Kennedy brothers had to be killed. Early on, Hoffa threatened to break Bobby Kennedy's back. But he later said President Kennedy would make a better target for death because "when you cut down the tree, the branches fall with it."[3]

In 1994, Hoffa's longtime lawyer, Frank Ragano, confessed that he had carried a 1963 message from Hoffa to New Orleans godfather Carlos Marcello and Florida godfather Santos Trafficante that Hoffa "wants you to get rid of the President right away." Significantly, Ragano added that Trafficante, on his deathbed in 1987, confessed that he and Marcello had, indeed, followed through on Hoffa's demand.[4]

How had such plotting escaped the attention of FBI chief Hoover? Apparently, it hadn't. In September 1972, America's top cop had already learned through electronic surveillance that Marcello "had put out a contract on the life of President Kennedy . . . Hoover did not inform his superiors within the Justice Department or warn the Secret Service," according to Hoover biographer Mark North.[5] Hoover's hand was firmly on the pulse of these organized crime proceedings, but he suspiciously did nothing with his knowledge.

If that weren't enough evidence of the godfathers' bloody intentions, Jose Aleman—a rich Cuban exile and an associate of Trafficante's—had tipped off two FBI agents that the Florida godfather had confided to him that President Kennedy was "going to be hit" before the 1964 election.

Whether J. Edgar Hoover had advance indications of an underworld plan to assassinate the president, he certainly knew about Lee Harvey Oswald before November 22, 1963. Yet he did nothing to keep Kennedy's alleged sole assassin from going to his job in a building overlooking the presidential motorcade route on that fateful day in Dallas. Hoover and his G-men had actually been keeping their eyes on Oswald since 1959, when the young ex-Marine defected to the Soviet Union. When the alleged defector returned to this country in 1962, several CIA divisions tracked his movements and regularly reported on this "possible security risk" to the FBI.

Lo and behold, however, it turns out that Oswald—upon his return—had become a paid FBI informant, according to author Burton Hersh:

Apart from the claim by former FBI security clerk William Walter that he processed documents to that effect, there was the revelation in chambers by Texas Attorney General Waggoner Carr and Henry Wade, the Dallas district attorney [to top Warren Commission officials] that Oswald had been on the FBI payroll for $200-a-month since September of 1962 with the informant number S-172.

The Hoover biographer adds that FBI "counterintelligence veterans have since confirmed Oswald's FBI employment." He notes that when Oswald was arrested for disturbing the peace in New Orleans in the summer of 1963, he demanded and was granted the right to see an FBI agent per the Warren Commission, Volume XXVII, Exhibit 2718, which was an FBI report dated April 6, 1964. Former BBC correspondent Anthony Summers later discovered a Dallas garage manager, Adrian Alba, who witnessed Oswald accepting a "good-sized . . . white envelope" from a G-man in a green FBI-owned Studebaker he serviced.[6] Oswald spent only one night in jail in New Orleans until a representative of none other than crime boss Carlos Marcello bailed him out.

As the chief investigator of the JFK assassination, Hoover failed to adequately probe many other ties between Oswald and Marcello, including these: Oswald buddy David Ferrie was a pilot for Marcello's drug-trafficking operations; Oswald's uncle and father figure Charles "Dutz" Murret was a major bookmaker for Marcello's gambling network; Oswald himself was a "runner" and "collector" for Marcello's gambling operation; and Oswald's mother, Marguerite, dated several members of Marcello's gang.

Why did Hoover ignore Marcello and other Mafia godfathers as suspects in his investigation of the JFK assassination? And why did he overlook even tighter connections between the Mob kingpins and Jack Ruby—the Dallas strip club owner who shot Oswald to death two days after the president's murder?

Like his favorite politician, Richard Nixon, J. Edgar Hoover was under the Mob's thumb. In the 1950s, the nation's top cop turned a blind eye toward the country's godfathers—even though Senate hearings chaired by Tennessee Democrat Estes Kefauver established proof of the existence of a rich, powerful, and murderous nationwide crime syndicate. Historian Mel Ayton says Hoover's early inattention to the Mob allowed it to expand and restructure:

> After the nationally televised Kefauver hearings, Hoover still insisted that there was no such thing as the Mafia, and as a consequence, there was a period of consolidation of the criminal organization, and a period of growth for Mafia "families" in every major city across the United States.[7]

Ayton, however, does not believe widespread rumors that Hoover laid off the Syndicate because Meyer Lansky had photos of Hoover and his top aide, Clyde Tolson, in a compromising sexual position. Ayton brands such evidence "flimsy" and quotes Hoover defender Richard Hack as saying, "It didn't matter that there were Mafia out there. [Unlike Hoover's Communist foes, they] were not going to bring the government down, they were just making money illegally and there were lots of cops to take care of that."

But could there be any grain of truth to the notion that the Mob was blackmailing Hoover over his reported gay relationship with his right-hand man at the bureau? Perhaps. Especially in light of the disclosure by highly respected investigative journalist Anthony Summers that Meyer Lansky had indeed obtained compromising photos of Hoover and Tolson. Summers quotes former Lansky associate Seymour Pollock as saying in 1990 that Hoover's homosexuality was "common knowledge" and that he had seen evidence of it for himself:

I used to meet (Hoover) at the racetrack every once in a while with lover boy Clyde, in the late forties and fifties. I was in the next box once. And when you see two guys holding hands, well come on! . . . They were surreptitious, but there was no question about it.

Top CIA counterintelligence official James Angleton reportedly possessed similar photos, and once showed them to CIA electronics expert Gordon Novel—who later exposed just what the photos revealed:

What I saw was a picture of [Hoover] giving Clyde Tolson a blowjob. There was more than one shot, but the startling one was a close shot of Hoover's head. He was totally recognizable. You could not see the face of the man he was with, but Angleton said it was Tolson. I asked him if they were fakes, but he said they were real, that they'd been taken with a fish-eye lens. They looked authentic to me . . .

Novel said Angleton displayed the pictures to him in 1967 and told him they were taken in 1946, at a time when the CIA biggie was engaged in a bureaucratic feud with Hoover.[8]

Adding to the sexuality theory: these two bachelors were inseparable for 40 years. They drove to work and ate lunch together every day (on the owner's tab at Harvey's in the Mayflower Hotel) and frequented racetracks (where reputed Mob tips on horses in fixed races enhanced their love of the Sport of Kings). The pair often wore matching suits, rejected the attention of women, and incessantly took photos of each other.[9]

Hoover willed his home and most of his estate to Tolson. And when Tolson died, he was buried just a few yards from

Hoover in DC's Congressional Cemetery. Being gay, of course, is not shameful in and of itself. Yet, if Hoover and Tolson were secret lovers, the FBI director's relentless hounding of homosexuals in government, and elsewhere, would make him a hyper-hypocrite.

The FBI boss was particularly active in hunting down homosexuals in the Johnson administration—and, after a bust by DC vice cops, he found that a top Johnson aide, Walter Jenkins, was caught performing oral sex on a stranger in the men's room of a YMCA near the White House. As a private citizen at the time— yet a "chronic campaigner," as LBJ once labeled him—Richard Nixon jumped on the incident. He stressed that Jenkins "was ill. But people with this type of illness cannot be in places of high trust."[10]

The Jenkins episode had little bearing on the outcome of the 1964 presidential campaign, mainly because President Johnson's GOP opponent, Barry Goldwater—a clean political fighter—to his great credit, refused to bring it up. It probably would not have changed the results anyway. LBJ won by a landslide.

For such a frequently crude man, Lyndon Johnson had a whimsical sense of humor—and being aware of Hoover's reputed homosexuality, the president seemed to be pulling Hoover's leg during a post–Jenkins Scandal phone conversation:

LBJ: Yeah, he worked for me for four or five years, but he wasn't even suspicious to me. I guess you're going to have to teach me something about this stuff. . . . I swear I can't recognize [homosexuals]. I don't know anything about them.
HOOVER: It's a thing that you can't tell sometimes. Just like in the case of the poor fellow Jenkins. . . . There are some people who walk kind of funny. That you might think [they're]

a little bit off, or maybe queer. But there was no indication of that in the Jenkins case.

While a number of biographers speculate that homosexual-hunter Hoover was a secret homosexual (and a cross-dresser with the pseudonym "Mary" according to one witness), there are just as many who doubt such rumors. Yet Richard Nixon was not a doubter. In fact, when the president was told of Hoover's 1972 death, he exclaimed: "Jesus Christ! That old cocksucker!"[11]

Two days later, however, at the FBI director's funeral, Nixon portrayed Hoover as a towering figure of morality and a selfless public servant: "One of the giants," Nixon declared, who "personified integrity, he personified honor, he personified principle, he personified courage, he personified discipline, he personified dedication, he personified loyalty, he personified patriotism."[12]

As Hoover's body lay in state in the Capitol Rotunda, a gaggle of Nixon's Bay of Pigs thugs up from Miami—egged on by G. Gordon Liddy—caused a minor ruckus at an antiwar rally on the National Mall. The demonstration drew a crowd of about 500, and Daniel Ellsberg was a main speaker.

Bebe Rebozo's friend and a future Watergate burglar, the mobbed-up Bernard Barker, interrupted Ellsberg's speech, shouting that he was a "traitor" and a "disgrace to the Jewish race." Future Watergate felon (and mobster) Frank Sturgis sucker-punched one demonstrator in the crotch, and broke another's clipboard in half. But the greatly outnumbered Nixon gang failed to disrupt the rally or harm Ellsberg. As Ellsberg biographer Tom Wells recounts: "The Cubans tried to break through a line of marshals at the stage to get to Ellsberg. But despite a good deal of pushing and shoving, they could not get their hands on their quarry."[13]

Liddy had promised to give the president the Viet Cong flag he imagined the protestors would be flying on the day of Hoover's funeral. But that part of the operation failed too: there was no such flag to be snagged. Ellsberg later asserted that he "faced assassination" in 1972 from the Nixon White House.[14] Liddy—who did plot to murder newspaper columnist Jack Anderson—eventually admitted only to planning to "befuddle" Ellsberg by dosing his soup with LSD.[15]

J. Edgar Hoover and Clyde Tolson may or may not have been blackmail-prone lovers, but they deeply shared one emotion—an avid hatred of Robert Kennedy. Author David Talbot reports that when RFK announced his run for the White House in 1968, Tolson shocked a group of FBI officials by declaring: "I hope that someone shoots and kills the son of a bitch."[16]

In an interview promoting his book about John and Robert Kennedy, Talbot concludes that John F. Kennedy was the victim of a cross fire in a choreographed ambush, and that Hoover conducted a cover-up of the crime. He adds that the conspiracy was not an all-Mob job, but "included the top people in the CIA and the Pentagon."[17] The author's inclusion of the Pentagon in the conspiracy to assassinate President Kennedy—something he does not do in his book—is a new twist that begs for amplification. Talbot specifically mentions former CIA director Allen Dulles—fired by President Kennedy after the ill-fated 1961 CIA-backed invasion of Cuba—as "probably an accomplice if not the master-mind" in a Mafia/CIA plot to murder JFK.

Curiously, Lyndon Johnson appointed Dulles to the presidential commission that rubber-stamped Hoover's fishy finding that President Kennedy was slain by a lone Communist nut with a cheap rifle—and that the murderer of the presidential assassin, Jack Ruby, was just another wacko acting on his own. A vast majority of Americans did not then—and still do not—believe the results of Hoover's investigation into one of the darkest days in our history.

Meanwhile, the CIA continues to withhold from public scrutiny thousands of pages of JFK assassination documents. As already noted, those documents are set to be released by the National Archives in 2017—unless President Donald Trump objects. While his opponent in the presidential race, Hillary Clinton, indicated she would not interfere with the process, it is less clear what Trump will decide.[18]

Richard Nixon's lies to the FBI about his whereabouts on the day President Kennedy was killed were not the first lies he ever told inquisitive G-men.

Nixon also lied, at least twice (about never having been arrested and about his job at a gas station while growing up in Whittier), on his 1937 application to be an FBI agent, and—as a result—was disqualified from consideration, according to recently released FBI documents. Ten years later, Nixon had become a U.S. Congressman and Hoover—despite the notation on Nixon's FBI application as "Not Qualified"—had become a major fan of the conservative anti-communist war vet from southern California. And there is ample evidence that Hoover helped Congressman Nixon "get" Alger Hiss, a suspected Soviet spy who was eventually convicted of perjury. Historian Tim Weiner points out that Nixon "had been studying the FBI's files for five months, courtesy of J. Edgar Hoover."[19]

Hoover, of course, had also been helping his newfound commie-hunting friend in Congress by staying away from top mobsters—Nixon's main sources of secret campaign money and secret personal slush funds.

Many years later, Hoover even assisted President Richard Nixon in covering up Nixon's inability to win an FBI badge. Both men publicly pretended that Nixon's application had fallen through bureaucratic cracks. Nixon even claimed he had "never heard" from the agency. In truth, the new documents show that Hoover's top aide, Clyde Tolson, scrawled "Not Qualified" on the future president's 1937 application. A rejection letter to Nixon *was* sent out. Also, contrary to Nixon's claim, Hoover *was* notified.

Yet these two masters of lies and deception put out a false public story during a joint appearance on May 28, 1969, in the ornate White House East Room. Hoover gave the president a gold badge that made him an honorary member of the FBI family. The long-time FBI boss called the badge "one of the most treasured possessions" of an FBI agent. It had an American eagle at the top and carried the agency's motto: "Fidelity, Bravery, Integrity."

Taking the stage to accept the object of honor he was once officially deemed unqualified to possess, Nixon told the audience of recent graduates from the FBI Academy: "In 1937, I submitted an application to become a member of the FBI [pause] . . . and I never heard anything from that application." Nixon said that when he was vice president, he decided to ask Hoover "what happened." "He did not know that I had applied [false] and said 'I'll check the files.' "

With Hoover sitting nearby, Nixon continued to lie—maintaining that Hoover reported back to him that "actually I had been approved as an agent of the FBI, except for the fact" that Congress did not approve the FBI's budget.[20]

For the man who went on to lead a criminal presidency and who was beholden to organized crime, Nixon's remarks at the 1969 ceremony include these words of stark, dark incongruity: "Our problem is to see to it that, all over America, our laws— the written laws—deserve respect of all Americans, and that those who carry out the law, who have that hard, difficult, grueling, sometimes dangerous task of enforcing the law, that they carry out their responsibilities in a way that deserves respect."[21]

When Hoover refused to go along with Nixon's power grab— devised by White House aide Tom Charles Huston—to make the White House the center of all U.S. spying (by the FBI, CIA, and NSA), Nixon was furious. Aside from forming the White House plumbers as a substitute for the Hoover-vetoed Huston Plan, Nixon seriously considered firing Hoover—though he worried that, in that case, a vengeful Hoover might spill some of Nixon's dirtiest secrets.

In the end, Nixon proved unable to fire the FBI chief. But that did not stop the president from bringing up that prospect from time to time—as in the following October 1971 conversations between Nixon and Hoover's boss, Attorney General John Mitchell:

NIXON: For a lot of reasons [Hoover] oughta resign. . . . He should get the hell out of there. . . . Now it may be, which I kind of doubt . . . maybe I could just call him and talk him into resigning. . . . There are some problems. . . . If he does go he's got to go of his own volition . . . that's why we're in a hell of a problem . . . I think he'll stay until he's a hundred years old.

MITCHELL: He'll stay until he's buried there. Immortality . . .

NIXON (in a later conversation): I think we've got to avoid

the situation where he can leave with a blast. . . . We may have on our hands here a man who will pull down the temple with him, including me. . . . It's going to be a problem.[22]

One reporter even claims that Nixon's White House plumbers aimed to kill Hoover. About a year after the Watergate burglary, reporter Mark Frazier said there were two break-in efforts at Hoover's home near Rock Creek Park, allegedly "directed by G. Gordon Liddy."

Writing in the *Harvard Crimson*, Frazier said the first attempt—aimed at finding incriminating evidence Hoover might have about Nixon—failed, but the second succeeded. "This time, whether through misunderstanding or design, a poison of the thiophosphate genre was placed on Hoover's personal toilet articles," he wrote. Frazier reported that three sources had referred to the break-ins in affidavits to the Senate Watergate Committee. Liddy later denied knowledge of any break-ins at Hoover's home.[23]

Thiophosphate, used in some insecticides, is incredibly toxic. It can cause a fatal heart seizure if ingested, inhaled, or absorbed. Detection is impossible unless an autopsy is performed within hours of death.

If the Nixon White House wanted to assassinate Hoover, irony is too weak a word to describe Hoover's own Watergate-era comment to friendly journalist Andrew Tully that Nixon's plumbers "think they can get away with murder."[24]

Hoover was right, it turns out, but he should not have limited his chilling assessment to the plumbers. In his famous post-resignation interview with David Frost, Nixon himself claimed that anything a president does—including murder—is legal:

FROST: So what in a sense, you're saying is that there are certain situations, and the Huston Plan or that part of it was one of them, where the president can decide that it's in the best interests of the nation or something, and do something illegal.

NIXON: Well, when the president does it that means that it is not illegal.

FROST: By definition.

NIXON: Exactly. Exactly. If the president, for example, approves something because of the national security, or in this case because of a threat to internal peace and order of significant magnitude, then the president's decision in that instance is one that enables those who carry it out, to carry it out without violating a law. Otherwise they're in an impossible position.

FROST: So, that in other words, really you were saying in that answer, really, between the burglary and murder, again, there's no subtle way to say that there was murder of a dissenter in this country because I don't know any evidence to that effect at all. But, the point is: just the dividing line, is that in fact, the dividing line is the president's judgment?

NIXON: Yes, and the dividing line and, just so that one does not get the impression that a president can run amok in this country and get away with it, we have to have in mind that a president has to come up before the electorate. We also have to have in mind, that a president has to get appropriations from the Congress. We have to have in mind, for example, that as far as the CIA's covert operations are concerned, as far as the FBI's covert operations are concerned, through the years, they have been disclosed on a very, very limited basis to trusted members of Congress. I don't know whether it can be done today or not.

Based on these views, it would not be too big a stretch to say Nixon may have believed he had all the godfather-like powers as his murderous Mafia sponsors.

And perhaps Vice President Spiro Agnew was right to fear for his life at the hands of the Nixon White House, as were other presidential enemies, including John Dean, Jack Anderson, Daniel Ellsberg, and Bob Woodward and Carl Bernstein.

ELEVEN

Nixon, Sparky, and Ozzie

Some historians say John F. Kennedy's assassination marked the end of innocence for the nation as a whole—the beginning of a streak of national violence that is still ongoing. Others see it as the time when television journalism took off, when live TV coverage became the key national information source. Certainly nothing demonstrated the power of live television more than the murder of Lee Harvey Oswald.

On November 24, 1963, two days after America's young and charismatic president had been assassinated in Dallas, a shocked and shattered public sat glued to television sets. Staring blankly at their screens, the nation watched live as Oswald was to be transferred from the Dallas city jail to a county holding facility. Flanked by two policemen, the handcuffed suspect emerged slowly into the basement garage of the Dallas police station. Radio reporter Ike Pappas shouted at the alleged assassin of President Kennedy, "Do you have anything to say in your defense?" Before Oswald could answer, Dallas nightclub owner Jack

"Sparky" Ruby darted out from behind a crowd of reporters and fired a shot into Oswald's stomach. "You rat, sonofabitch!" Ruby screamed. "You shot the President!"[1]

More television viewers than any time in history watched the murder of Oswald and there can be no doubt about the perpetrator. But the motivation for the murder—the why—remains a subject of debate today, more than five decades after the fact.

Jack Ruby insisted he killed Oswald out of affection for Jacqueline Kennedy and her children. But that seems ridiculous to most observers, including Richard Billings, a top investigator for the House committee that probed the JFK assassination in the late 1970s:

> The pattern of activity from the associations in his [Ruby's] background argue to me overwhelmingly that Ruby didn't just go kill Oswald because he was a patriot or on a whim, or for any reasons other than the reasons he was directed to do it by the people for whom he worked. . . . And they were the organized crime people, the bosses in Dallas, Texas and Louisiana.

Billings said Ruby reported to underworld figures in Dallas who were, in turn, associates of Carlos Marcello, the Mob kingpin who oversaw a $1-billion-dollar-a-year criminal empire in both New Orleans and Dallas.[2] Marcello, a prime target of Robert Kennedy, was deported from Louisiana to Guatemala during the Kennedy administration.

Jack Ruby ran the Carousel Club, a seedy Dallas strip joint filled with black plastic booths from which you could buy a beer for 60 cents a glass, or buy one of Ruby's strippers a bottle of cheap champagne for $17.50 a bottle. Initial press reports portrayed Jack Ruby as a small-time gangster whose spur-of-the-moment patriotic fervor caused him to murder Oswald to protect Mrs. Kennedy from testifying at Oswald's trial.

Ruby also had a reputation for being temperamental and prone to violence. He frequently packed heat as well as brass knuckles. At his sleazy upstairs strip club in Dallas, Jack was famous for throwing drunk or obnoxious patrons down the steep flight of stairs. Cops on the take (Ruby was the Mob's payoff man for a massively corrupt police department in Dallas), sipping Jack's complimentary booze in the closest booths to the stage, looked the other way at Sparky's incendiary barroom rages and badly battered victims. In one alleged incident, Ruby reputedly threw Lee Harvey Oswald himself down the club's stairs for spouting pro-communist slogans. (A staged CIA trick?) Yet, in a separate Oswald-Ruby sighting at the Carousel, a visiting nightclub singer said Ruby introduced her to Oswald as "Lee" and stressed his pal worked for the CIA.

More than a dozen credible people say these two alleged lone nuts—Oswald and Ruby—knew each other. If that were so, there was almost certainly a plot to kill our thirty-fifth president, for it takes only two individuals to make a conspiracy.

There is still more to uncover concerning Ozzie and Sparky. One of the most fascinating and most underreported stories in the JFK assassination mystery deals with the Jack Ruby dope courier who not only attested to Jack's friendship with Lee Harvey Oswald but who also accurately predicted the president's murder.

Two days before John F. Kennedy was killed in Dealey Plaza, 34-year-old Rose Cherami (sometimes spelled Cheramie)—a sex worker, drug runner, and ex-stripper at Ruby's Carousel Club—was on a Florida-to-Texas heroin run for Ruby, Congressman

Richard Nixon's one-time paid snitch on such Mafia activities. Sally Kirkland portrayed Rose in Oliver Stone's 1991 movie *JFK*.

In rural Louisiana, a violent argument with two Ruby-connected drunken male traveling companions broke out both inside and outside a seedy roadside tavern/house of prostitution. The clash continued during the next leg of their car ride. Rose was ultimately tossed out of the gangsters' vehicle and then run over by another car near Eunice, Louisiana.

On the way to a hospital, the cut and bruised Cherami told Louisiana State Police lieutenant Francis Fruge that her pending business in Dallas included picking up cash for eight kilos of heroin she'd been assigned by Ruby to purchase in Houston. She said her fellow travelers were out to kill President Kennedy. At the hospital, she told doctors, nurses, and others JFK would soon be murdered in Dallas.

After the crime that shook the world on November 22, 1963—and after Ruby had gunned down alleged Kennedy assassin Lee Harvey Oswald two days later—Cherami told Fruge that Ruby and Oswald were such close friends that they were homosexual lovers.[3] She said Oswald had visited Ruby's striptease joint. As reported earlier, two emcees at the Carousel Club had also spotted Oswald there, as had a sizeable number of Ruby's employees and customers.

In 1967, Dr. Victor Weiss—who treated Rose at the Louisiana hospital—told New Orleans district attorney Jim Garrison's investigators that he too had heard her predictions about the planned Kennedy slaying. And he confirmed that, after Ruby shot Oswald, Rose had told him in the hospital that she had seen Oswald sitting with Ruby at a table in the Carousel prior to the JFK assassination.

Another doctor at the same hospital, Wayne Owen, later told

the *Madison Capital Times* that Cherami informed him and other hospital interns of the coming assassination. Cherami even predicted the role of her drug-trafficking boss. Dr. Owen was quoted as saying that one intern was told "that one of the men involved in the plot was a man named Jack Rubenstein." Owen said that when they learned Rubinstein was Ruby they grew quite concerned. "We were all assured that something would be done about it by the FBI or someone. Yet we never heard anything."[4]

Lieutenant Fruge told the House Select Committee on Assassinations that Cherami seemed "quite lucid" during her talks with him. The panel found that Rose was "without psychosis" during her hospitalization, but that, because of her withdrawal from heroin, she "might have a mild integrative and pleasure defect." House investigators confirmed major elements of Cherami's story—even key details of the drug run—giving her intriguing tale fresh plausibility among conspiracy theorists.

Earlier, while working for Jim Garrison's JFK assassination investigation, Lieutenant Fruge had tracked down the roadside bar where Cherami and her fellow Ruby-linked cohorts had feuded and tussled. Mac Manuel, owner of the Silver Slipper Lounge—once operated by Ruby—vividly recalled and verified the incident. He also picked out a mug shot of one of Rose's companions as Cuban exile Sergio Arcacha-Smith.

Such a link would be highly significant, according to House assassination investigators, who pointed out in 1979 that Arcacha-Smith was an anti-Castro Cuban refugee who had been active in 1961 as the head of the New Orleans Cuban Revolutionary Front. (Author's note: The CRF—a CIA-backed outfit—was located in the same Camp Street building in the French Quarter where assassination suspects Oswald, Ferrie, Guy Banister, and

E. Howard Hunt hung out.) Arcacha-Smith had befriended anti-Castro activist and former commercial pilot David Ferrie, who was named as a suspect in the Kennedy assassination within days of the president's death.

The committee did not know that Oswald was a friend and former Civil Air Patrol student of Ferrie. Nor did the panel know that Ferrie and Arcacha-Smith were part of Carlos Marcello's underworld empire. Oswald and Ruby, of course, also had ties to Marcello. As we know, the New Orleans godfather later confessed in prison that he knew Oswald and Ruby, had set up Ruby in the striptease club business, and that he—Marcello—had been behind the JFK assassination.

Marcello had once offered Arcacha-Smith money in return for gambling concessions in a post-invasion Cuba; in October 1961, Arcacha-Smith introduced Marcello errand boy and pilot Ferrie to Carlos Bringuier; On August 9, 1963, Oswald was handing out Fair Play for Cuba leaflets when he became involved in a fight (or fake fight) with Bringuier.

Oswald was arrested, and on August 12, he was found guilty and fined ten dollars. (While in jail, Oswald was visited by FBI agent John Quigley.) Five days later, Oswald debated the Cuba issue with Bringuier on a New Orleans radio show.

On November 26, 1963, Lieutenant Fruge tried to interest Dallas police in Rose's astonishing tale—but they turned him down. When Cherami refused Fruge's suggestion that she talk to the FBI, she was released from the hospital and Fruge went back to his regular police beat. JFK assassination expert Jim Di-Eugenio thinks the Dallas cops passed up a prime opportunity:

So, just four days after the assassination, with an extremely and provably credible witness alive, with her potentially

explosive testimony able to be checked out, the Cherami testimony was now escorted out to pasture. Eyewitness testimony that Ruby knew Oswald, that Ruby was somehow
involved in an international drug circle, that two Latins were
aware of and perhaps involved in a plot to kill Kennedy, and
that Ruby probably knew the men; this incredible lead—the
type investigators pine for—was being shunted aside by
[Dallas Police Captain Will] Fritz.

As DiEugenio further observed: "It would stay offstage until
Jim Garrison began to poke into the Kennedy case years later."[5]

On September 4, 1965, Rose Cherami died in a car crash near
Big Sandy, Texas. While her death certificate suggests she was
killed at the crash scene, hospital records indicate she might have
first been shot in the head at close range: "The driver said that
Cherami was lying on the road and, although he tried, he couldn't
avoid running over her skull. While her death certificate reads
'DOA,' official hospital records indicate she was operated on
for eight hours for a 'deep punctate stellate' wound to her right
forehead, which could indicate a gunshot wound at point blank
range."[6]

Oswald and Ruby appeared to be polar opposites, at least politically. "Ozzie"—sometimes known derisively to his fellow marines
as "Oswaldovich"—was a fluent Russian-speaking American
Marxist military man with top secret clearances and questionable loyalty. While in captivity of his own accord, he offered to
spill sensitive intelligence about the U.S. spy plane, the U-2.

Installed by Chicago Mafia boss Sam Giancana as his man in
Dallas in the fifties, Jack Ruby had been running errands for the

Chicago "Outfit" since he was a kid. Publicly a professed JFK fan, Sparky said he killed Mrs. Kennedy's husband's killer to save Jackie a mournful trip back to Dallas to give Oswald trial testimony. As confessionals go, this warranted an "F": In fact, Jack Ruby was a man with lifelong ties to the Mafia, a man Luis Kutner, a former staff lawyer for a 1950 Senate inquiry into organized crime, described as "a syndicate lieutenant who had been sent to Dallas to serve as a liaison for Chicago mobsters."[7]

Born in March 1911 in Chicago, Jack Ruby grew up surrounded by the Mafia lifestyle. In his youth he made extra money as a ticket scalper and by running numbers for the infamous Al Capone. In the thirties, Ruby worked at Santa Anita racetrack, which was operated at that time by Chicago Labor racketeer, extortionist, and eventual JFK assassination suspect Johnny Roselli. According to columnist Jack Anderson, Ruby's connections with Roselli continued throughout his life.[8] Assassination authority Mark Lane contends that Ruby "had been a hit man for organized crime as early as 1939 in Chicago, and [went on to serve] as an FBI informant in Dallas since 1959."[9]

Because of Jack's strong ties to corrupt union leaders—and the fact that the strippers in his club belonged to the Mafia-dominated AGVA union—when a congressional committee held hearings investigating organized crime in 1947, Ruby was called to testify. Anxious to prevent its labor racketeering secrets from being spilled, the Mafia exerted pressure upon a friend in Congress (guess who?) to keep Ruby from testifying.

A 1947 FBI memo sent to the congressional committee— possibly released by mistake—was discovered in 1975. In the "sensitive" memo an FBI assistant states: "It is my sworn testimony that one Jack Rubenstein [Ruby's original last name] of Chicago . . . is performing information functions for the staff of

Congressman Richard Nixon, Republican of California. It is re-
quested Rubenstein not be called for open testimony in the aforementioned hearings."[10]

Nixon's role in helping the Mob see to it in 1947 that Jack
Ruby did not have to testify was confirmed in *Double Cross*, a
book by Chicago godfather Sam Giancana's brother and godson,
published in 1992. In the book, Giancana said he and Nixon had
enjoyed a long, warm, and mutually rewarding relationship
going back to Nixon's vice presidential days:

> Nixon's done me some favors, all right . . . got us some high-
> way contracts, worked with the unions and overseas. And
> we've helped him and his CIA buddies out, too. Shit, he even
> helped my guy in Texas, [Jack] Ruby, get out of testifying in
> front of Congress back in forty-seven. . . . By sayin' Ruby
> worked for him.

The truth is, as outlined earlier in this book, Richard Nixon's
ties to the Mafia went back almost as far as Jack Ruby's.

Richard Nixon and the Chicago hoodlum who killed President Kennedy's alleged murderer would be difficult to tell apart
in a police lineup. They were both white males, about the same
age—and they both had five o'clock shadows, widow's peaks,
and large noses. The physical similarities ended there, but these
two men had something else in common, something in addition
to their links to the Mafia: both were big supporters of the CIA's
anti-Castro activities in Cuba.

In 1998, investigative reporter Gus Russo—a researcher on
the three-hour 1993 documentary, *Who Was Lee Harvey
Oswald?*—joined several other JFK assassination experts in con-

cluding that Vice President Nixon was the original instigator of assassination plots against Castro:

> Recent interviews strongly suggest that Nixon, along with his military aide, General Robert Cushman, secretly undertook an anti-Castro operation that ran outside of presidential and Security Council controls. He enlisted trusted power brokers in Washington and exiles in Miami to hatch not only a Cuban peso-counterfeiting scheme, but also to assemble an assassination squad. The goal was to invade Cuba while Castro was being executed—all prior to the November 1960 election— thus aiding Nixon's presidential bid.
>
> Originally known as "Operation Pluto," this concept of invading Cuba while Castro was being executed later became infamously known as "the Bay of Pigs."

The primary interest of Pluto's director-in-chief, Richard Nixon, was a deeply felt hatred of communism. He first visited Cuba before World War II, and was close to Florida senator George Smathers, Castro's predecessor Fulgencio Batista's champion in Washington, and to Bebe Rebozo, the aforementioned Miami businessman whose partners on several occasions included organized crime figures. Smathers, Rebozo, and Nixon reportedly invested in Cuba. Smathers himself was such a fan of Batista, he was known as "the Senator from Cuba."

As for Jack Ruby, he was an ardent foot soldier in CIA/Mob efforts to topple Cuba's next dictator, Fidel Castro. He ran guns to anti-Castro forces and worked to free Santos Trafficante, the Florida mob boss jailed by Castro, from the clutches of the commie dictator. Ruby met with Trafficante in 1959, in a Cuban prison, to try to arrange for his release. Indeed, soldier of fortune Gerry Patrick Hemming credits Ruby and his talks in Havana "with an American close to Castro" as being instrumental in freeing Trafficante a short time later.

One of Sam Giancana's gunmen who turned government informant, Charles Crimaldi, has said mobbed-up Teamsters president Jimmy Hoffa was the "original liaison" between the CIA and the underworld in the Nixon-led assassination plots against Castro. A government official who used Crimaldi's information about numerous drug deals describes the former Syndicate figure as "absolutely reliable."[11] Hoffa was another associate that Jack Ruby and Richard Nixon had in common. Both had close and longstanding ties to the Teamsters' president. In his Chicago days, Ruby was an officer in a union dominated by Paul Dorfman, a man who helped Hoffa expand his influence with Chicago mobsters.

Author Anthony Summers quotes James P. "Junior" Hoffa as saying, "I think my dad knew Jack Ruby, but from what I understand, he [Ruby] was the kind of guy everybody knew. So what?" Given Hoffa's record of threats against the lives of both John and Robert Kennedy, "the potential significance of such a [Ruby] connection is immense," Summers emphasizes.[12]

In the early years of the Nixon presidency, Teamsters official Murray "Dusty" Miller's help for a Nixon-favored politician had prompted Nixon aide Chuck Colson to send a memo to Chief of Staff Bob Haldeman noting, "'Duster' [sic] Miller, who heads the Southern Region for the Teamsters, is actively backing [Texas senatorial candidate] George Bush with money and political support. Be sure this guy is in our labor book and rewarded appropriately."[13]

One of the first social invitations Nixon accepted after the

Watergate scandal forced him from the presidency was from the Teamsters. As mentioned earlier, on October 9, 1975, he came out of a yearlong self-exile to play golf with President Frank Fitzsimmons and other top Teamsters officials. The setting was a Mob-owned country club in Southern California. Among club owners was Bebe Rebozo's old Mafia pal Moe Dalitz. Among those who attended a post-game party for Nixon were Anthony Provenzano, Allen Dorfman, and the union's executive secretary, Murray "Dusty" Miller. Miller, a seemingly minor character in this story, may have played a bigger role than many experts think: records show that Jack Ruby telephoned Dusty Miller several days before the JFK assassination.[14]

Meanwhile, Moe Dalitz biographer Michael Newton reports that during a 1962 Nixon-Rebozo visit to Paradise Island in the Bahamas, the two men were given the "red carpet treatment" by top Meyer Lansky associate, Seymour "Sy" Alter. Newton says Alter did business with Bebe's bank, where Rebozo told his staff, "Alter is a friend of ours. Treat him well."

Was the man Jack Ruby murdered in front of a national audience a total stranger? Evidence indicates he was not. It is not a stretch to imagine that Ruby and Lee Harvey Oswald had met before Oswald's murder, and, as already noted, more than a dozen people claim to have seen the two men together during the four months prior to the Kennedy assassination.

For example, two strippers at the Carousel say the two were friends. And a singer from a nearby nightclub says Jack introduced her to Oswald at the Carousel and said his pal "Lee" was with "the CIA." A mind-reader at the club recalls Oswald as an audience member who participated in his act. And a cashier and a waitress claim to have seen Oswald and Ruby in a deep pre-assassination conversation in a booth at their diner.

In 1979, House assassination investigators found that Oswald's uncle and father figure, Charles "Dutz" Murret, had "worked for years in an underworld gambling syndicate affiliated with the Carlos Marcello crime family." Oswald was also a friend of David Ferrie, a Marcello employee believed by many researchers to be a key figure in the JFK assassination. In November 1963, Ruby's phone bill suspiciously skyrocketed. Among those he talked with on the phone were some individuals who were connected to Oswald by one or two degrees. Ruby spoke with Robert "Barney" Baker, a strong-arm man for Hoffa in Chicago, and Nofia Pecora Sr., a key aide to New Orleans godfather Carlos Marcello. Most portentous of all, Ruby called David Yaras, a Teamsters hit man.

In addition to Oswald's ties to Ruby, a long-secret document released by a presidential assassination review board in 1998 lends credibility to an old claim that Lee Harvey Oswald was seen in Dallas with a CIA agent about two months before the Kennedy assassination. And former House assassination investigator Robert Tanenbaum told the same board that CIA director Allen Dulles headed off a Warren Commission probe about information from "unimpeachable sources that Lee Harvey Oswald was a contract employee of the CIA and the FBI."

Ex-CIA agent Victor Marchetti has linked chief Nixon White House spy E. Howard Hunt and one of his Watergate burglars, Frank Sturgis, with David Ferrie—a man who, in addition to knowing Lee Harvey Oswald, had indisputable Mafia and CIA connections in the sixties. New Orleans district attorney Jim Garrison identified Ferrie as a key suspect in the JFK assassination. Six witnesses saw Ferrie and Oswald (and assassination suspect Clay Shaw) together in Louisiana in the summer of 1963.

More damning, photographic evidence demonstrates that Ferrie knew Oswald since at least 1955.[15]

Biographers of mobster Johnny Roselli say there was an association between Roselli and Hunt in 1961 "when the Dominican dictator Rafael Trujillo was assassinated with weapons supplied by the CIA." CIA operative, Mob associate, and Watergate burglar Frank Sturgis has claimed that he knew Oswald; that documents existed at the CIA detailing the role of Ruby in the Kennedy killing; and that Oswald and Ruby once met in a hotel in New Orleans. Sturgis has also asserted that Nixon asked Helms "several times" for "the files on the Kennedy assassination, but Helms refused to give it to him, refused a direct order from the President." (Senate Watergate investigator Howard Baker once said Nixon and Helms "had so much on each other, that neither could move.")

Those particular statements by Sturgis sound credible, but his words should never be taken as gospel. After all, he was a CIA agent well versed in the art of disinformation. He told too many conflicting tales to be considered a fully reliable source. Yet even compulsive liars sometimes tell accurate tales—and perhaps there's a kernel of truth or two in Sturgis's claims. The same goes for Sturgis's Watergate supervisor, E. Howard Hunt.

In a rare interview, the dying 86-year-old Hunt told *Slate* magazine in 2004 that he orchestrated the 1954 Eisenhower/Nixon administration–backed overthrow of Jacobo Arbenz, the elected president of Guatemala; he revealed that he took a secret spying trip to Cuba after Castro took power in 1959; and Hunt disclosed his role in the killing of Che Guevara in Bolivia (Hunt said Che's hands were cut off "so he couldn't be identified by fingerprints" after he was shot to death.) As talkative with *Slate* as Hunt was on such subjects, he declined to answer several significant questions:

> SLATE: I know there is a conspiracy theory saying that David Atlee Phillips—the Miami CIA station chief—was involved with the assassination of JFK.
> HUNT: [Visibly uncomfortable] I have no comment.
> SLATE: I know you hired him early on, to work with you in Mexico, to help with Guatemala propaganda.
> HUNT: He was one of the best briefers I ever saw.
> SLATE: And there were even conspiracy theories about you being in Dallas the day JFK was killed.
> HUNT: No comment.

On his deathbed two years later, however, Hunt acknowledged he was a "benchwarmer" for the Dallas murder of Kennedy—a conspiracy he says was led by Vice President Lyndon Johnson and consisted mostly of veteran CIA agents. Hunt's son, St. John Hunt, said in recent years his mother told him his dad was in Dallas "on business" on the day Kennedy was slain. St. John tells me he wouldn't be surprised if his dad knew Lee Harvey Oswald because both "traveled in the same circles."

Onetime CIA operative Robert Morrow argues that Oswald went to the Soviet Union as a CIA agent, and that—on his return—became an FBI informant. That fits with the disclosure, in recent years, that the FBI used Oswald as an underworld informant nine times in 1959 "to furnish information" on criminal activities. Morrow also asserts that, as vice president, Nixon sanctioned and ordered a number of political assassinations—including a secret "Operation Forty" plan to kill leftist Cuban exile leaders. Morrow claims a Mob-CIA conspiracy to murder JFK involved mob leaders Giancana, Marcello, and Trafficante.

According to Morrow, David Ferrie planned the assassination, with help from a prominent New Orleans businessman named Clay Shaw. Recently, it has been discovered that both Ferrie and Shaw had CIA ties. Ferrie knew Shaw and was also friends with Oswald—as well as with Marcello. Like many other assassination suspects, Ferrie died under mysterious circumstances in 1967. When Jack Ruby died, police found that his final address book carried the name "Ferris," an alias frequently used by Ferrie.

TWELVE

Did Oswald Know Ruby?

In the early morning of November 22, 1963, a stranger entered the Lucas B&B Restaurant in Dallas and told head waitress Mary Lawrence and the night cashier that he was waiting for regular customer Jack Ruby. After Ruby's arrival, Mary said the two men talked at a table for an hour or so. Jack picked up the check—and they left together.

After Oswald's arrest for President Kennedy's murder, Mary told the FBI that the man Ruby met in the early morning of the final day of John Kennedy's life "appeared very similar to Lee Harvey Oswald." She later told Dallas Police that the man with Jack Ruby "was positively Lee Harvey Oswald."[1]

Did Richard Nixon's onetime underworld stool pigeon, Jack Ruby, know Lee Harvey Oswald? There's no hard evidence that he did, but numerous witnesses say they saw the two men together before the JFK assassination. If there was such an association, of course, the odds of an assassination plot rise greatly.

On November 24, 1963, ex–vice president Nixon was watching

TV in his Manhattan apartment. With him was aide Nick Ruwe, who later described Nixon's shock when Jack Ruby shot Lee Harvey Oswald: "The Old Man was white as a ghost," Ruwe told former Nixon aide Roger Stone. "I know that guy," Nixon declared. Stone says Ruwe asked no further questions of Nixon.

Stone, also a former adviser to Donald Trump, says Nixon told him in 1983:

> It's a hell of a thing. I actually knew this Jack Ruby fella. Murray Chotiner brought him in back in '47. Went by the name of Rubenstein. An informant. Murray said he was one of Lyndon Johnson's boys. . . . We put him on the payroll.[2]

Nixon, according to Stone, thought President Johnson was behind the murder of President Kennedy—a theory that has little credibility among assassination researchers. In fact, in recent years, after just one showing, the History Channel yanked from future lineups a documentary, Nigel Turner's *The Men Who Killed Kennedy,* with the LBJ-did-it thesis. As with his idol (Stone has a huge tattoo of Nixon's head on his back), Stone is a veteran of political mud baths whose credibility has more than once been challenged.

Yet, due to other evidence, there is some reason to believe Stone's story about Nixon knowing Ruby. Chicago godfather Sam Giancana, who said Congressman Nixon got Ruby, his "guy in Texas," out of testifying before a House committee in 1947, had already highlighted a possible Nixon-Ruby connection.[3] Giancana's statement is backed by a "sensitive" 1947 FBI memo saying that Ruby was "providing information functions" to Nixon.[4] So Stone is not alone in making the case for such a relationship.

Nixon and Ruby could well have met in California in the forties, when Ruby was hanging out in Los Angeles with Nixon's first Mob financial supporter, Mickey Cohen. An interesting side note: twelve hours after Ruby killed Oswald, FBI agents quizzed Cohen and stripper Candy Barr.[5] Cohen and Ruby were very much alike. Ruby's lawyer, the mobbed-up Melvin Belli, referred to his client as "a junior version of Mickey Cohen."[6] To say the least, if Jack Ruby knew Lee Oswald *and* Richard Nixon, the implications would be highly significant to our understanding of the many remaining JFK assassination mysteries.

Soon after Ruby murdered Oswald, Carousel emcee Bill DeMar (Bill Crowe in real life) publicly identified Oswald as a recent patron. "I have 20 customers call out various objects in rapid order," DeMar told the Associated Press. "Then I tell them at random what they called out. I am positive Oswald was one of the men that called out an object about nine days ago." Carousel patron Harvey Wade backed up DeMar's account.

Comedian Wally Weston—who preceded DeMar as an emcee earlier in November 1963—claimed Oswald was at the Carousel "at least twice" before the assassination. Weston made the revelation in an exclusive July 19, 1976 interview with the New York *Daily News*. The same article reported that:

> Dallas lawyer Carroll Jarnigan told FBI agents he saw Oswald and Ruby together in the Carousel on the night of October 4, 1963, and overheard them discussing plans for Oswald to assassinate Texas Governor John Connally, who was wounded in the fusillade that killed Kennedy.

The connections of Ruby and Oswald in the Carousel are even further supported by one of the other employees. At 20,

"Little Lynn" (in private life, Karen Carlin) was Jack's youngest stripper. With long locks of artificially colored gray hair, Lynn had the body of a swimsuit contestant—but, on stage, she wore little other than a big smile, pink heels, and a matching G-string.[7]

On November 24, 1963, Little Lynn told U.S. Secret Service agent Roger Warner that she, in his words, "was under the impression that Lee Harvey Oswald, Jack Ruby, and other individuals unknown to her, were involved in a plot to assassinate President Kennedy and that she would be killed if she gave any information to authorities." Lynn, predicting her own death with near pinpoint accuracy, reportedly died of a gunshot wound in Houston in 1964.[8]

By some accounts, even before her boss killed Oswald, Jack's featured stripper, 27-year-old "Jada" (real name, Janet Conforto) told reporters that Ruby and Oswald were acquainted. Described by Ruby biographer Seth Kantor as "supercharged with animalism," the orange-haired Jada had been recruited by Ruby from a club in New Orleans. That joint was partly owned by the underworld's biggest bigwig in Louisiana and Texas, prime JFK assassination suspect Carlos Marcello.[9]

In Dallas, even offstage, Jada acted the part of a star . . . and of a wild exhibitionist. Usually wearing only a mink coat and high-heeled shoes, she spun around town in a new gold Cadillac convertible with "JADA" embossed on the door. After one notable visit to Mexico, the brazen stripper returned with 200 pounds of weed in the Caddy's trunk, according to Dallas sports reporter Gary Cartwright.[10] She got through customs by diverting the attention of border agents. Jada pretended to fall out of her car, and then fell out of her coat—purposely exposing herself to border officers.

The number of individuals who saw Oswald at the Carousel

only grows larger. Beverly Oliver sang at the Colony Club, a parking lot away from the Carousel. Years later, Oliver said that about two weeks before the assassination, when visiting the Carousel, she spotted Jada at a table with Ruby and another man. "Ruby introduced me: 'Beverly, this is my friend, Lee.'" That man, she later realized, was President Kennedy's accused murderer. But Beverly kept mum on her Ruby-Oswald sighting at first, she said, because she feared for her life. Oliver did not want to end up like Jada, who she implied had died a mysterious death.[11] These were not the only Carousel employees or customers to have linked President Kennedy's reputed assassin with Ruby. Frances Irene Hise said she met "Ozzie" in the company of her friend Ruby several times at the Carousel in the summer and fall of 1963.[12]

In 2007, sports reporter Gary Cartwright confirmed key elements of the accounts of both Jada and Beverly: "After the assassination, Jada told us Ruby once introduced her to Lee Oswald at the Carousel. While they were having drinks, Beverly Oliver, a singer from the Colony Club next door, stopped by and was also introduced. . . . Jada is dead now, but I phoned Beverly not long ago and asked if she remembered. 'Sure do,' she said. Ruby introduced him as 'my friend Lee from the CIA.'"[13]

Jada, unlike many others connected to Ruby and Oswald, did not die mysteriously. She was killed, at 44, in a 1980 highway accident in New Mexico when a school bus ran over her motorcycle, according to researcher Mark Colgan. She is buried under the name "JADA" in a cemetery in New Orleans.[14]

And how about Beverly Oliver's tale? It is open to question, according to many assassination experts. Renowned researcher

John McAdams concludes, "No account of [Jada] saying she saw Ruby and Oswald together appeared in any newspapers, nor anywhere else. And [Jada] explicitly told the FBI that she had never seen them together."[15]

The late Gary Mack, onetime curator of the Sixth Floor Museum at Dealey Plaza in Dallas, also thought Beverly Oliver's claim was dubious. As for a Ruby-Oswald connection, Mack told this author, "[T]here's no hard evidence they were acquainted and it's hard to imagine either man linked to the other. Oswald didn't drink, he was never out at clubs, he wasn't cheating on his wife, and Oswald certainly offered nothing of significance for Ruby to advance either himself or his club."[16]

Mack is correct: there is no hard evidence—like a photograph or a letter—linking these two disturbed loners history has forever joined at the hips. But there are additional reputed Ruby-Oswald sightings that go beyond the confines of the Carousel.

In the mid-1970s, congressional assassinations investigator Gaeton Fonzi thought the most promising of "hundreds" of such reports dealt with a man named George Feraldo. The general manager of the Key West International Airport, Feraldo told the investigator he saw Ruby and Oswald at the airport in the summer of 1963.

Fonzi said one reason he traveled to Key West to interview Feraldo (who had telephoned his information to U.S. senator Richard Schweiker) is that Fonzi had seen an FBI report linking Ruby to gun-smuggling operations in the Keys. During a multiple-day stay in Key West, Fonzi found Feraldo "intelligent and credible" as well as a "generally well-respected family man." But Fonzi left the Keys with an uneasy feeling after his interviewee eventually admitted that he had done some work for the CIA. Fonzi said that revelation left him feeling "as though I had just been slapped across the face."[17] Of course, the CIA and the Mafia were known as two sides to the same coin back then—so perhaps the investigator should not have questioned the plausibility of Feraldo's story. But Fonzi concluded he was being fed CIA disinformation.

More famous names in JFK assassination history have weighed in on the possible Oswald-Ruby linkage. In 1964, General Edwin Walker told Dallas reporter Jim Marrs, "[The Warren Report] was ridiculous and a sham as well as an insult to the public intelligence. Rubenstein knew Oswald. Oswald knew Rubenstein. The report would have to start all over on this basic fact." And New Orleans district attorney Jim Garrison said that "there is simply no question about it. We didn't even have to do a great deal of investigative digging; connections popped up everywhere we scratched the surface."[18]

In the end, however, it doesn't really matter whether Ruby knew Oswald. Their mob connections are enough to make an argument that they could have both been a part of a plot.

What if there was a plot to murder President Kennedy that included two men who did not know each other? Ruby and Oswald could well have been part of this conspiracy; and Ruby could have been activated to kill Oswald after Oswald's arrest. This could be what Oswald was indicating when he insisted, "I'm a patsy." And it could have been what Ruby was referring to when he declared, "I have been used for a purpose."

There is a stack of circumstantial evidence that both Ruby and Oswald were connected to New Orleans Mafia boss Carlos Marcello. And many JFK assassination experts believe Marcello played some role in the president's murder.

According to an FBI-planted cellmate of Marcello's, the New

Orleans godfather actually engineered the JFK slaying. In recently released prison files from 1985, Jack Van Laningham quotes Marcello as admitting, "Yeah, I had the son of a bitch killed. I'm glad I did. I'm sorry I couldn't have done it myself!" A note from Van Laningham's FBI handler confirms Marcello's words.[19]

In the FBI files—based on bugs secretly placed in Marcello's cell—the mobster confessed that he used an associate, Jack Ruby, to kill Oswald. Marcello also admitted that he had set up Ruby "in the bar business in Dallas." The godfather said he'd brought Oswald into the JFK assassination plot via David Ferrie, a Marcello operative who had known Oswald in New Orleans.[20]

In 1956, informant Eileen Curry told the FBI that her boyfriend, James Breen, had gotten permission from Jack Ruby to join what was described as "a large narcotics setup operating between Mexico, Texas and the East."[21] During a post-assassination interview, former Dallas county sheriff Steve Guthrie told the FBI he thought Ruby operated prostitution and other illegal activities.[22]

And, under oath, Dallas disc jockey Kenneth Dowe told the Warren Commission that Ruby was known around his radio station, KLIF, for procuring women for visiting record promoters "who had very large expense accounts."

Dowe also testified that Ruby phoned KLIF on the afternoon after the assassination, claimed he was friendly with District Attorney Henry Wade, and offered to cover Oswald's transfer from the city to the county jail the next day.[23] Late that night, Ruby, pretending to be a reporter, corrected Wade when the D.A. informed a press conference that Oswald was a member of the anti-Castro Free Cuba Committee. Standing on the top row of a camera platform. Ruby shouted out: "Henry, that's the Fair Play for Cuba Committee," a pro-Castro outfit with only one member in Dallas—Lee Larry Oswald.

Mob hit man Frank Sheeran said he was told by Jimmy Hoffa that Ruby was tasked by the Mob to get some of his police officer friends to kill Oswald while he was in their custody. Hoffa explained to Sheeran what happened next:

> Jack Ruby's cops were supposed to take care of Oswald, but Ruby bungled it. That's why he had to go in and finish the job on Oswald. If he didn't take care of Oswald, what do you think they would have done to him—put Ruby on a meat hook.

Hoffa also disclosed to Sheeran that Marcello, Trafficante, and Giancana were involved in the hit on Kennedy. Indeed, in the late 1970s, the House Select Committee on Assassinations came to a similar conclusion.

The disclosure about Marcello in the newly released FBI files supports the conclusions of one of the most qualified experts on the JFK assassination, G. Robert Blakey, who was chief counsel and staff director to the mid-1970s House Select Committee on Assassinations. In 1981, Blakey found that Marcello and two other godfathers—Santos Trafficante of Florida and Chicago boss Sam "Mooney" Giancana—were complicit in planning Kennedy's slaying in Dallas.[24]

Oswald had Mob ties in New Orleans through Charles "Dutz" Murret, who was a bookie for Sam Saia, a gambling kingpin and Marcello sidekick. In 1963, when Oswald was living in New Orleans, he worked for Saia as a runner at Felix Oyster House—one of Saia's French Quarter bookmaking parlors—according to Blakey. John H. Davis interviewed Joseph Hauser, a witness in a federal criminal investigation of Marcello, for his Marcello biography, *Mafia Kingfish*. Hauser reconstructed for Davis a statement Marcello made to him:

> Oswald? I used to know his [expletive] family. His uncle he work for me. The kid work for me too. He worked for Sam outta his place downtown. . . . The feds came . . . askin' about him, but my people didn't tell 'em nothing. Like we never heard of the guy . . . [25]

As for Jack Ruby's ties to the boss of America's oldest crime family, back in the 1970s Blakey's panel established links between the nightclub owner "and several individuals affiliated with the underworld activities of Carlos Marcello. Ruby was a personal acquaintance of Joseph Civello, the Marcello associate who allegedly headed organized crime activities in Dallas . . . [and] a New Orleans nightclub figure, Harold Tannenbaum, with whom Ruby was considering going into partnership in the fall of 1963."

Shortly after the assassination, Jack Ruby's headliner, Jada—rightly, it turns out—threw cold water on Ruby's initial excuse for killing Oswald. Ruby claimed he was a super-patriot who loved President Kennedy, and that his action was politically motivated. Not so fast, said the orange-haired stripper during an interview with ABC's Paul Good: "I believe he disliked Bobby Kennedy . . . I didn't think he loved [President] Kennedy that much" to kill Oswald. And dogged assassination reporter Jefferson Morley recently discovered an exotic dancer with the stage name Gail Raven who became a close Ruby friend. Raven told Morley that Jack "was not in love with the Kennedys and he did not like Robert Kennedy by no means." Raven described Ruby's claim that he killed Oswald to spare Jackie Kennedy from having to return to Dallas to attend a trial of Oswald as "absolutely made up."[26]

A pre-assassination indication that Ruby might be part of a conspiracy to kill the president came at around noon on November 21, 1963. A number of Dallas police officers were meeting in the office of Assistant District Attorney Ben Ellis when Ruby entered and passed out business cards advertising Jada's gig at the Carousel. According to Lieutenant W. F. Dyson, Ruby introduced himself to Ellis and added: "You probably don't know me now, but you will."[27]

Before Ruby pulled the trigger on his .38-caliber Colt Cobra in the basement of the Dallas Police Department, did he have second thoughts? Or did he want to get caught before he actually carried out his mission?

Billy Grammer, a Dallas Police dispatcher, says he received a telephone threat against Oswald's life the night before Oswald's murder. He said the tipster did not identify himself, but he did greet the officer by name. The caller advised police to change their plans for Oswald's transfer to another jail the next day. The voice on the other end was urgent, asserting, "We are going to kill him!"

Only after Jack Ruby murdered Oswald did Grammer realize he had been talking to a local striptease club operator he knew well. "It had to be Ruby," he later disclosed. Grammer says that phone call convinced him the Oswald slaying was "not spontaneous," but rather a "planned event."[28]

While Ruby's stunning crime was witnessed by millions of baffled viewers on live TV, Reuters's Ralph Harris was one of the first reporters in the basement to grab a phone and dictate a bulletin to his wire service's editors: "The fatal shot, fired by Jack Ruby into Oswald's abdomen at point-blank range, in the presence of armed police and reporters, had such a stunning impact that the scene froze into a moment of paralyzed amazement, then pandemonium as Oswald dropped to the concrete floor."[29]

Shortly before his death from cancer in 1967, Ruby secretly slipped a note to Dallas deputy sheriff Al Maddox. In a July 1996 TV interview, Maddox revealed that, in the note, Ruby confessed that there "was a conspiracy" to murder JFK and that Ruby's motive in killing the alleged presidential assassin was not patriotism, but rather to "silence Oswald."[30]

As soon as he saw the slaying of Oswald on TV, Attorney General Robert Kennedy drew that very same conclusion. Ruby, he felt, had Mob written all over him, so he immediately dispatched his top Justice Department investigator, Walt Sheridan, to Dallas to look into Ruby's background. Within only hours, Sheridan "turned up evidence that Ruby had been paid off in Chicago" by a close associate of mobbed-up Teamsters Union president Jimmy Hoffa, a mortal enemy of the Kennedy brothers. Sheridan said Ruby "picked up a bundle of money from Allen M. Dorfman," a chief Hoffa henchman.

When the attorney general examined Jack Ruby's many pre-assassination phone calls to key Mafia figures, the organized crime expert declared, "The list was almost a duplicate of the people I called before the [Senate] Rackets Committee," he told author David Talbot.[31]

Perhaps partly out of fear for his own life, Bobby Kennedy kept his investigation into his beloved brother's murder to himself. And he refused to cooperate with the Warren Commission's probe. Talbot says Bobby intended to reopen the investigation if he became president. Talbot speculates that, in Los Angeles in 1968, White House hopeful Robert Kennedy may have been gunned down by the same conspirators who killed his brother Jack in Dallas.

THIRTEEN

Mob Assassination Connections

In 1994, Jimmy Hoffa's former lawyer Frank Ragano disclosed Hoffa's version of how President Kennedy was killed. On July 24, 1963—four months before the assassination—Ragano claimed he met in New Orleans with Trafficante and Marcello. He said he carried the message that Hoffa "wants you to do a little favor for him. You won't believe this, but he wants you to kill John Kennedy. He wants you to get rid of the President right away." Ragano said the facial expressions of the two mobsters "were icy. Their reticence signaled that this was an uncomfortable subject, one they were unwilling to discuss."

But Ragano further claimed Trafficante, on his deathbed in 1987, confessed that he and Marcello had, indeed, followed through on Hoffa's "favor." He quoted the ailing Mob boss as saying: "Who would have thought that some day he would be President and he would name his goddam brother attorney general? Goddam Bobby. I think Carlos fucked up in getting rid of Giovanni [John in Italian] maybe it should have been Bobby."

Ragano admitted that he should have taken the message Trafficante passed more seriously:

> In my loyalty to the three men, I had ignored basic logic and
> obvious hints: each of them had participated actively or
> behind the scenes in the assassination. They had been part of
> a conspiracy, or knew that one had been hatched against
> Kennedy's life. Most probably, Carlos and Santos plotted
> against the president for their own selfish reasons—not just
> to aid Jimmy Hoffa. Jimmy could not have intimidated or
> given orders to these powerful bosses. His personal war with
> the Kennedys may have influenced them, but was not the sole
> factor guiding them.[1]

Mob and CIA experts Warren Hinckle and William Turner
report that, during the Nixon administration, pressure from
Washington "eased off" on Chicago Mafia boss Sam Giancana.
They add that "long-standing deportation proceedings against
CIA-connected mobster Johnny Rosselli were dropped. Government lawyers explained in court, without going into specifics,
that the Mafia soldier had performed 'valuable services to the
national security.' "[2]

Was Ruby told to kill Oswald by the Mob? Why would he
have done so? Did he think he'd be treated as a national hero?
Was there a CIA or FBI or Dallas police connection? How else
could Ruby have gotten past dozens of FBI agents and police
officers to shoot the alleged presidential assassin in TV's first live
murder? Why did the Warren Commission and the FBI withhold
vital information about Ruby's unsavory background? And why,
even before the assassination, didn't the FBI and CIA warn their
ranks that Ozzie was a violence-prone Marxist who worked on

an upper floor of a building along the president's motorcade route in Dallas?

In 1997, Robert Blakey, the chief counsel of the 1970s-era House Assassinations Committee, told a TV program that Jack Ruby "is the Rosetta stone for the assassination. And once you connect Ruby immediately to organized crime, do you then turn back and say: 'Can I connect Oswald to organized crime?' And the answer is 'yes.' "[3]

As we have seen, Ruby was not your ordinary low-level hoodlum. He had high-level Mob and Teamsters contacts. And, as recounted by former CIA operative Robert Morrow, Ruby seemed to be everywhere at once on the day of President Kennedy's slaying:

> In Dallas, Jack Ruby would be quite busy [on November 22, 1963] but the Warren Commission would deem his activities and associations unimportant. The Mob's man in Dallas, the man former Vice President Richard Nixon excused from testifying before a congressional committee, the man identified by CIA personnel as a gunrunner to Cuba, the man who was identified in 1956 as an informant for the Federal Narcotics Bureau and the Los Angeles Police Department as a key figure in a major narcotics operation between Mexico, Texas and the East, the man the Warren Commission would dismiss as a simple night club operator with no involvement in organized crime, would kill Lee Harvey Oswald.[4]

Keeping in theme with the Warren Commission's level of accuracy, the panel didn't seem to have that right either.

On November 28, 1963—just four days after Ruby shot Lee

Harvey Oswald to death—the CIA sent this highly classified message to the White House and the State Department:

> On 26 November 1963 a British journalist named John Wilson, and also known as John Wilson-Hudson, gave information to the American Embassy in London which indicated that an "American gangster-type" named Ruby visited Cuba around 1959. Wilson himself was working in Cuba at the time and was jailed by Castro before he was deported.
>
> In prison in Cuba, Wilson says he met an American gangster gambler named Santos who could not return to the USA because there were several indictments outstanding against him. Instead he preferred to live in relative luxury in a Cuban prison. While Santos was in prison, Wilson says, Santos was visited frequently by an American gangster type named Ruby. His story is being followed up. Wilson says he had once testified before the Eastland Committee of the U.S. Senate, sometime in 1959 or 1960.[5]

This document was not made public until mid-1976, when an intrepid JFK assassination researcher pried it loose from the CIA through the Freedom of Information Act. The document had been kept from the Warren Commission—which allowed the panel to mistakenly claim, in its final report, that it "could not establish a significant link between Ruby and organized crime."[6]

In 1979, a House investigating committee found that Jack Ruby associates Trafficante, Marcello, Giancana, and Hoffa were probably behind the 1963 assassination of President John F. Kennedy. At the same time, a Cuban exile associate of Trafficante's disclosed that the Mob boss certainly had foreknowledge of plans to assassinate JFK.

Jose Aleman—who was also an FBI informant—said Trafficante had complained to him about Jack and Robert Kennedy in early 1963. He said the brothers were not honest, they took graft, and did not keep a bargain. The godfather further charged that the Kennedys had attacked his good pal: "Have you seen how [the president's] brother is hitting Hoffa, a man who is a worker, who is not a millionaire, a friend of the blue collars? He doesn't know that this kind of encounter is very delicate. Mark my words, this man Kennedy is in trouble, and he will get what is coming to him." Aleman said he countered that JFK would be re-elected in 1964, and Trafficante responded, "No, Jose, he is going to be hit."[7]

Did Richard Nixon know what his criminal buddies knew about the Mafia's obvious involvement in the 1963 JFK assassination? With myriad ties to Santos Trafficante and others reputedly involved, Nixon must, at the very least, have connected some of the dots. Sam Giancana, who confessed to his own leading role in Kennedy's slaying, even claimed he met beforehand with Nixon in Dallas—and that the former vice president "knew about the whole thing."[8] Furthermore, Giancana boasted of having sent a team of Chicago hitmen to Dallas, and he claimed the fatal shot was fired by one of his lieutenants—a man named Richard Cain—from the sixth floor of the Texas School Book Depository.

Both Giancana and Cain were killed "gangland style" in the 1970s. Giancana's death was particularly grisly. The Mob boss was murdered in his own Oak Park, Illinois, home while under police protection just before he was slated to testify before the

Senate Intelligence Committee about the JFK assassination. Seven .22-caliber bullets were blasted into his mouth and neck—a Mob signature for those who fail to heed "omerta," the Mafia's code of silence on illegal actions.

Even Jack Ruby's own lawyer, Melvin Belli, doubted his client's explanation as to why he murdered Lee Harvey Oswald: "Clearly his story of trying to protect Mrs. Kennedy from a harrowing court appearance at a final trial for Oswald did not add up, although it was a story he persisted on to the end. . . . I am sure the story was false because it didn't square with everything else we knew."[9]

In 1976, Johnny Roselli—a key figure in the CIA-Mafia assassination plots against Castro—offered an easier-to-believe explanation for Oswald's killing: "When Oswald was picked up, the underworld conspirators feared he would crack and disclose information that might lead to them. This almost certainly would have brought a massive U.S. crackdown on the Mafia. So Jack Ruby was ordered to eliminate Oswald . . ."[10]

During a June 7, 1964, interview with the chairman of the Warren Commission, Jack Ruby himself seemed to say that the real reason he shot Oswald was to silence him. During the half-hour session, the gangster begged Chief Justice Earl Warren several times to fly him to Washington, where he could talk freely. At one point, Ruby declared: "Gentlemen, unless you get me to Washington, you can't get a fair shake out of me." At another, he stated, "I want to tell the truth, and I can't tell it here." Oswald's killer coupled a later plea with a dramatic announcement: "Gentlemen, my life is in danger."

Warren rebuffed each request, finally issuing a lame excuse for not taking Ruby to Washington: "Well, the public attention that it would attract, and the people who would be around.

We have no place there for you to be safe when we take you out, and there are not law enforcement officers, and it isn't our responsibility to go into anything of that kind."[11]

Ruby got the death sentence for murdering Oswald, but his conviction was reversed on October 5, 1966, and a retrial was ordered. It also came to light that the judge was writing a book about the case during the trial—a book that would have sold better had the trial been over quickly. Before a new trial could take place, Ruby died of cancer while still a prisoner in Dallas. He told family members, he'd been "injected with cancer cells."

Assassination expert Jim Marrs has observed that, in the winter of 1967, "just as a new trial had been ordered and it seemed that Ruby might become accessible to the news media, he developed a sudden case of cancer and died in less than a month. It seemed Ruby's fear of death in Dallas—as expressed to the Warren Commission—was justified."[12]

Pointing to Ruby's Cuba ties, which linked him to both the CIA and the Mafia, author Anthony Summers writes: "Ruby's apparent connections led to the very core of the most enduring suspicions as to who really killed Kennedy. Yet, the CIA and the FBI withheld some links from the Warren Commission. The rest were ignored or given minimal weight in [the commission's] official report. These were indefensible omissions."[13] The commission's finding that Ruby "had no significant link" to organized crime is astonishing at best and damning at its worst.

And Hoffa, well, he was inextricably tied to the mob from his earliest days in the Teamsters Union. The man's alliance with the Mafia began in 1941, when the Mob helped the Teamsters drive a rival union from Detroit. This helped bring about what organized crime expert Dan Moldea describes as Hoffa's "rapid descent from working-class hero to labor racketeer."

In the wake of this deal, according to Moldea, "The Mafia owned Jimmy Hoffa." As just one seamy aspect of this early Teamsters-Mafia relationship, Moldea found a narcotics connection: "When mobsters Jimmy Quasarano and Peter Vitale needed a façade of legitimacy for their Detroit-based narcotics operation, Hoffa created a dummy Teamsters local for them to run."[14] A recent history of the Bureau of Narcotics concurs, saying that Hoffa had "protected Detroit's major drug traffickers by assigning them to a certain [Teamsters] local."[15]

FOURTEEN

The Watergate-Assassination Connection

Could Richard Nixon have had inside information on the assassination of President John F. Kennedy—and then, nine years later, as president, have used that information to try to blackmail CIA director Richard Helms into halting an FBI investigation into Nixon's involvement in the Watergate cover-up? Possibly. Fresh evidence, coupled with previously published accounts, illustrate a startling new perspective on the events that left America stunned 54 years ago.

One major piece of evidence is a declassified tape recording of a May 18, 1973, meeting between President Nixon and his top aide discussing their earlier efforts to conceal White House links to the attempted June 1972 burglary of documents from the Democratic National Committee in Washington's Watergate office building. That conversation, together with existing quotes from the same aide, finger Nixon as the very source of the rumor that the CIA participated in and conducted a massive cover-up of the JFK assassination.

Curious "national security" deletions in recordings released after Nixon's 1994 death, along with the declassification of one crucial CIA document—an internal report on the 1961 Bay of Pigs invasion of Cuba—point to the likelihood Nixon may have known, and suppressed, blockbuster secrets about the November 22, 1963, murder of his archrival. This material adds credibility to the theory that the CIA and organized mobsters killed President Kennedy.

Other documents released in recent years, such as an FBI memo in which an informant describes a huge mob payoff to the Nixon White House "to guarantee the release of Jimmy Hoffa from the Federal penitentiary" seem to confirm this theory. As discussed earlier, many assassination researchers have linked Hoffa and Mob leaders to JFK's murder.

Regardless of the validity of claims that Nixon blackmailed Helms, the aforementioned Nixon-Ford relationship certainly did prove to be useful to both men in later years. When Nixon was president, Ford served as his top congressional agent in a failed effort to impeach liberal Supreme Court justice William O. Douglas. At Nixon's direction, Ford later succeeded in stopping the first congressional Watergate probe. And in the summer of 1973, the heavy pressures of Watergate forced President Nixon to start thinking aloud about an eventual resignation.

The crime itself—when five burglars, all CIA-connected individuals, dressed in suits and wearing surgical gloves, were arrested for breaking into the Watergate on June 17, 1972—had Richard Nixon worried the trail of guilt would lead to him. The apprehended burglars had been recruited and supervised by Nixon's own top White House spy and "dirty trickster," E. Howard Hunt. Enraged by the bungled job, Nixon made a series of frenzied phone calls to Hunt's boss, Chuck Colson, becoming so agitated he threw an ashtray against the wall. Behind the anger lay fear that his own tangled web would be exposed.

Recordings show that Nixon clearly coached his chief of staff, Bob Haldeman, to scare CIA director Helms into believing that if Hunt were implicated in the Watergate affair he might blab to authorities about CIA involvement in "the Bay of Pigs." Haldeman subsequently disclosed that the term was a secret code name—not for the 1961 Cuban invasion, but for the JFK assassination, two years later.

On June 23, 1972, Nixon instructed Haldeman to tell Helms in a meeting later that day that "Hunt knows too damned much. . . . If this gets out that this is all involved . . . it would make the CIA look bad, it's going to make Hunt look bad, and it's likely to blow the whole Bay of Pigs thing . . . which we think would be very unfortunate for both the CIA and the country . . . and for American foreign policy."[1]

The CIA chief reacted violently to Nixon's attempt to intimidate him. "Helms gripped the arms of his chair, leaned forward and shouted: 'The Bay of Pigs had nothing to do with this! I have no concern about the Bay of Pigs!' " Haldeman recalled in a post-Watergate book.[2] "He [Helms] yelled like a scalded cat when Haldeman mentioned the Watergate trail might lead to the 'Bay of Pigs,' " Nixon aide, John Ehrlichman, who attended the meeting, recalled in his own book.[3]

In his book, Haldeman was explicit that such mentions had nothing to do with the disastrous 1961 invasion of Cuba by CIA-trained exiles:

It seems that in all those Nixon references to the Bay of Pigs, he was actually referring to the Kennedy assassination. (Interestingly, an investigation of the Kennedy assassination was a project I suggested when I first entered the White House. I had always been intrigued with the conflicting theories of the assassination. Now I felt we would be in a position to get all the facts. But Nixon turned me down.)

Haldeman went on to declare that the CIA pulled off a "fantastic cover-up" that "literally erased any connection between the Kennedy assassination and the CIA."[4] If Haldeman knew of such involvement, Nixon almost certainly did. Whatever made Haldeman conclude that Nixon and the CIA were privy to JFK assassination secrets logically had to come from Nixon himself. It is ridiculous to think that Nixon's chief of staff would have known more about such sensitive subjects than the president.

Nixon aide John Ehrlichman later underlined the logic of such a conclusion: "Virtually nothing Nixon did was done without Haldeman's knowledge. That is not to say that Haldeman approved everything Nixon said or did; but it was essential that he know, and have a chance to object, before it happened."[5]

But Nixon's threat is only one piece of evidence connecting the president to Helms and a possible CIA role in the Kennedy assassination. In a tape dated May 18, 1973, Nixon and Haldeman recall Haldeman's delivery of the warning to Helms from the previous June.[6] In this conversation, Haldeman reminds the president what Helms had said:

HALDEMAN to NIXON: Oh, we have no problem with the Bay of Pigs, of anything. And that [Helms's statement] surprised me, because I had gotten the impression from you that the CIA did have some concern about the Bay of Pigs.
NIXON: [no objection to the statement]
HALDEMAN to NIXON (at another point in the tape): He

[Helms] says the CIA has nothing to hide in the Bay of Pigs. Well, now, Ehrlichman tells me in just the last few days that isn't true. CIA was very concerned about the Bay of Pigs, and in the investigation apparently he was doing on the Bay of Pigs stuff. At some point, there is a key memo missing that CIA or somebody has caused to disappear that impeded the effort to find out what really did happen on the Bay of Pigs.

In another tape,[7] made only four days earlier, Nixon pressured his press secretary, Ron Ziegler, to try to accomplish what Haldeman and Ehrlichman could not:

NIXON: Listen. I've been after this Goddamn staff for a long time. I'm going to ask you to do something. Haldeman never did it, Ehrlichman never did it, nobody else, because this Goddamn [National Security Adviser Henry] Kissinger is always stopping them. Now, look, I want the Diem [Nixon suspected President Kennedy ordered the assassination of South Vietnam president Ngo Dinh Diem] and the Bay of Pigs [documents] totally declassified and I want it done in 48 hours. . . . This is ten years old. [Note: The Kennedy assassination was, at the time, ten years old, while the Bay of Pigs invasion took place twelve years earlier.] Declassify it.

Seconds later, a section of the Nixon-Ziegler discussion is deleted for reasons of "national security." When the non-classified part of the conversation picks up, the two men are discussing President Kennedy's biggest mistakes.

These White House tapes are replete with such "national security" redactions when the subjects of Hunt, Kennedy, or "the Bay of Pigs" come up.

For example, during a 15-minute Oval Office talk between Nixon and Colson on July 1, 1972, the two were discussing items discovered in Hunt's White House safe:

NIXON: Of course, the gun and the walkie-talkie, well, Christ, the guy just probably didn't put it in his briefcase. He's that kind of guy . . .

COLSON: He's carried a gun for years. Well, he kept it—he didn't keep it in his desk. He had it locked in a safe.

[Withdrawn item. National Security]

COLSON: The tragedy of it, Mr. President, was that I never have been in his office, so I didn't know whether the story that ran in the [WASHINGTON] DAILY NEWS [about the contents of Hunt's safe] was true or not . . .

[A second redaction occurs after Colson reassures the president Hunt can be trusted with "sensitive" documents.]

COLSON: I mean, he's a true believer, a real patriot. My God, the things he's done for his country. It's just a tragedy that he gets smeared with this [Watergate burglary]. Of course, the other story that a lot of people have bought is that Howard Hunt was taken out of the country by the CIA. Well, he's certainly done a lot of hot stuff . . . Oh Jesus. He pulled a lot of very fancy stuff in the sixties.

[Withdrawn Item. National Security]

NIXON: Well, I don't agree. If anything ever happens to him [Hunt], be sure he blows the whistle, the whole Bay of Pigs.

COLSON: He wrote the book.

NIXON: Blow their horn . . . [8]

The numerous "National Security" deletions in the Watergate tapes are sad reminders of Chief Justice Earl Warren's 1964 answer to the question of whether his commission's JFK assassination files would ever be made public: "Yes, there will come a time. But it might not be in your lifetime. I am not referring to anything especially, but there may be some things that would involve security. This would be preserved but not made public."[9]

On August 9, 1974, another Warren Commission member, President Gerald Ford—the man who owed both his seat on the commission and his desk in the Oval Office to Nixon—went on national television to announce an unconditional pardon of his presidential predecessor. He read a proclamation granting Nixon "a full, free and absolute pardon . . . for all offenses against the United States which he . . . has committed or may have committed or taken part in during the period from January 20, 1969, through August 9, 1974."[10]

On January 16, 1975, President Ford was considering the appointment of what became known as the Rockefeller Commission to investigate CIA abuses. He told a small group of journalists he "needed trustworthy citizens who would not stray from the narrow confines of their mission because they might come upon matters that could damage the national interest and blacken the reputation of every president since Truman."

Ford was asked, "Like what?" His response: "Like assassinations!" Then he quickly added: "That's off the record!"[11]

HOOVER AND THE JFK ASSASSINATION

J. Edgar Hoover was in the hip pocket of America's godfathers, reputedly because they had pictorial proof of his homosexuality. So the FBI director put the Mafia on a low level of his crime-fighting priorities. That is until 1961, when John and

Robert Kennedy put potent muscle behind the government's drive against organized crime—and Hoover reluctantly began paying more than just lip service to battling the Mob.

As President John F. Kennedy's attorney general, Robert Kennedy became a menace to the Mafia—and his take-no-prisoners tactics trickled down not only to Hoover, but also to top local and state cops, district attorneys, and judges. Kennedy expert Matthew Smith observes: "Never before had such success been obtained by the forces of law against mobsters who, for years, had evaded prosecution. It had also a gathering momentum, for law enforcement agents in many cities in the United States were so impressed by Robert Kennedy's campaign they began bringing cases against their local mobsters [whose] past experience of failures had made them reluctant to prosecute."[12]

Of course, this angered the godfathers, who had played a key role in John Kennedy's ascent to the White House. The dons of the Cosa Nostra felt deeply betrayed. Because he was a major rumrunner during Prohibition, Kennedy family patriarch Joseph Kennedy rubbed elbows and shared handsome illegal profits with some of the nation's most notorious mobsters. And Old Joe turned to some of these same men in 1960, when his son, Senator John Kennedy, faced Vice President Richard Nixon for the presidency. There was evidence of massive voter fraud by mobsters in Illinois and Texas. Those states threw the election to JFK. The Mafia was now looking for major favors, or at least leniency, from the Kennedys. But, under Bobby, by 1964, the Justice Department had increased Cosa Nostra convictions by 700 percent over 1960.[13]

Bobby had federal agents arrest New Orleans godfather Carlos Marcello and physically deport him to Guatemala. And he initiated action that landed mobbed-up Teamsters boss Jimmy Hoffa in a prison cell. As historian Anthony Summers notes: "If top Mafia bosses felt double-crossed, their law—the law of the Mob—might demand vengeance."[14] Thus did angry Mob bosses and Hoffa conclude that one or both of the Kennedy brothers had to be done away with.

In 1994, Hoffa's longtime lawyer, Frank Ragano, confessed that he had carried a 1963 message from Hoffa to New Orleans godfather Carlos Marcello and Florida godfather Santos Trafficante that Hoffa "wants you to get rid of the President right away." Significantly, Ragano added that Trafficante, on his deathbed in 1987, confessed that he and Marcello had, indeed, followed through on Hoffa's demand.[15] How had such plotting escaped the attention of FBI chief Hoover? Apparently, it hadn't. In September 1972, according to Hoover biographer Mark North, America's top cop had already learned through electronic surveillance that Marcello "had put out a contract on the life of President Kennedy. . . . Hoover did not inform his superiors within the Justice Department or warn the Secret Service."[16]

Whether J. Edgar Hoover had advance indications of an underworld plan to assassinate the president, he certainly knew about Lee Harvey Oswald before November 22, 1963. And yet he did nothing to keep Kennedy's alleged sole assassin from reporting to his job in a building with a good shot at the presidential motorcade route on that fateful day in Dallas.

Hoover and his G-men had actually been keeping their eyes on Oswald since 1959, when the young ex-Marine defected to the Soviet Union. After he returned to this country in 1962, several CIA divisions tracked Oswald's movements and regularly reported on this "possible security risk" to the FBI. Lo and behold, however, it turns out that Oswald had become a paid FBI informant on his return, according to author Burton Hersh:

Apart from the claim by former FBI security clerk William Walter that he processed documents to that effect, there was the revelation in chambers by Texas Attorney General Waggoner Carr and Henry Wade, the Dallas district attorney [to top Warren Commission officials] that Oswald had been on the FBI payroll for $200-a-month since September of 1962 with the informant number S-172.[17]

Hersh adds that FBI "counterintelligence veterans have since confirmed Oswald's FBI employment." And the author notes that when Oswald was arrested for disturbing the peace in New Orleans in the summer of 1963, he demanded and was granted the right to see an FBI agent.

Former BBC correspondent Anthony Summers later discovered a Dallas garage manager, Adrian Alba, who witnessed Oswald accept a "good-sized . . . white envelope" from a G-man in a green FBI-owned Studebaker he serviced.[18] Oswald spent only one night in jail in New Orleans. A representative of none other than crime boss Carlos Marcello bailed him out.

As the chief investigator of the JFK assassination, Hoover decided only two hours after Ruby gunned down Oswald that there was a need to "issue something so we can convince the public that Oswald is the *real* assassin."[19] So Hoover failed to adequately probe many other ties between Oswald and Marcello, including these: Oswald buddy David Ferrie was a pilot for Marcello's drug-trafficking operations; Oswald's uncle and father figure Charles "Dutz" Murret was a major bookmaker for Marcello's gambling network; Oswald himself was a "runner" and "collector" for Marcello's gambling operation; and Oswald's mother, Marguerite, dated several members of Marcello's gang.

Why did Hoover ignore Marcello and other Mafia godfathers as suspects in his investigation of the JFK assassination? And why did he overlook even tighter connections between the Mafia kingpins and Jack Ruby? Could it be that the Mob was black-mailing Hoover over his reported homosexual relationship with his right-hand man at the bureau, Clyde Tolson? Sounds plausible.

Especially in light of the disclosure by Anthony Summers that gangster Meyer Lansky had obtained compromising photos of Hoover and Tolson. Summers quotes former Lansky associate Seymour Pollock as saying in 1990 that Hoover's homosexuality was "common knowledge" and that he had seen evidence of it for himself:

> I used to meet (Hoover) at the racetrack every once in awhile with lover boy Clyde, in the late forties and fifties. I was in the next box once. And when you see two guys holding hands, well come on! . . . They were surreptitious, but there was no question about it.

Summers says top CIA counterintelligence official James Angleton possessed similar photos, and once showed them to CIA electronics expert Gordon Novel, who later reported:

> What I saw was a picture of [Hoover] giving Clyde Tolson a blowjob. There was more than one shot, but the startling one was a close shot of Hoover's head. He was totally recogniz-able. You could not see the face of the man he was with, but Angleton said it was Tolson. I asked him if they were fakes, but he said they were real, that they'd been taken with a fish-eye lens. They looked authentic to me . . .

Novel said Angleton displayed the photos to him in 1967 and told him they were taken in 1946, at a time when Angleton was engaged in a bureaucratic feud with Hoover. It should also be noted that Angleton had very friendly relations with a key Mafia figure, New York lawyer Mario Brod, who reportedly brokered drug deals for Angleton.[20] The Mafia and the CIA were so tight back then they were known as two sides of the same coin.

J. Edgar Hoover and Clyde Tolson may or may not have been blackmail-prone lovers, but they deeply shared one emotion—an avid hatred of Robert Kennedy. In *Brothers*, David Talbot reports that when RFK announced his run for the White House in 1968, Tolson shocked a group of FBI officials by declaring, "I hope that someone shoots and kills the son of a bitch."

Talbot concludes that John F. Kennedy was the victim of a cross fire in a choreographed ambush, and that Hoover conducted a cover-up of the crime. He adds that the conspiracy was not an all-Mob job, but also "included the top people in the CIA and the Pentagon." Talbot's inclusion of the Pentagon in the conspiracy to assassinate President Kennedy—something he omits from his book—is a new twist that begs for amplification.

Talbot specifically mentions former CIA director Allen Dulles, who was fired by President Kennedy after the ill-fated 1961 CIA-backed invasion of Cuba and simultaneous attempt to assassinate Cuban leader Fidel Castro, as "probably an accomplice if not the mastermind" in the CIA/Mafia plot.

Ironically, Lyndon Johnson appointed Dulles to the presidential commission that rubber-stamped Hoover's fishy finding that President Kennedy was slain by a lone Communist nut with a cheap rifle—and that the assassin of the president's assassin was just another wacko acting on his own. A vast majority of Americans did not then—and still do not—believe the results of Hoover's investigation into one of the darkest days in our history.

It now turns out that Hoover's investigation—relied upon by the Warren Commission—failed to tell the commission that the CIA and FBI had uncovered a major assassination clue: seven weeks before the assassination, an unknown person had falsely claimed to be Oswald in a local phone call to the Soviet Embassy in Mexico City.[21] Likewise, the two agencies did not inform the commission of Mafia-CIA plots against Cuba's Castro.

Meanwhile, the CIA and FBI continue to withhold from public scrutiny more than 1,000 JFK assassination documents. These are mandated by Congress to be declassified by October 2017, unless the president at the time objects. Two of Richard Nixon's Watergate burglars—E. Howard Hunt and Frank Sturgis—have among the thickest files to be piled onto the coming document dump. Both former spooks (Sturgis was also a Santos Trafficante lieutenant) admitted collaborating on what Hunt called "the Big Event" in Dallas. Sturgis boasted to a girlfriend and later to a detective—and to almost anyone who would listen—that he was a proud conspirator. In a deathbed admission, Hunt confessed he was part of the plot, but just a "benchwarmer," a term he failed to further explain.

E. HOWARD HUNT: JFK ASSASSINATION SUSPECT

Was a key Richard Nixon cohort in past and future covert intelligence operations—then-CIA agent E. Howard Hunt—in Dallas the day President Kennedy was killed? During a 1985 libel trial brought by Hunt against *Spotlight*—a newsletter owned by right-wing Liberty Lobby—for publishing an article in August

1978 by former CIA agent Victor Marchetti titled "CIA to Admit Hunt Involvement in Kennedy Slaying," CIA operative Marita Lorenz swore she saw Hunt in Dallas. Hunt co-worker at the CIA Walter Kuzmuk said he could not recall having seen Hunt between November 18 and sometime in December of 1963. Furthermore, Joseph Trento, a reporter for the *Wilmington News & Journal*, insisted he had once seen an internal CIA memo that said, "Someday we will have to explain Hunt's presence in Dallas on November 22, 1963." Hunt lost the case.

Most notorious for directing Nixon's Watergate burglary, Hunt died at 88 in January 2007 in Miami. And Hunt's son, Howard St. John (known as "St. John") Hunt of Eureka, California, was soon peddling a story that his dad *rejected* an offer to take part in a plot to kill President Kennedy.

In an interview with the *Los Angeles Times*, St. John Hunt did admit to telling previous lies about his dad's whereabouts on that fateful day. He said he was instructed by Hunt in 1974 to back up an alibi for his whereabouts. "I did a lot of lying for my father in those days," St. John confessed. E. Howard Hunt's most frequently used alibi for that day was that he was at his Potomac, Maryland, home watching TV with his children.

Yet, asked in a *Slate* interview in 2004 about "conspiracy theories about your being in Dallas the day JFK was killed," E. Howard Hunt nervously replied "No comment."

In his "deathbed" confession ("Howard Hunt and deathbed interview") on which St. John's book is based, Howard Hunt does not elaborate on the specifics of his benchwarmer duties for what he termed "the Big Event." Could he have been the paymaster? After all, a CIA agent has testified under oath she saw Hunt give a cash-filled envelope to Jack Ruby at a CIA safe house in Dallas on assassination eve.[22]

In his final, final confession, Howard Hunt also implicated Lyndon Johnson as the mastermind behind the assassination plot. Though Johnson disliked the Kennedys—especially Bobby—and profited most from President Kennedy's murder, few scholars believe LBJ was in on the hit.

In a *Rolling Stone* article, St. John said his dad even revealed the names of other figures with alleged knowledge of the events in Dallas:

> David Atlee Phillips, a Hunt friend and CIA propaganda expert who first worked with Hunt in helping to overthrow a leftist government in Guatemala in 1954. He was the chief of covert action in Mexico City in 1963. Phillips later ran President Nixon's successful CIA-led campaign to overthrow Chilean President Salvador Allende.
>
> Cord Meyer, a CIA agent and disinformation specialist. Meyer's beautiful bohemian ex-wife, Mary Pinchot Meyer, had had an affair with JFK. At age 43, Mary was killed by two professionally placed bullets, fired from up close, as she took an afternoon stroll on a canal towpath near the Potomac River in Washington.
>
> Bill Harvey, a CIA veteran with connections to the failed CIA-backed Bay of Pigs invasion in 1961, and to Mafia godfathers Santos Trafficante and Sam Giancana.
>
> Frank Sturgis, a CIA operative and Hunt pal who once boasted to another CIA operative, Marita Lorenz, that "We killed Kennedy." In 1972, Sturgis was arrested as one of Nixon's Hunt-supervised Watergate burglars.
>
> David Morales, a CIA agent who helped train Cuban exiles for the Bay of Pigs. He also ran CIA-assassination programs in South America and Vietnam. In a drunken tirade in

1973, he said to his close friend Ruben Carbajal, "We took care of that son of a bitch [President Kennedy], didn't we?"

Antonio Veciana, a Cuban exile and the founder of the militant CIA-backed "Alpha 66." Veciana told a Senate investigator he once saw alleged JFK assassin Lee Harvey Oswald talking with a CIA man he knew as "Maurice Bishop"—widely believed to have been David Atlee Phillips's CIA code name.

In *Rolling Stone*, St. John Hunt said his dad told him there was a "French gunman" firing from the famed grassy knoll in Dealey Plaza. And he clearly recalled his mother telling him, on November 22, 1963, that his dad was on a business trip to Dallas.[23]

Does St. John's tale ring true? Perhaps in that last crucial area—his dad's whereabouts on that dark day. For the most part, however, it could just be that E. Howard Hunt was practicing what was known during Watergate as a "modified limited hang out." John Ehrlichman, the Nixon aide who dealt with the CIA, coined that term. It has come to mean a reluctant partial release of information while managing to withhold the most damaging facts of the case. In addition, why didn't Howard even dare to implicate the most obvious killers of John Kennedy—his biggest enemy—the Mafia, whose godfathers thought he had betrayed them? The Mafia is good at murder, but it takes the government to cover up a crime many top mobsters themselves have confessed to over the last several decades.

Until his last "confession," E. Howard Hunt was destined to be remembered by history mainly as President Nixon's chief White House spy—a former senior CIA officer who served 33 months in prison for his role as a leader of the Watergate burglary. Now, however, it becomes much easier to at least believe that Hunt was in Dallas on November 22, 1963—just as the jury at the libel suit concluded in that 1985 trial.

In 2009, St. John Hunt completely changed his tune—conceding that his dad had not told him the entire truth about the JFK assassination. In what he termed "probably the last interview I'll do," E. Howard Hunt's son said the longtime CIA spy had disclosed only "some of what he knew," and that "it's quite possible" his dad did "minimalize [sic] his role in the JFK hit."

"If only I had been able to stay with him longer and we were able to keep our project a secret from the rest of the family I would have been able to get the whole story," St. John told Waking the Midnight Sun, a website devoted to "magic and realism, high weirdness and everyday life."

Aside from possibly hiding his own role in the JFK assassination, E. Howard Hunt may have "left out" the involvement of CIA director Richard Helms, St. John said. "My father's loyalty to Helms is well known, and of course we all know that Helms was a master at getting the dirty work done while keeping his own involvement above suspicion."

St. John Hunt also confirmed that his father set up a CIA front called the Cuban Revolutionary Council in New Orleans, and said his father might have met Lee Harvey Oswald in the office building both men reportedly used there. "Certainly their paths crossed very closely and my father was training Cubans for the invasion in Guatemala around New Orleans."

That question about a possible Hunt-Oswald association, as well as many others related to the JFK assassination, could soon be answered if the CIA releases the 3,603 secret documents on the JFK assassination in October 2017. Many are related to Hunt, Morales, Phillips, Harvey, and others named by Hunt.

(The list of the files was first made public by the investigative news site WhoWhatWhy.org on February 4, 2016, by reporter Russ Baker.)

Another key question about Howard Hunt and the JFK assassination could be buried in the CIA files slated for declassification: Did Hunt ever work on a still top-secret CIA program with Clay Shaw? In 1969, Shaw became the only man ever tried as part of an alleged conspiracy to murder President Kennedy. After a 39-day trial, a New Orleans jury took less than an hour to find the wealthy local businessman not guilty. But the jury did not know what was disclosed by the CIA after Shaw's death: he had repeatedly committed perjury at his trial.

Then 55, the tall, white-haired, distinguished-looking Shaw was indicted and tried by a rather flamboyant ex-FBI agent—the parish's controversial district attorney, Jim Garrison. The D.A. and his staff produced enough evidence to convince the jury there was a conspiracy—but the jurors said Shaw did not participate in it. Could the jury have been mistaken on Shaw? Looking at the case through history's rearview mirror, yes indeed.

Shaw was a military intelligence officer in World War II. His first postwar job was with a CIA proprietary, the Mississippi Shipping Company. At the time of his trial, Shaw was a director of Permindex, a Swiss firm suspected of not only being a CIA front but also of laundering money for the Mafia. Shaw was also the director of the International Trade Mart in New Orleans—a position that entailed extensive foreign travel. It was not until 1996 that the CIA disclosed Shaw had obtained an agency security clearance as far back as 1949.

We now know the defendant (played by Tommy Lee Jones in Oliver Stone's 1991 film *JFK*) lied under oath when he answered the most critical question of his trial: "Mr. Shaw, have you ever worked for the Central Intelligence Agency?" His response: "No, I have not." Shaw lied yet again—and even more boldly—after the trial, telling *Penthouse*, "I have never had any connection with the CIA." In 1979, however, former CIA director Richard Helms acknowledged under oath that Shaw had been a contact in the CIA's Domestic Contact Service.

As a CIA contact, Shaw used his cover as a businessman to feed the agency intelligence from his frequent foreign travels. JFK assassination researcher Martin Shackelford reports that Shaw's CIA activities included a still-secret conspiracy that involved a future Watergate felon:

> As late as 1967, Shaw had a "covert security" classification for a top secret program called QKENCHANT. The program remains so highly classified that we are still unable to learn anything about its nature, but Shaw's classification was approved by the CIA's then covert operations chief, Richard Helms ... Former CIA official Victor Marchetti said that QKENCHANT was most likely run out of the Domestic Operations Division of the Clandestine Services, run by Tracy Barnes. Support for this comes from recently-released documents identifying Barnes' then-deputy, E. Howard Hunt, as another individual involved with QKENCHANT.[24]

A top CIA spy before he became a secret agent for President Nixon's "black projects," E. Howard Hunt has long been a JFK assassination suspect.

Nonetheless, if Hunt and Shaw had worked together on QKENCHANT, it seems fair to ask whether they might also have been key players in the murder of our thirty-fifth president. At Shaw's trial, the defendant was shown a picture of the late

David Ferrie—another prime suspect in the JFK assassination—and was then asked "whether you have ever known this man?" Shaw declared, "No, I never have."

Once a man perjures himself on the stand, there is reasonable suspicion to suspect he will do so again, and according to many credible witnesses, he did in this case. Several prominent citizens of Clinton, Louisiana, testified that they had seen Shaw in the company of Ferrie and Lee Harvey Oswald. Longtime Ferrie friend Raymond Broshears said he saw Shaw and Ferrie together a number of times; and a Ku Klux Klan member named Jules Ricco Kimble said Ferrie introduced him to Shaw. (Photographic evidence has since turned up showing that Ferrie and Oswald were friends.)

Vernon Bundy told the Shaw jury he had seen the defendant meet with Oswald at a seawall on Lake Pontchartrain in June 1963. (Shaw also swore at his trial that he never knew Oswald.) Mailman James Hardiman testified that he had delivered letters addressed to "Clay Bertram" to a forwarding address for Clay Shaw—and that none of the letters was ever returned.

Standing six-foot-six in socks, "Big Jim" Garrison was an imposing figure with a booming voice. His key witness was Perry Russo—then a 21-year-old insurance agent. Russo positively identified a photo of Clay Shaw as "Clay Bertrand." He testified that, in September 1963, he had overheard Shaw discussing plans to assassinate Kennedy. Russo said others present were Ferrie and a man introduced to him as "Leon Oswald."

Shaw's defense team, led by F. Irvin Dymond, undercut Russo's testimony by saying Garrison had drugged and hypnotized the witness to obtain his statement. The D.A. insisted Russo was hypnotized and given "truth serum" only to make certain of his honesty. The speedy not-guilty verdict strongly indicates the jurors bought the Shaw legal team's major contentions, including this one. All the jurors agreed, however, that Garrison had proved that the president's death resulted from a conspiracy.

For the rest of his life, Russo stuck to his story about being at a pre-assassination meeting attended by Shaw, Ferrie, and Oswald. Years after the trial, in a videotaped interview, Russo remembered that "Ferrie was in control of the gathering. . . . He was in one of his obsessive evenings concerning his hatred of the President of the United States."

Ferrie died on February 22, 1967—just as Garrison was about to indict him. Ferrie was found lying on a couch in his apartment with a sheet pulled over his still-bewigged head. Two typed but unsigned suicide notes were found nearby. The first began, "To leave this life, to me, is a sweet prospect." The second simply said that "when you read this I will be quite dead and no answer will be possible." Metro Crime Commission director Aaron Kohn believed Ferrie was murdered. But the coroner ruled his death was natural—caused by a cerebral hemorrhage.

Clay Shaw did not live to bear the added burden of being exposed as a perjurer when the CIA, in 1979, finally admitted he had worked for them. He was carrying a heavy enough load when he died: despondency over a stack of unpaid legal bills and depression over his outing as a homosexual. A chain smoker, Shaw died in 1974—apparently of lung cancer. He was buried before an autopsy could be performed.

In time, historians may piece together more hidden fragments of the truth about Richard Nixon, the CIA, the Mob, and the death of John F. Kennedy. But their task will be made far easier if Earl Warren's "national security" strictures are removed—and if the "national security" deletions on the Watergate tapes are restored.

FIFTEEN

"The Bay of Pigs"

How might Richard Nixon and the CIA have come up with the "Bay of Pigs" to secretly refer to the JFK assassination?

When Nixon was vice president, he and then-CIA agent Hunt were principal secret planners of the invasion of Cuba that failed so miserably when President Kennedy ordered it. Nixon and Hunt were also key leaders of an associated—and also ill-fated—plot to assassinate Cuban leader Fidel Castro. As Kennedy scholar Richard Mahoney has noted, Nixon "was pushing hard in secret councils for Castro to be forcibly removed, either by invasion or 'executive action.' . . . By mid-summer 1960, the drive to eliminate Castro countenanced assassination."[1]

Richard Bissell, a top CIA official at the time, later recalled, "Assassination was intended to reinforce the [Bay of Pigs] plan. There was the thought that Castro would be dead before the landing. Very few, however, knew of this aspect of the plan."[2] For the "executive action" mission, potential assassins were recruited from Mafia ranks, so that if any of their activities were disclosed, organized crime could be blamed.

President Kennedy publicly accepted full responsibility for the April 17, 1961, invasion in which 1,400 exiles were quickly overwhelmed by some 20,000 Cuban troops. But, convinced he was set up by the CIA, Kennedy fired CIA chief Allen Dulles— an old Nixon friend—and, in a fit of rage, swore to dismantle the agency.

Nixon, Hunt, and many CIA and exile leaders pinned almost complete blame for the military catastrophe on Kennedy for not providing adequate air cover. At the time, Nixon told a reporter it was "near criminal" for Kennedy to have canceled the air cover.[3] In one of his many books, Hunt later accused the president of "a failure of nerves."

Mafia bosses were angry with Kennedy too. Already enraged by his anticrime crusade in this country, they were equally upset that their lucrative gambling casinos—shuttered by Castro— would not be returning to Cuba. What if the Mob and renegade elements of the CIA decided to send their hired guns against Kennedy instead of Castro? More importantly, did Nixon know? After all, he and Hunt had come up with the original ideas they thought JFK later bungled. And Nixon's tight CIA and Mafia contacts undoubtedly kept him completely up-to-date on major related developments.

L. Fletcher Prouty, a former Air Force officer who regularly worked with the CIA on covert operations, has said Nixon "may very well have realized" that such a killing team "was involved" in the Kennedy murder.

In his book, Helms denied knowing what Haldeman was talking about during their June 23, 1972 meeting: "The Bay of

Pigs hasn't got a damned thing to do with this . . . And what's more, there's nothing about the Bay of Pigs that's not already in the public domain."

Helms's response, however evasive, points to the probability that the subject Nixon raised to him through Haldeman actually dealt with something other than the invasion. Indeed, the CIA's own top-secret postmortem on the invasion—when it was finally declassified in 1998—discloses major agency blunders and criticizes the failure to inform President Kennedy that "success had been dubious."[4]

But the report contains absolutely nothing that could be interpreted as sensitive to national security.

In a 1992 TV interview with Larry King, former president Richard Nixon said he'd never had any interest in digging into the JFK assassination: "I don't see a useful purpose in getting into that and I don't think it's frankly useful for the Kennedy family to constantly raise that up again."

His closed-lip approach on the subject is unsurprising, but there's good reason to doubt the truth of Nixon's professed disinterest in the subject: it came from the most paranoid chief executive in history, a guy who relished investigations, spying, secrets, and conspiracies. As John Ehrlichman observed in a mid-1990s interview, "He was a conspiracy buff. He liked intrigue, and he liked secret maneuverings of the FBI, and he liked to hear about what the CIA did, and so on. He just couldn't leave that stuff alone."

As for Nixon's stated compassion for the Kennedys, evidence shows he deeply despised them. So much so that, as president, he ordered E. Howard Hunt to forge diplomatic cables to make it look like President Kennedy ordered the murder of South Vietnamese leader Ngo Dinh Diem. He darkly suggested at a news conference that if Robert Kennedy, as attorney general, had placed more wiretaps on mobsters, perhaps his brother would not have been killed in Dallas. Nixon dispatched White House spy Anthony Ulasewicz to Chappaquiddick, Massachusetts, to investigate the 1969 crash of a car driven by Edward Kennedy that killed the senator's female companion.

In a 1990 TV interview with journalist Morton Kondracke, Nixon said, "I don't know," when asked whether he thought Oswald acted alone in killing Kennedy. As usual, he gave the impression he had no interest at all in the topic: "And I refuse to read the new books and see the docudramas and so forth."

Kondracke also wanted to know whether, as president, Nixon ever saw any evidence suggesting that JFK's "attempts to kill Castro inspired Castro to kill him, or any such thing." Not arguing with his questioner's determination that JFK had tried to bump off the Cuban leader and failing to mention any of his own secret vice presidential efforts to do the same, Nixon responded, "No. No, I have never seen any information of that type. All I know is what I read in books [which he forgot he just said he refused to read] and the newspapers and what I have seen, a modest amount, on TV."

The remarks register "Whopper" on what might be called the "Buzhardt Test." Nixon's closest Watergate lawyer, Fred Buzhardt, once called Nixon "the most transparent liar" he'd ever met. "Almost invariably when the president lied, he would repeat himself, sometimes as often as three times—as if he were trying to convince himself," he added.

Perhaps a truer gauge of Nixon's interest in, and feelings toward, political assassinations is contained in his almost cavalier

1991 assessment of what should be done about the troublesome Iraqi dictator, Saddam Hussein: "If I could find a way to get him out of there, even putting a contract out on him, if the CIA still did that kind of thing, assuming it ever did, I would be for it."

SIXTEEN

Blackmailing the CIA Chief

In the dark, early hours of June 17, 1972, from inside the offices of the Democratic National Committee at the Watergate office building in Washington, DC, burglar James McCord radioed an alarm to his two supervisors. Monitoring the operation from their command post in the Watergate Hotel, E. Howard Hunt and G. Gordon Liddy heard McCord's electronic whisper that he and the four other burglars might have been detected.

"Scratch it," Hunt advised.

But instead Liddy commanded to McCord: "Let's go! Everybody's here [meaning the four Cuban-American burglars from Miami] . . . Go!"

"So they went . . . filed off into history," Hunt later recalled.[1]

Minutes after the men heeded Liddy's order, DC police nabbed McCord and the burglars, dressed in suits and ties and wearing surgical gloves. Hunt and Liddy hastily fled the scene, but were eventually tied to the crime.

These men would become the first known participants in the

nation's biggest political scandal. Two summers later, "Watergate" forced President Richard Nixon to resign in disgrace.

This was no ordinary burglary team: Ex–CIA agent Hunt was Nixon's chief White House spy; ex–CIA agent McCord and ex–FBI agent Liddy were top officials of the president's 1972 campaign committee. The Cuban-Americans had CIA ties and—with Hunt as their supervisor—had been involved in planning the failed CIA-backed Bay of Pigs invasion of Cuba eleven years earlier. All of the men had been involved in previous clandestine Nixon White House operations against the president's enemies.

Hunt and Liddy had also participated in a particularly sordid affair—planning the assassination of newspaper columnist Jack Anderson, one of Nixon's preeminent foes in the media. Anderson had been a thorn in Nixon's side ever since he worked for columnist Drew Pearson and wrote a story in the 1950s about large contributions to early Nixon campaigns by one of the leading mobsters in Los Angeles—Meyer Lansky. Anderson's stories during Nixon's presidency about mobster Johnny Rosselli (the Mafia's liaison with the CIA) and various Mob-CIA plots infuriated the president. He worried that Rosselli, a loose cannon, would become too friendly with Anderson. Nixon knew Rosselli had plenty of secrets to divulge, some of them personal . . . such as Rosselli's work on the Nixon-Hunt plan to kill Castro. These factors had led to White House discussions about the columnist's murder.

The plot against Anderson only came to light in 1975 when the *Washington Post* reported that, "according to reliable sources," Hunt told associates after the Watergate break-in that he was ordered to kill the columnist in December 1971 or January 1972. The plan allegedly involved the use of poison obtained from a CIA physician. The *Post* reported that the assassination order came from a "senior official in the Nixon White House," and that it was "canceled at the last minute."[2]

Hunt never publicly acknowledged that the anti-Anderson effort included murder, or that the order came from the president. However, in an affidavit about a key meeting on the matter of how to get back at Anderson with his White House boss, Charles Colson, Hunt said, "Colson seemed more than usually agitated, and I formed the impression that he had just come from a meeting with President Nixon."[3]

For his part, Liddy acknowledged that he and Hunt were assigned the task of "stopping" Anderson: "We examined all the alternatives and very quickly came to the conclusion that the only way you're going to be able to stop him is to kill him. . . . And that was the recommendation."[4]

President Nixon chose to be out of the country the day of the Watergate break-in. He was visiting a private island in the Bahamas owned by his old drinking buddy Robert Abplanalp, a wealthy businessman. Nixon had choppered there from his Key Biscayne home. Hot-tempered even under normal conditions, the chief executive went ballistic when Colson told him by phone that his men had been arrested at the Watergate. Nixon grew so enraged, that, as mentioned earlier, he threw an ashtray against one of the walls in Abplanalp's luxurious Caribbean retreat.[5]

Knowing his presidency was threatened, Nixon moved quickly to save himself. His major weapons were lies, cover-ups, and blackmail. He first instructed his press secretary, Ron Ziegler, to inform reporters back in Florida that it was beneath the White House to even comment on a "third-rate burglary attempt."

On June 22, after returning to the White House, Nixon made his first public comment on the burglary. He flatly asserted that "the White House has had no involvement whatever" in the break-in. And he declared, convincingly, that such an event "has no place in our electoral process or in our governmental process."

On the twenty-third, in an effort to get the CIA to stop the FBI's initial Watergate probe, Nixon tried to blackmail CIA director Richard Helms by using his knowledge of CIA participation in the JFK assassination to keep the lid on Watergate.

He coached his chief of staff, Bob Haldeman, on what he could say to plant fear in Helms about Hunt in a key Watergate meeting scheduled for later that day:

> Of course, this Hunt, that will uncover a lot of things. You open that scab, there's a lot of things, and we just feel that it would be very detrimental to have this thing go any further. This involves the Cubans, Hunt and a lot of hanky panky that we have nothing to do with ourselves.

The message he wanted to get across to Helms, Nixon told Haldeman, was that under pressure, an apprehended Hunt would start blabbing to authorities about the "Bay of Pigs."

> Hunt knows too damned much. . . . If this gets out that this is all involved . . . it would make the CIA look bad, it's going to make Hunt look bad, and it's likely to blow the whole Bay of Pigs thing . . . which we think would be very unfortunate for both the CIA and the country . . . and for American foreign policy.[6]

At another point in the conversation, Nixon instructed Haldeman to tell Helms that "the President believes this is going to open up the whole Bay of Pigs thing again. And that they [the

CIA] should call the FBI in and [unintelligible] don't go any further into this case. Period."

The "Bay of Pigs" phrase drew an immediate and furious reaction from the CIA chief. Helms gripped the arms of his chair, leaned forward and shouted: "The Bay of Pigs has nothing to do with this! I have no concern about the Bay of Pigs," Haldeman later recalled in a post-Watergate book. He remembered being "absolutely shocked by Helms's violent reaction" when he delivered Nixon's message.[7]

Nixon aide John Ehrlichman, who had sat in on the meeting, corroborated Haldeman's story. "When Haldeman hinted that the trail might lead to the Bay of Pigs, Richard Helms yelled like a scalded cat. 'We're not afraid of that!' he said with more animation than I'd ever seen in that urbane gentleman before. Richard Helms was not attractive when he got excited. I thought at the time, the Bay of Pigs was obviously a very touchy subject."[8]

That's because Helms knew the phrase "Bay of Pigs," used in this context by Nixon, did not refer to the 1961 Cuban invasion. Rather it referred to the secret Nixon-CIA code name for JFK's assassination.

Haldeman himself revealed the meaning of the phrase in his book. Haldeman never revealed his source, but evidence points to Nixon, since, as John Ehrlichman put it, "[v]irtually nothing Nixon did was done without Haldeman's knowledge. That is not to say that Haldeman approved everything Nixon said or did; but it was essential that he know, and have a chance to object, before it happened."

As for Ehrlichman, he went to his grave without spilling any "Bay of Pigs" secrets. He did, however, write a novel about a president and a CIA chief trying to blackmail each other over a previous assassination plot that involved both men.[9]

If Haldeman knew about the CIA's alleged involvement in the Kennedy murder, Nixon had to be his source. The president would have had to tell his top aide what was truly behind his "Bay of Pigs" threat against the agency.[10] That conclusion gains solid support from a recently released Watergate tape—from May 18, 1973—in which Nixon and Haldeman recall the "Bay of Pigs" warning Haldeman delivered to Helms the previous June, and Haldeman reminds Nixon that Helms said he had no concern about the Bay of Pigs.

> HALDEMAN to NIXON: And that surprised me, because I had gotten the impression from *you* that the CIA did have some concern about the Bay of Pigs.

On the tape, Nixon raises no objections to the accuracy of Haldeman's memory.[11]

Watergate expert and National Public Radio correspondent Daniel Schorr also believes that Nixon's Watergate threat to the CIA about the "Bay of Pigs" was "about some deeply hidden scandal . . . an assassination or something on that order. It was supposed to involve the CIA and President Kennedy."

Schorr also says that, to this day, "Helms vows that he has no idea what dark secret Nixon was alluding to. But, whatever it was, it led Nixon into trying to enlist the CIA in an attempted obstruction of justice that became his final undoing."[12]

And although Helms has denied knowing what Haldeman meant by "Bay of Pigs," the expression was enough to get him to cave in to the blackmail threat initially and order the FBI to back off in its Watergate investigation. A CIA memo written by him five days after the June 23 meeting said the agency will "adhere to" its request to the FBI "to desist from expanding the investigation into other areas which may well, eventually, run afoul of our operations."[13]

Speculating separately, JFK assassination expert Jim Marrs—without knowing about Haldeman's revelation—asks two perceptive questions about taped "Bay of Pigs" conversations between Nixon and his most trusted adviser:

> Could they have been circuitously referring to the interlocking connections between CIA agents, anti-Castro Cubans, and mobsters that likely resulted in the Kennedy assassination? Did they themselves have some sort of insider knowledge of this event?[14]

Audiotapes ran on all of Nixon's office and telephone conversations. The president would not want to refer to John F. Kennedy murder secrets as "Dallas" or "the whole JFK thing."

How, logically, could the JFK assassination become known to Nixon and Helms and a few others as the "Bay of Pigs," and how would it become so significant?

As already mentioned, some historians are convinced Nixon and Hunt were key leaders of an associated—and also ill-fated—plot to assassinate Cuban leader Fidel Castro. For that mission, potential assassins were recruited from Mob ranks, so that if any of their activities were disclosed, organized crime could be blamed. As then-director of the CIA's covert operations, Helms was a key participant in the Castro assassination plots.

Fronting for Hughes, Robert Maheu approached mobsters Johnny Rosselli, Sam "Mooney" Giancana, and Santos Trafficante. One report says 15 professional killers ultimately made up the "ultra-black" (deep undercover) Castro assassination team, consistent with a typical mob hit, as summarized by author

David Scheim: "A mob murder is usually a methodical job, performed by a coordinated team of specialists. Up to 15 gunmen, drivers, spotters, and other backup personnel, plus several cars, are used on some jobs."[15]

President Kennedy's former press secretary Pierre Salinger says Maheu told him (in 1968 when Salinger was trying to get a contribution from Maheu's boss, Howard Hughes, for Robert Kennedy's presidential campaign) that the CIA-Mafia plots against Castro were authorized by Nixon: "I knew Maheu well. He told me about his meetings with the Mafia. He said he had been in contact with the CIA, that the CIA had been in touch with Nixon, who had asked them to go forward with this project. . . . It was Nixon who had him [Maheu] do a deal with the Mafia in Florida to kill Castro."[16]

Nixon White House counsel John Dean confirms that Maheu was "the point of contact for the CIA's effort to have the Mafia assassinate Fidel Castro in the early 1960s." Dean said he was told by fellow Nixon aide Jack Caufield that the Hughes empire "was embroiled in an internal war, with two billion dollars at stake, private eyes swarming, nerve-jangling power plays going on, and Mafia figures lurking in the wings."[17]

Longtime Mob lawyer Frank Ragano disclosed in the 1990s that the assassination plot against Castro was hatched in the summer of 1960. He reported that "Maheu's search for Mob killers began with Johnny Roselli who brought in Sam Giancana, the Chicago boss, and Santo [Trafficante] . . . The CIA operatives told Maheu he could offer $150,000 to the assassins, and that Castro's murder was a phase of a larger plan to invade Cuba and oust the Communist government."[18]

Sam "Mooney" Giancana confided to his brother, Chuck, in 1966, that the CIA had offered him $150,000 to hit Castro. "I told 'em I couldn't care less about the money. We'll take care of Castro. One way or another. I think it's my patriotic duty."

Giancana said that CIA director Allen Dulles had come up with the idea and that two top CIA officials—Richard Bissell and Sheffield Edwards—were chosen to make the arrangements. And, he said, the agency made contact with him through Maheu.

Mooney also said that, after holding a Rosselli-arranged meeting with Maheu, he instructed Rosselli "to tell Santo Traffi- cante and Carlos Marcello he wanted them to provide the assis- tance necessary—their Cuban connections—to pull off the CIA assassination plan." Giancana designated Rosselli as the plan's Mafia-CIA liaison.

The Mafia had both longstanding "Cuban connections" and good reasons for wanting to get rid of Fidel Castro. Before the Castro revolution, Havana had been the Las Vegas of the Carib- bean, studded with lucrative gambling casinos owned primarily by the American Syndicate and operating with the complete ap- proval of Cuban dictator Fulgencio Batista—who was, in fact, "owned" by the American Syndicate, particularly by early Nixon supporter Meyer Lansky.

In that 1966 conversation with his brother, Chuck, Sam Gian- cana also mentioned a number of other conspirators in the plot on Castro's life: "Mooney said he put Jack Ruby back in action supplying arms, aircraft, and munitions to exiles in Florida and Louisiana, while the man who had served as Castro's top gam- ing official [during the short time after the revolution that Castro had allowed the casinos to remain open], Frank Fiorini [also known as Watergate burglar Frank Sturgis], joined Ruby in the smuggling venture along with a [Guy] Banister CIA associate, David Ferrie."[19]

Banister was a retired FBI agent with close Mob and CIA

connections. He worked as a private detective while Lee Harvey Oswald lived in New Orleans. An associate of Banister, Ferrie served as an adult leader of the Civil Air Patrol in New Orleans when Oswald was a teenage member. Ferrie, who also worked for Marcello, was the chief suspect in New Orleans district attorney Jim Garrison's investigation of the JFK assassination.

Ex-Watergate burglar and CIA agent Frank Sturgis testified before Congress in 1975 that the Mob offered him $100,000 for the hit on Castro, but he went with the CIA because the agency came through with a higher offer: $150,000. In an interview several years later, Sturgis said he knew Oswald claimed to have CIA connections. He said Oswald had a fistfight with a Sturgis associate when Oswald visited Miami to try to infiltrate an anti-Castro organization there.[20]

Did Nixon know? After all, he and Hunt had come up with the original ideas for the Bay of Pigs invasion they felt JFK had bungled. And Nixon's tight CIA and Mob contacts undoubtedly kept him completely up to date on major related developments.

Former CIA director Richard Helms is very cagey in responding to the "Bay of Pigs" issue in a recent interview for an oral history of the Nixon administration. He denies knowing what Haldeman was talking about. Helms's response, however evasive, lends weight to the probability that the subject Nixon raised with him, through Haldeman, actually dealt with something other than the 1961 CIA-backed invasion of Cuba.[21]

Indeed, the CIA's own top-secret postmortem on the invasion—when it was finally declassified in 1998—disclosed major agency blunders and criticized the failure to inform President Kennedy that "success had been dubious."[22] But the report contains absolutely nothing that could be interpreted as sensitive to national security.

The 150-page document, authored by the agency's inspector general, Lyman Kirkpatrick, followed a six-month internal probe. It blamed the fiasco on "serious mistakes in planning" and found that top CIA officials wrongly blamed the disaster on Kennedy for failing to provide air support for the invaders.

CIA hostility to President Kennedy is underscored in a rebuttal to the report written by the CIA's deputy director of intelligence, Charles Cabell, in which he states the president's "unmitigated and almost willful bumbling" was motivated by his personal malice toward the agency. (Cabell's brother was the mayor of Dallas at the time of the JFK assassination). Cabell's remarks square with the views of Hunt, who charged that Kennedy tried "to whitewash the New Frontier by heaping guilt on the CIA"—guilt, he said, that was "unearned excrement."[23]

The Kirkpatrick Report included one startling disclosure: that the CIA realized the Soviet Union had somehow learned the exact date of the amphibious landing in advance—but went through with the invasion anyway. There are no indications the CIA warned the president of the leak before the invasion took place. The report also showed that CIA director Dulles expressed strong doubts about such operations only three weeks after the failed invasion—in which Castro's forces easily turned back the rebels, killing 200 and capturing 1,200 before they could get off the beach.

The declassified document quotes Dulles as saying he was "the first to recognize that I don't think that the CIA should run paramilitary operations of the type in Cuba. I think we should limit ourselves more to secret intelligence collection and operations of the non-military category."[24]

Several days before the invasion, the Miami correspondent for the *New York Times*, Tad Szulc, wrote a story about the planned landing. But, after a personal appeal from President Kennedy, senior *Times* editors toned it down. Two months later, Szulc told the Senate Foreign Relations Committee that information about the supposedly secret invasion had been available in Miami in March to any interested reporter.

Kennedy later told *Times* editors, "If you had printed more about the operation, you would have saved us from a colossal mistake."[25]

Apart from the suspicious interactions between Nixon and the CIA dealing with the Bay of Pigs, the president's Watergate warning to Helms about the dangerous CIA secrets Hunt could tell—and the events leading up to it—deserves a closer look.

As far back in his presidency as September 18, 1971, Nixon contemplated ordering the CIA to turn over to him its complete files on the "Bay of Pigs." This happened at a White House meeting of Nixon, Attorney General John Mitchell, and Nixon aides Haldeman, Ehrlichman, and Egil Krogh. Ehrlichman's hand-written notes have Ehrlichman telling the group: "Bay of Pigs—order to CIA—President is to have the FULL file or else—nothing withheld. President was involved in Bay of Pigs—must have the file—theory—deeply involved—must know all."

The president personally followed up at a meeting with Helms on October 8, 1971. Ehrlichman sat in. His notes quote Nixon as saying, "Purpose of request for documents: must be fully advised in order to know what to duck; won't hurt Agency, nor attack predecessor."

Helms answered: "Only one president at a time; I only work for you."

Nixon then said: "Ehrlichman is my lawyer—deal with him on all this as you would me."

After Ehrlichman tells Helms he'll be making requests for more material, Helms responds: "OK, anything."[26]

Watergate burglar and former CIA agent Frank Sturgis supports the possibility that these conversations, too, actually dealt with the JFK assassination. Sturgis has said Nixon asked Helms "several times" for "the files on the Kennedy assassination but Helms refused to give it to him, refused a direct order from the President." Backing Sturgis's assertion that the CIA failed to obey Nixon's order is a newly released Watergate tape of a May 18, 1973, conversation in which Haldeman tells Nixon: "[Helms says the CIA] has nothing to hide in the Bay of Pigs. Well, now, Ehrlichman tells me in just the last few days that isn't true. CIA was very concerned about the Bay of Pigs, and in the investigation apparently he was doing on the Bay of Pigs stuff. At some point, there is a key memo missing that CIA or somebody has caused to disappear that impeded the effort to find out what really did happen on the Bay of Pigs."[27]

Haldeman claimed the CIA cover-up of the JFK assassination included failing to tell the Warren Commission about agency assassination attempts against Fidel Castro, an accusation also leveled against Commission member Gerald Ford.[28] And he disclosed that the CIA's counterintelligence chief James Angleton phoned the FBI's Bill Sullivan to rehearse their answers to possible commission questions. Haldeman gave these samples:

Q. Was Oswald an agent of the CIA?
A. No.
Q. Does the CIA have any evidence showing that a conspiracy existed to assassinate Kennedy?
A. No.

Haldeman pointed out that Sullivan was Nixon's "highest-ranking loyal friend" at the FBI.

In the early days of the Watergate cover-up, according to Ehrlichman, Nixon "knew a great many things about Hunt that I didn't know." He quotes the president as saying, "His lawyer is Bittman. . . . Do you think we could enlist him to be sure Hunt doesn't blow national secrets?"

As late as March 21, 1973, as powerful congressional Republicans started expressing serious backroom doubts about the president's credibility and survivability, Nixon was still deeply concerned about keeping Hunt quiet. He told aide John Dean that Hunt's demands for an additional $120,000 in hush money must be met. And the two men then had this exchange:

NIXON: Well, your major guy to keep under control is Hunt.
DEAN: That's right.
NIXON: I think. Because, he knows . . .
DEAN: He knows so much.
NIXON: . . . about a lot of other things.[29]

Nixon's blackmailing efforts even extended to former president Lyndon Johnson. A 1994 book based on Haldeman's personal diaries shows that, in January 1973, Nixon tried to coerce LBJ into using his influence with Senate Democrats to derail the Watergate investigation.[30]

Haldeman said Nixon threatened to go public with information that LBJ bugged the Nixon campaign in 1968. When Johnson heard of the threat, "he got very hot and called Deke [DeLoach, number-three man at the FBI] and said to him that if the Nixon people are going to play with this, he would release information" that would be even more damaging to Nixon.

In reviewing Haldeman's book, the *San Francisco Chronicle* noted that the "information that Mr. Johnson was going to release was deleted from Mr. Haldeman's diary by the National Security Council during the Carter administration, which scrutinized it for sensitive national security material. It is the only such deletion in the entire book."

Whatever it was, it worked. Nixon dropped the blackmail plan after LBJ's counterthreat. The *Chronicle* quoted Nixon historian Stephen Ambrose as saying that Johnson "obviously had something powerful enough on Nixon to make him back off."

Did LBJ have some evidence that Nixon knew in advance of the plan to kill JFK?

Attorney General Robert Kennedy himself suspected CIA/Mob involvement in his brother's assassination.

Kennedy learned the identity of Howard Hughes operative (and onetime Nixon dirty trickster) Robert Maheu when he was told about the Maheu-arranged CIA-Mafia murder conspiracy against Castro. Hughes expert Michael Drosnin reports that RFK was "shocked. Not about the failed attempt to kill Castro, which he and his brother almost certainly approved in advance, but about the CIA's choice of hit men. Especially Giancana."[31]

Jack Newfield, producer of the 1998 Discovery Channel documentary *Robert F. Kennedy: A Memoir*, said that Robert Kennedy had a firm idea about who killed his brother: "Bobby told [JFK adviser] Arthur Schlesinger he blamed 'that guy in New Orleans'—which meant (mob boss) Carlos Marcello. Bobby was intense about prosecuting Marcello as attorney general. He deported him in 1961, indicted him when he returned, and tried him in 1963."[32]

In 1998, the Assassination Records Review Board declassified a January 4, 1975, memo in which Secretary of State Henry

Kissinger reported that, as attorney general, "Robert Kennedy personally managed the operation on the assassination of Castro."

The memo, involving a conversation between Kissinger and President Gerald Ford, centered on a potentially harmful CIA scandal. Kissinger told Ford that former CIA director Richard Helms was warning that press reports surfacing about CIA "dirty tricks" were "just the tip of the iceberg" and that if more information came out "blood will flow."

Newsweek editor Evan Thomas, the first to write about the previously secret document in the *Washington Post*, cautioned that it does not make clear whether Kissinger "believes the story that he is passing along from Helms or, for that matter, whether Helms is truly alleging that Robert Kennedy ran the assassination program or just that the press is cooking up a story about Kennedy's involvement."

During the Lyndon Johnson presidency, Jack Anderson wrote a column about an "unconfirmed report" that RFK "may have approved a plot which backfired against his late brother." Drosnin said this "was Bobby's worst nightmare, the fear that he confided to a few close friends that Castro or the Mafia or the CIA itself ordered his brother's murder."[33]

DALLAS

Everyone who lived through the JFK assassination knows exactly where he or she was on November 22, 1963 . . . with one exception: Richard Nixon, who actually happened to be in Dallas that fateful day, could not recall this fact when he was questioned by the FBI only months later. The interview dealt with an apparently erroneous claim by Marina Oswald that her husband had targeted Nixon for death during an earlier 1963 trip to Dallas. A February 28, 1964, FBI report on the interview said Nixon "advised that the only time he was in Dallas, Texas, during 1963 was two days prior to the assassination of President John F. Kennedy."

In fact, Nixon had arrived in Dallas two days before the assassination, but he had stayed until the day Kennedy was assassinated. At the time, Nixon was Pepsi's chief counsel. He had been defeated in the 1962 race for governor of California, had moved to an Upper East Side apartment in what he termed "the fast track" of New York City—and was still considered a top Republican who had not abandoned his White House ambitions.

On the morning of November 22, Nixon was up early in his suite at the Baker Hotel in Dallas—a city seething with strong anti-Kennedy feelings. He read a *Dallas Morning News* report on a meeting he'd held with local reporters the previous day. The story quoted him as saying, "I am going to work as hard as I can to get the Kennedys out." President Kennedy, who was in a hotel suite in nearby Fort Worth, "was reportedly irritated by this comment, the latest of several Nixon outbursts, as he scanned the newspapers that last morning." JFK may not have read the part of the story where Nixon did express the hope Kennedy would be granted a "courteous reception in Dallas."

Nixon had arrived on November 20 to attend a Pepsi Cola Company board meeting. Dallas reporter Jim Marrs says Nixon and actress Joan Crawford, a Pepsi heiress, "made comments to the effect that they, unlike the President, didn't need Secret Service protection, and they intimated the nation was upset with Kennedy's policies. It has been suggested that this taunting may have been responsible for Kennedy's critical decision not to order the Plexiglas top placed on his limousine on Nov. 22."

Once adviser Stephen Hess saw Nixon when the former vice president had returned to his New York apartment after the assassination, he said Nixon was "pretty shook up." Hess later portrayed his boss to political reporter Jules Witcover as unusually defensive about his pre-assassination comments in Dallas: "He had the morning paper, which he made a great effort to show me, reporting he had held a press conference in Dallas and made a statement that you can disagree with a person without being discourteous to him or interfering with him. He tried to make the point that he had tried to prevent it. . . . It was his way of saying, 'Look, I didn't fuel this thing.' "

Years later, Hess was more blunt about Nixon's paranoia over the newspaper piece when he told author Anthony Summers, "He was saying to me, in effect, 'You see, I didn't have anything to do with creating this.' He was very concerned that Kennedy had been assassinated by a right-winger and that somehow Nixon would be accused of unleashing public hatred."

What Nixon apparently failed to tell Hess was that the major story from his meeting with reporters in Dallas was certain to fuel the anger of some Texans toward Kennedy (as well as the anger of both JFK and LBJ). The headline in the *Dallas Morning News* on November 22 said: "Nixon Predicts JFK May Drop Johnson." Vice President Johnson was, of course, a Texan.

While Nixon eventually came clean regarding his whereabouts on that fateful day, he seemed touchy whenever the matter was raised. For example, in a 1992 interview with CNN's Larry King, Nixon interjected he was in Dallas "In the morning!" when King cited the presumed geographical coincidence. Nixon claimed to have left Dallas on a flight to New York several hours before Kennedy's noontime arrival at Love Field.

But L. Fletcher Prouty, a top military-CIA operative during

the Eisenhower and Kennedy years, has questioned Nixon's assertion. Prouty says former Pepsi Cola Company general counsel Harvey Russell told him that Russell and several other company executives were meeting with Nixon in Dallas when they heard the news of JFK's assassination. Russell said the group knelt in a brief prayer before Nixon was driven to the airport.

Not only did Nixon misremember where he was on November 22, he made at least three conflicting statements about how he first learned his archenemy had been shot to death. In a 1964 *Reader's Digest* article, he recalled hailing a cab after his Dallas–New York flight: "We were waiting for a light to change when a *man* ran over from *the street corner* and said that the President had just been shot in Dallas." In November 1973, however, Nixon said in *Esquire* that his cabbie "missed a turn somewhere and we were off the highway . . . a *woman* came *out of her house* screaming and crying. I rolled down the cab window to ask what the matter was and when she saw my face she turned even paler. She told me that John Kennedy had just been shot in Dallas."

In his post-presidential memoirs, however, Nixon changed his story yet again. He said nothing about the driver missing a turn or being off the highway. By then, Nixon had somehow recalled his exact location: in Queens near the 59th Street Bridge. He said that while the cab stopped for a light, a *man rushed over from the curb and started talking to the driver*—not to Nixon, as he had most recently claimed about the screaming woman who had run from her house.

In yet another curious twist, a November 22 wire service photo of Nixon indicates he might even have learned of the shooting *before* his cab ride. In the photo, a glum-looking Nixon, hat in lap, is sitting in what appears to be an airline terminal. The caption on the United Press International photo reads: "Shocked

Richard Nixon, the former vice president who lost the presidential election to President Kennedy in 1960, is shown Friday after he arrived at Idlewild Airport in New York following a flight from Dallas, Tex., where he had been on a business trip."

Nixon's actions often contradicted his words when it came to discussing the Kennedy assassination. In the 1992 Larry King interview, Nixon said he'd never had any interest in digging into the JFK assassination: "I don't see a useful purpose in getting into that and I don't think it's frankly useful for the Kennedy family to constantly raise that up again." Yet, as president, there are strong indications that he tried very hard secretly—but unsuccessfully—to obtain the CIA's JFK assassination files.

New tapes show Nixon also pressed aides to plant a false story in the press linking Senator Kennedy to the 1972 assassination attempt against Alabama governor George Wallace.

Even the tiniest tidbit about the Kennedys would greatly excite the president. Chief presidential spy E. Howard Hunt has said Nixon was especially keen on new JFK assassination-related information—if it could be used for "possible political advantage, i.e. if it could be shown ex-post-facto that Mr. Castro and President Kennedy had a working relationship, this might have been of some potential value . . ."

In congressional testimony delivered in the 1970s but only released in recent years, Hunt offered an example of just such information. Nixon's spymaster said that in late 1971 or early 1972 he interviewed a woman (whose name he conveniently could not remember) who had been brought to him in a Miami hotel by fellow unofficial White House spies who carried out unsavory—and frequently illegal—activities for Nixon, such as the Watergate burglary—Bernard Barker and Eugenio Martinez. The woman claimed she was in Cuban leader Fidel Castro's home on November 22, 1963. "The burden of her story was that a pall of gloom had settled over the Fidel Castro household on the [radio] announcement of President Kennedy's death because, according to her—and, again, this is unverifiable information, as far as I know—Mr. Kennedy and Mr. Castro were on the verge of working out some sort of an agreement, a détente, if you will, an arrangement which would permit both countries to live without the tensions that had existed."

Though Hunt stressed the unverifiable nature of this woman's allegation in his testimony, he thought highly enough of it at the time to file a report on his interview with her to the CIA—as well as to his White House boss, Charles Colson, who undoubtedly passed it along to the president. In fact, newly released records show Kennedy and Castro may have been nearing a détente that was aborted by the JFK assassination.

Nixon, of course, as well as the CIA and the Mafia and anti-Castro exiles in the United States, opposed any accommodation with Castro. Many of them were more extreme: they wanted Fidel dead.

Who else was in Dallas on that fateful day? Boasting that he was the mastermind of a Mob/CIA plot to kill President Kennedy, Chicago godfather Sam Giancana told relatives that he, too, was in Dallas to supervise the plot. Giancana claimed that Nixon "knew about the whole damn thing"—adding that he had met with Nixon in Dallas "immediately prior to the assassination."

Giancana had never been adept at keeping secrets. When Mob/CIA hit teams were planning to assassinate Cuban leader Fidel Castro in 1960—an operation reportedly overseen by then-vice president Richard Nixon—Giancana's loose lips allowed FBI director J. Edgar Hoover to discover the plans.

Former CIA contract agent Robert Morrow claims Hoover had also learned about the JFK assassination conspiracy from FBI wiretaps on Mafia chieftains, and had tipped off Nixon—Hoover's favorite politician—in advance. Researcher Mark North contends that Hoover's taps allowed the FBI director to learn of the plot in September 1962. Hoover knew the contract called for the assassination to take place before the next presidential election, which was November 4, 1964, but, Mark North says, he kept all this from his superiors (President Kennedy and Attorney General Robert Kennedy).

Nixon was not the only unsavory character present in Dallas that day; Jack Ruby was there as well. Ten days earlier Ruby had met with Paul Jones, known as the Chicago Mob's "paymaster"—in Syndicate parlance, a trusted individual who passes out envelopes of cash in Mob bribes and/or payoffs. Ruby and Jones hadn't seen each other since the 1940s, but Jones and a Teamsters' organizer named Alexander Gruber, a man with known connections to hoodlums who worked for racketeer Mickey Cohen, stopped by Ruby's apartment for talks on both November 12 and 13. More might have been on the visitors' agenda than talking, however, since when Jack Ruby was arrested for killing Oswald on the twenty-fourth, the debt-ridden striptease club operator had $2,000 on his person, and authorities found $10,000 in his apartment.

Jack Ruby was one busy man on November 22. Shortly after Kennedy was shot, Ruby showed up at Parkland Hospital, where the president had been taken.

Former Dallas reporter Seth Kantor, who was then working for Scripps-Howard newspapers out of Washington and traveling with the presidential party, actually spoke with Ruby at Parkland. Ruby tugged on Kantor's suit jacket, called him by his first name and the two men shook hands. Kantor said Ruby "looked miserable. Grim. Pale. There were tears brimming in his eyes. He commented on the obvious—how terrible the moment was—and did I have any word on the President's condition?" Kantor had no more time for banter with Ruby, and rushed off to hear JFK press aide Mac Kilduff announce to the world that the President was dead.

Jack Ruby later denied being at Parkland at that critical time. Could Ruby, had he been at Parkland then, have planted the "magic bullet" on a stretcher—therefore connecting the crime with the rifle alledgedly used by Oswald?

Though the Warren Commission concluded that Kantor must have been mistaken about his encounter with Ruby at Parkland, this author knew Kantor as a fine, meticulous, and believable reporter. Kantor died of cancer several years ago, but not before a key Warren Commission attorney, Burt Griffin, declared that "the greater weight of the evidence" indicates Kantor did, indeed, see Ruby at Parkland. Some JFK assassination conspiracy buffs think Ruby may have been responsible for planting the bullet on a stretcher at the hospital.

Minutes after Kilduff's announcement of Kennedy's death, Jack Ruby phoned Alex Gruber—the very same Alex Gruber who had dropped by to see Ruby with the Mafia "paymaster" just days earlier.

On the evening of November 22, Ruby was hanging around on the same floor of the police station where Oswald was being questioned. He even attended the midnight police station press conference at which Oswald was trotted out briefly for the world to see. Ruby was apparently armed that night—adding weight to the theory that he had been "stalking" Oswald ever since the alleged assassin's arrest. Ruby originally admitted to police that he was packing a pistol as he mingled with the journalists and policemen that night, but later withdrew the statement because it indicated premeditation on his part.

While he was in jail, Ruby told a reporter: "It is the most bizarre conspiracy in the history of the world. It'll come out at a future date . . ." Ruby also told the reporter—future *Los Angeles Times* and CNN executive Tom Johnson—that he was flying high just before he fired his .38 Colt Cobra into Oswald's gut. "I'd taken thirty antibiotic and Dexedrine pills. They stimulate you."

In the course of the police station press conference, Ruby corrected the Dallas district attorney when he told reporters that Oswald belonged to the Free Cuba Committee, an anti-Castro outfit. Ruby pointed out that the D.A. had meant Fair Play for Cuba, a pro-Castro group.

In fact, the Fair Play for Cuba Committee had only one member in New Orleans: Lee Harvey Oswald. And he was not exactly recruited; Oswald had practically begged to join the outfit in an April 1963 letter to the group's headquarters in New York. He bragged that he had handed out pro-Castro leaflets, but needed more. He told the organization that he had worn a placard around his neck saying HANDS OFF CUBA! VIVA FIDEL!

Was Oswald trying to join the pro-Castro group as a CIA mole? Did Ruby know this and feel it was necessary for reporters to hear his correction at the news conference in order to keep the public characterization of Oswald as a Marxist consistent? Whether he did it for the CIA or not, Oswald certainly had worked hard to define himself that way.

Lee Harvey Oswald was working as an order-filler at the Dallas Texas School Book Depository on November 22. Shortly after shots rang out in Dealey Plaza, Oswald fled the crime scene. Later that afternoon, a policeman trying to arrest Oswald was shot to death. After a struggle with the armed Oswald in a movie theater, police apprehended him and charged him with the murders of both President Kennedy and the policeman.

In 1964, the Presidential Commission headed by Chief Justice Earl Warren concluded that Oswald—firing a rifle from a sniper's nest on the sixth floor of the depository—was Kennedy's sole assassin. The commission portrayed Oswald as a "discontented" loner whose "avowed commitment to Marxism and Communism" might have contributed to his deed.

THE NEW ORLEANS CONNECTION

But the Warren Commission had not looked carefully at the alleged assassin's ties to the Syndicate.

Oswald was murdered two days after the JFK assassination by a local mobster he probably knew, Jack Ruby. After his death, Marina Oswald also linked Oswald to the unsuccessful April 1963 murder attempt in Dallas on former major general Edwin Walker, a right-wing zealot. (Walker had been forced to retire from the army in 1961 after it was discovered he was showing right-wing films to his troops.)

But there are many good reasons to doubt Oswald's involvement in the Walker shooting and to wonder whether linking him to this attempted murder might have been designed to strengthen the belief that he was President Kennedy's assassin by underscoring Oswald's leftist reputation—while once again camouflaging his ties to the Mafia and the CIA. Additionally:

- An eyewitness saw at least two men leave the shooting scene in two cars. He said neither man resembled Oswald—who only learned to drive many months later.
- Four days before the incident, one of Walker's bodyguards spotted two men prowling around Walker's house.
- Walker's name and phone number were found in Oswald's address book.
- Walker may have known both Oswald and Ruby.
- Walker had numerous links with anti-Castro Cubans.

Marina Oswald—a major source for the Warren Commission's conclusion that Lee was involved in the Walker shooting—is not a reliable witness. She also claimed, for example, that she kept her husband from shooting Nixon in Dallas earlier in 1963. Yet Nixon was in Dallas that year only once—for his November visit. (Marina also claimed to have locked Lee in the bathroom to keep him from shooting Nixon. Like most bathrooms, however, theirs locked from the inside.)

In addition to his Mob ties, did Lee Harvey Oswald have connections to the CIA?

The answer, we now know, is "probably yes."

In the 1950s and 1960s, the CIA was a frighteningly potent and, for the most part, unaccountable spy agency. Among its top priorities was ousting Fidel Castro as leader of Cuba. And it certainly appears that Lee Harvey Oswald was a double agent in those efforts.

Oswald's good friend in New Orleans, David Ferrie, was once a CIA pilot, and in 1963, when Oswald spent some time in New Orleans, Ferrie worked for Carlos Marcello's gang and was active in anti-Castro activities.

Both men, Ferrie and Oswald, worked out of the same office building as Guy Banister—a right-wing former head of the Chicago office of the FBI. Banister was seen in his New Orleans office in 1963 having meetings with Ferrie and Oswald. Oswald used Banister's Camp Street address on his supposedly pro-Castro Fair Play for Cuba Committee leaflets. The CIA's E. Howard Hunt had occasion to be in and out of the same building.

THE CIA CONNECTION

Former CIA operative Robert Morrow—who claims Jack Ruby was one of President Kennedy's murderers—blames the assassination on Kennedy's failure to fully support the Bay of Pigs invasion. Morrow also asserts that Oswald went to Russia for the CIA "and was an FBI informant by the summer of 1963, was brought into an assassination plot led by New Orleans resident and CIA consultant Clay Shaw, using right-wing CIA operatives and anti-Castro Cubans headed by Jack Ruby in Dallas and Guy Banister in New Orleans."

In 1976, Congressman Don Edwards—a former FBI agent—concluded from his work as the chairman of a subcommittee on constitutional rights that the FBI and CIA were "somewhere behind [the JFK assassination] cover-up."

In 1978, Senator Richard Schweiker, a Pennsylvania Republican, used words similar to Nixon's private comments in the Oval Office when he described the Warren Commission's findings as "one of the biggest cover-ups in the history of our country." Schweiker maintained that Oswald "was playing out an intelligence role. This gets back to him being an agent or a double agent. . . . I personally believe that he had a special relationship with one of the intelligence agencies; which one, I'm not certain. But all the fingerprints I found . . . point to Oswald as being a product of, and interacting with, the intelligence community."

As a kid, Lee Harvey Oswald seldom missed an episode of his favorite TV show, *I Led Three Lives*, a program about an FBI agent who had infiltrated the Communist Party. Was he already preparing himself for the life of a spy or counterspy?

Just before he joined the Marines, Oswald wrote the Youth League of the Socialist Party of America, seeking information. In the Marines, because of his widely professed interest in Communism—and his constant public practice of Russian—Lee was given the nickname of "Oswaldovich."

Were the leftist actions designed to cover up rightist tendencies that the U.S. Intelligence network used to its advantage? The fact that "Oswaldovich" was granted a "confidential" clearance at Atsugi Air Force Base in Japan—a top-secret installation that was home to the U-2 spy plane—supports that possibility.

CONCLUSION

With crucial help from Richard Nixon, a crooked politician the Mafia got its hooks into early, the godfathers shot to the top of their murderous power and influence during Nixon's presidency.

An early indication that there were connections between Nixon, the Mob, and the Mafia-connected Teamsters Union came when an alternative newspaper, *Sundance,* published a piece by Jeff Gerth, who later became a top investigative reporter for the *New York Times.* In 1972, after a six-month study, Gerth concluded that during Nixon's presidency the Mob "prospered almost unrestricted" by the federal government: "From its base in the gigantic resources of heroin traffic, gambling, prostitution, 'protection,' and a host of other enterprises of violence against society, organized crime has moved like a bulldozer into the world of legal, 'respectable' business," Gerth found. He rightly concluded that his probe of Nixon's connections to organized crime was "merely the top of a dirty iceberg that will slowly become visible over the coming years."[1]

One of the few mainstream newspapers to probe the then president's ties to the Teamsters and the Mob, the *Los Angeles Times*, urged the Justice Department to pursue an unfettered investigation. A June 1, 1973, editorial criticized the feds for dropping wiretaps that were starting to show a Mafia plot to loot Teamsters' pension funds. The newspaper said some federal officials "of unquestioned integrity" suspected that the decision was politically motivated: "One can understand how dispiriting to federal investigators it has been to observe [Teamsters president Frank] Fitzsimmons one day in the company of known criminal chieftains and the next aboard Air Force One with Mr. Nixon."

A much clearer picture of that iceberg is now emerging, thanks to decades of talkative Mafia dons, thousands of books, and two government investigations, as well as new research, fresh interviews, and the release of additional Nixon tapes and documents.

In March 2017, Judge John Tunheim—who headed the Assassination Records Review Board in the 1990s—repeated his call for declassification of the JFK documents. Tunheim declared: "It's time to release them all. There is no real reason to protect this information."[2]

With history cementing him as a front man for the Syndicate, is it a stretch to speculate that Nixon might somehow have been associated with—or at least known in advance—of a Mob contract on President Kennedy's life? After all, since 1946, Nixon had been in the Syndicate's hip pocket, and he was a leading beneficiary of JFK's 1963 murder.

Did the godfathers put out a contract on Kennedy that would ultimately result in the second coming of their favorite godson?

One further question: Is the Mafia still the menace to society and clean government that it was during the Age of Nixon? Well, it is not as murderous now, and it has largely moved to the suburbs—where Mob authority Selwyn Raab says typical Mafia pursuits, such as gambling, drugs, and extortion, have also moved. He adds, however, that the Mafia has lost an important asset: political clout. Raab opines that it will be hard for the godfathers to ever return to the level of influence they exercised during the twentieth century.[3]

ACKNOWLEDGMENTS

Because this book took so long to write, I have lots of fine people to eagerly thank.

The best literary agent in D.C., Ron Goldfarb, gets first mention for convincing Thomas Dunne of St. Martin's Press that this book was worthy of his prestigious imprint. Ron's top assistant, Gerrie Sturman, was invaluable throughout the process.

At St. Martin's, the list of standout contributors is long, beginning with editors Emily Angell and Stephen Power and Emily's terrific assistant Lisa Bonvissuto. Others at St. Martin's genuinely worthy of mention: Eagle-eyed copy editor Ryan Masteller; skillful publicist Joe Rinaldi; production manager Jason Reigal; production editor Ken Silver; marketing expert Danielle Prielipp; and designer Kathy Parise.

I also want to express appreciation to those who have helped me research, think through, and mold the manuscript over the past few years: Jenna Jachles, Alex Brown, and Kilian Korth—sharp former students of mine at American University. And I'm grateful for outstanding suggestions from veteran publishing pros Linda Cashdan and Pat O'Connor.

Supportive family members were led by my sister Deanna Nowicki and my brother-in-law Frank Nowicki.

Close friends who offered encouragement and advice include Jay Bell and Mary Mariani, Rob and Romani Thaler, Jane Berger and Roger Gittines, Fred Tracy, Ted and Cornelia McDonald, Tom Foty, Paula Cruickshank, Tina and Igor Rafalovich, Rick and Nancy Boardman, the Rael Family, Bob and Nancy Sloan, William Klein, Carol and Max Hershey, Kim Mealy, Bill Stoffel, Al Schumm, Liz Specter, Steve and David Toth, David and Patti Victorson, Dan Deutsch, Rob Enelow. Frank Sciortino, Bill Wilson, Bill Scott, Penny Pagano, Greg Clugston, James Cave, Traykia Moore, Mary Chamberlayne, Nicole Hollander, Gladis Reyes, Rowena Gear, and Margaret Southern.

On the same list of dandy friends go the names of old reporting and writing pals Muriel Dobbin, Pat Sloyan, Jim McManus, Dan Moldea, Gus Russo, Bob Moore, Ford Rowan, Sid Davis, David Rosso, Tom Gauger, Tom DeLach, Warren Corbett, Bill McCloskey, Bill Greenwood, David Taylor, Mary Belcher, Denise Gamino, Bonnie Angelo, Craig Smith, Al Spivak, Robert Frishman and Jeanne Shinto, Bill McCulloch and Carolyn Cooper, Howard Dicus, Charlotte Astor—and the late Tom Girard, Pye Chamberlayne, Bob Pierpoint, and Stanley Kutler.

NOTES

Author's Note

1. Chris Matthews, *Kennedy & Nixon: The Rivalry That Shaped Postwar America* (New York: Simon and Schuster, 2011), 289.

Timeline of Events

1. Jim Marrs, *Crossfire: The Plot that Killed Kennedy* (New York: Carroll & Graf, 1989), 268.
2. E. Howard Hunt, *American Spy: My Secret History in the CIA, Watergate and Beyond* (New Jersey: John Wiley and Sons, 2007), 111
3. Frank Ragano and Selwyn Raab, *Mob Lawyer: Including the Inside Account of Who Killed Jimmy Hoffa and JFK* (New York: Charles Schribner's Sons, 1994), 144.
4. Patrick Howley, "Roger Stone: Nixon thought LBJ killed Kennedy," *The Daily Caller*, November 22, 2013.
5. Pat Sloyan, interview with author, 2016.

One: The Mob in the Age of Nixon

1. Editorial, *Life*, October 18, 1963, 6.
2. "Kefauver Crime Committee Launched," U.S. Senate.gov. https://www.senate.gov/artandhistory/history/minute/Kefauver_Crime_Committee_Launched.htm.

3. Ibid.

4. G. Robert Blakey and Richard N. Billings, *Fatal Hour: The Assassination of President Kennedy by Organized Crime* (New York: Berkley Books, 1992), 216.

5. Bryan Bender and Neil Swidey, "Robert F. Kennedy saw conspiracy in JFK's assassination," *The Boston Globe*, Nov. 24, 2013.

6. David Scheim, *Contract on America: The Mafia Murder of President John F. Kennedy* (Zebra Books, 1989), 53.

7. Seth Kantor, *The Ruby Cover-up* (Kensington Publishing Corporation, 1992), 25.

8. Jack Nelson and Bill Hazlett, "Teamsters Ties to Mafia—and to White House," *Los Angeles Times*. May 21, 1973.

Two: The Nixon-Mafia Relationship

1. L. Fletcher Prouty, *JFK: The CIA, Vietnam, and the Plot to Assassinate John F. Kennedy* (Secaucus, NJ: Carol Publishing Group, 1992).

2. Gerald Home, *Class Struggle in Hollywood, 1930–1950, Moguls, Mobsters, Stars, Reds, and Trade Unionists* (Texas: University of Texas Press, 2001), 103.

3. HSCA "Security Classified" testimony released by the Assassination Records Review Board in 1990s.

4. The records were disclosed in a 2003 Discovery Channel TV documentary, *Kennedy and Castro: The Secret History*. The program was based on work conducted by the National Security Archive, a private research group in Washington that collects and publishes declassified documents.

5. Sam Giancana and Chuck Giancana, *Double Cross: The Explosive Inside Story of the Mobster Who Controlled America* (New York: Little, Brown, 1992).

6. Hank Messick, *Lansky* (Mattituck, NY: Amereoh Ltd., 1999), 293.

7. Lance Morrow, *The Best Year of Their Lives: Kennedy, Johnson, and Nixon in 1948: The Secrets of Power* (New York: Basic Books, 2005).

8. Paul Hoffman, "Tiger in the Court" (Playboy Press), 81.

9. Kantor, *The Ruby Cover-Up*.

10. Jeff Gerth, "Richard M. Nixon and Organized Crime," *Penthouse*, July 1974.

11. Number apparently missing from text, but likely refers to the quote on page 29 from Mark Feldstein, *Poisoning the Press: Richard Nixon,*

Jack Anderson, and the Rise of Washington's Scandal Culture (New York: Picador, 2010), 100

12. Herbert Mitgang, "Nixon Enemy in 1950 Had the Last Laugh in '74," *New York Times*. May 25, 1992.

13. *Godfathers Collection: The True History of the Mafia,* The History Channel, 2003.

14. Blakey and Billings, *Fatal Hour,* 262

Three: Dick and Bebe

1. Morrow, *Best Year of Their Lives.*

2. Anthony Summers, *Not in Your Lifetime: The Defining Book on the J.F.K Assassination* (New York: Open Road, 2013).

3. "Nixon's Friend: Charles 'Bebe' Rebozo," *Chicago Tribune,* May 9, 1998.

4. According to JFK Assassination expert A. J. Weberman. See ajweberman.com/medulex13.pdf.

5. Anthony Summers, *The Arrogance of Power,* 101.

6. Arthur Schlesinger, *Journals: 1952–2000.*

7. Seymour Hersh, *The Atlantic,* May 1982; and Rick Perlstein, *Nixonland: The Rise of a President and the Fracturing of America* (New York: Scribner, 2008).

8. Anthony Lukas, *Nightmare: The Underside of the Nixon Years* (Athens: Ohio University Press, 1999), 363.

9. Bob Woodward, *The Last of the President's Men* (New York: Simon and Schuster, 2013), 96–100.

10. Anthony Summers, *The Arrogance of Power: The Secret World of Richard Nixon* (New York, Penguin, 2001), 100.

11. John Ehrlichman, *Witness to Power: The Nixon Years* (New York: Pocket, 1982), 51.

12. *San Francisco Examiner,* June 22, 1973.

13. Carl Oglesby, *The Yankee and Cowboy War: The Astonishing Link Between the JFK Assassination and the Deposing of Nixon* (New York: Berkley Pub Group, 1976).

14. Summers, *Arrogance of Power,* 112.

15. Ibid., 114.

16. Drew Pearson and Jack Anderson "Washington Merry-Go-Round," *Life,* October 31, 1968.

17. Summers, *Not in Your Lifetime.*

18. Bill Bonanno, *Bound by Honor: A Mafioso's Story* (New York: Armeda Ltd., 1999).

19. *Miami News*, June 25, 1974.

20. H. R. Haldeman, *The Ends of Power* (New York: New York Times Books, 1978).

21. Alan Block, *Masters of Paradise: Organized Crime and the Internal Revenue Service in the Bahamas* (New Brunswick: Transaction, 1991), 126.

22. *The Victoria Advocate*, May 18, 1962.

23. Bauder, "Nixon's Swiss Stash," *San Diego Reader*, July 18, 2012.

24. Summers, *Arrogance of Power*, 256.

25. Ibid.

26. Ibid., 258.

27. Ibid., 242.

28. White House guest list, November 4, 1969.

Four: Mobsters in Cuba

1. George Crile, "The Mafia, the CIA and Castro," *The Washington Post*, May 16, 1976.

2. "60 Minutes." In *JFK, Hoffa, and the Mob*. CBS. November 17, 1992.

3. Howard Kohn, "Strange Bedfellows: The Hughes-Nixon-Lansky Connection," *Rolling Stone*, May 20, 1976.

4. Summers, *Arrogance of Power*, 127.

5. Ibid., 125–27.

6. Gus Russo, *Live by the Sword: The Secret War Against Castro and the Death of JFK* (Baltimore, MD: Bancroft Press, 1998), 51.

7. Scott Deitche, *The Silent Don: The Criminal Underworld of Santo Trafficante Jr.* (Fort Lee, NJ: Barricade, 2007), 142–43.

8. Daniel Sheehan, *The People's Advocate: The Life and Legal History of America's Most Fearless Public Interest Lawyer* (Berkeley, CA: Counterpoint, 2013). Daniel Sheehan, "Daniel Sheehan," https://www.youtube.com/channel/UCnrShHXCboC6fNzFFTOCCog/videos. Youtube.

9. John Newman, *Where Angels Tread Lightly: The Assassination of President Kennedy*, vol. 1 (North Charleston, SC: Createspace, 2015), 112–13.

10. Ragano and Raab, *Mob Lawyer*, 67.

11. Ibid., 47.

12. Deitche, *Silent Don*, 87.

13. Summers, *Arrogance of Power*, 243.

14. John A. Andrew III, *Power to Destroy: The Political Uses of the IRS from Kennedy to Nixon* (Chicago, IL: Ivan R. Dee, 2002), 229; and Jeff Gerth, "Nixon and the Mafia," *Rolling Stone*, November 1, 1972.

15. Dan Moldea, *The Hoffa Wars: Teamsters, Rebels, Politicians, and the Mob* (Paddington Press, 1978), 106.

16. Andrew, *Power to Destroy*, 234.

17. Block, *Masters of Paradise*, 12.

18. *Sundance*.

19. Michael Newton, *Mr. Mob: The Life and Crimes of Moe Dalitz* (Jefferson, NC: McFarland, 2009), 227.

20. Summers, *Arrogance of Power*, 244.

21. Block, *Masters of Paradise*, 99–100.

22. James Hogan, *Spooks: The Haunting of America: The Private Use of Secret Agents*, (New York: William Morrow and Company, 1978), 180.

23. Summers, *Arrogance of Power*, 244.

24. Block, *Masters of Paradise*, 294.

25. Deitche, *Silent Don*, 102.

26. Robert Kirkconnell, *American Heart of Darkness*, vol. 1, (Bloomington, IN: Xlibris, 2013), 147.

27. Alan J. Weberman and Michael Canfield, *Coup d'Etat in America: The CIA and the Assassination of John F. Kennedy*, (San Francisco, CA: Quick American Archives, 1992), 84.

28. Dan Baum, *Harper's*, "Legalize It All," April 2016, and Adam Edelman, "Top adviser to Richard Nixon admitted that 'War on Drugs' was policy tool to go after anti-war protesters and 'black people,'" New York *Daily News*, March 23, 2016.

29. Newman, *Where Angels Tread Lightly*, 61–64.

Five: Nixon's Mafia Web

1. Joseph Trento, *Prelude to Terror: The Rogue CIA and the Legacy of America's Private Intelligence Network* (New York: Carroll and Graf, 2005), 9.

2. Douglas Valentine, *The Strength of the Wolf: The Secret History of America's War on Drugs* (Brooklyn, NY: Verso Books, 2006), 260.

3. David Kaiser, *The Road to Dallas*, (Cambridge, MA: Belknap Press, 2009), 302.

4. David Talbot, *Brothers: The Hidden History of the Kennedy Years* (London: Simon and Schuster, 2007), 187.

5. Michael Drosnin, *Citizen Hughes: The Power, the Money, and the Madness* (New York: Holt, Rinehart, and Winston, 1985), 296.

6. Frank McCullough, conversation with author, December 2010.

7. Howard Kohn, "The Hughes-Nixon-Lansky Connection: The Secret Alliances of the CIA from World War II to Watergate," *Rolling Stone*, May 30, 1976.

8. "Robert Maheu, 90; Tycoon's Aide, CIA Spy," *Washington Post*, August 6, 2008.

9. "Hughes Bribe of Nixon Alleged," *Las Vegas Sun*, February 28, 2005.

10. Ibid.

11. Jack Anderson column, August 28, 1974.

12. Summers, *Arrogance of Power*, 109.

13. Block, *Masters of Paradise*, 126.

14. Drosnin, *Citizen Hughes*, 360.

15. Ibid., 260.

16. Sally Denton and Roger Morris, *The Money and the Power: The Making of Las Vegas*, (New York: Vintage 2002), 284.

17. Carl Sifakis, *Mafia Encyclopedia*, 362.

18. Denton and Morris, *The Money and the Power*, 284.

19. Drosnin, *Citizen Hughes*, 505, 506.

20. "Charles Rebozo FBI File," FBI Records: The Vault, 1974. Accessed May 14, 2017, https://vault.fbi.gov/Charles%20Rebozo/Charles%20Rebozo%20Part%201%20of%206/view.

21. Ronald Kessler, *The Richest Man in the World: The Story of Adnan Khashoggi* (New York, Warner Books, 1986), 12.

22. Olivia Goldhill, "Expensive Divorces: The Biggest Settlements in Legal History," *The Telegraph*, June 5, 2015.

23. William K. Knoedelseder Jr. and Ellen Farley, "Billion Dollar Divorce," *Penthouse*, August 14, 1979.

24. Donald L. Barlett and James B. Steele, *Howard Hughes: His Life and Madness* (New York: W. W. Norton, 2004), 494.

25. Summers, *Arrogance of Power*, 283.

26. *Pittsburgh Post-Gazette*, "Nixon Ruled Out as Witness in Divorce," Associated Press, December 20, 1979.

27. Summers, *Arrogance of Power*, 283.

28. Ibid.

29. Michelle Green, "Unveiling Adnan Khashoggi: A Provocative Biography Tells of His Deals, His Wealth, and His Women," *People*, February 24, 1986.

30. James Neff, *Mobbed Up: Jackie Presser's High-Wire Life in the Teamsters, the Mafia, and the FBI* (New York: Dell, 1990), 189.

31. Scheim, *Contract on America*, 300, 301.

32. Fred Emery, *Watergate: The Corruption of American Politics and the Fall of Richard Nixon* (New York: Times Books, 1994), 434.

33. "Richard D. Kleindienst, Figure in Watergate Era, Dies at 76," *The New York Times*, February 4, 2000.

34. Anthony Summers and Robbyn Swan, *Sinatra: The Life* (New York: Vintage, 2006), 516.

35. Chris Rojek, *Frank Sinatra* (Cambridge: Polity Press, 2004), 142.

36. J. Randy Taraborrelli, *Sinatra: Behind the Legend* (Seacaucus, NJ: Carol Publishing Group, 1997), 399.

37. Stanley Kutler, *Abuse of Power: The New Nixon Tapes* (New York: Free Press, 1997), 621.

38. Facts, 224.

39. Kelley conducted the interview with Lawford for her book, *His Way*.

40. Don Fulsom, *Nixon's Darkest Secrets: The Inside Story of America's Most Troubled President* (New York: Griffin, 2013), 77.

41. John H. Davis, *Mafia Kingfish: Carlos Marcello and the Assassination of John F. Kennedy* (New York: Signet, 1989), 397.

Six: Hoffa and Clemency

1. Davis, *Mafia Kingfish*, 409.

2. Robert Kennedy, *The Enemy Within: The McClellan Committee's Crusade Against Jimmy Hoffa and Corrupt Labor Unions* (New York: Da Capo Press, 1994), 75.

3. Howard Kohn, "Strange Bedfellows—The Hughes-Nixon-Lansky Connection: The Secret Alliances of the CIA from WWII to Watergate," *Rolling Stone*, May 20, 1976.

4. Mark North, *Act of Treason: The Role of J. Edgar Hoover in the Assassination of President Kennedy* (New York: Carroll and Graf, 1991), 56.

5. Gus Russo, *Supermob: How Sidney Korshak and His Criminal Associates Became America's Hidden Power Brokers* (New York: Bloomsbury, 2006), 261.

6. Richard Reeves, *President Nixon: Alone in the White House* (New York: Touchstone, 2001), 90.

7. James Neff, *Vendetta: Bobby Kennedy versus Jimmy Hoffa* (New York: Little, Brown and Company, 2015), 165–66.

8. William Sullivan, a former top FBI official has verified the Hoffa-Marcello meeting.

9. Dan Moldea, *The Hoffa Wars: Teamsters, Rebels, Politicians, and the Mob* (New York: Paddington, 1978), chapter 1.

10. Ragano and Raab, *Mob Lawyer*, 258–59.

11. Ibid., 370.

12. James Warren, "Nixon's Hoffa Pardon Has on Odor," *Chicago Tribune*, April 8, 2001.

13. Charles, Brandt, *"I Heard You Paint Houses": Frank "the Irishman" Sheeran and the Inside Story of the Mafia, the Teamsters, and the Last Ride of Jimmy Hoffa* (Hanover: Steerforth Press, 2005).

14. Phone call between Charles Colson and Richard Nixon, 016–053, from December 1971; transcription by the author's editorial assistant, Claire Mattingly.

15. Ragano and Raab, *Mob Lawyer*, 382.

16. *Los Angeles Times*, August 17, 1985.

17. *Palm Beach Sentinel*, June 19, 1987.

18. Scheim, *Contract on America*.

19. Dan Moldea, *Dark Victory: Ronald Reagan, MCA, and the Mob* (New York: Penguin, 1986), 260.

20. Bill Bonanno, *Bound by Honor: A Mafioso's Story* (New York: Armeda Ltd., 1999).

21. According to a 1999 statement by Chairman Pete Hoekstra of the House Subcommittee on Oversight and Investigations.

22. Based on the findings of House investigators.

23. "Payoff to Nixon For Hoffa Pardon Is Alleged Anew," *Washington Post*, November 17, 1979.

24. Douglas Brinkley and Luke Nichter, *The Nixon Tapes: 1973* (New York: Houghton Mifflin Harcourt, 2015), 111.
25. Associated Press Philadelphia Bulletin, December 20 1973.
26. Neff, *Mobbed Up,* 181.
27. Ibid.
28. Jack Nelson and Bill Hazlett, "Teamsters Ties to the Mafia—And to the White House," *Los Angeles Times*, May 31, 1973.
29. D. J. R. Bruckner, "Watching for Hoffa," *Chicago Sun-Times*, July 15, 1971.
30. Stanley I. Kutler, *The Wars of Watergate: The Last Crisis of Richard Nixon* (New York: Knopf, 1990), 245.
31. Tape transcriptions by the author and Claire Mattingly.
32. Brandt, *"I Heard You Paint Houses,"* 284–85.
33. *Los Angeles Times*, December 13, 1988.
34. Howard Abadinsky, *Organized Crime* (Belmont: Wadsworth, 1980), 337.
35. "A Book by Hoffa Accuses Fitzsimmons of Mob Link," *New York Times*, September 12, 1975.
36. Neff, *Mobbed Up*, 190.
37. Ibid., 204.
38. Joseph B. Treaster, "Mob Killer Says Hoffa Told Him to Slay Successor," *New York Times,* June 23, 1982.
39. "Hoffa's Body Was Dumped in Glades, Ex-mobster Says," United Press International, April 1, 1985.
40. History Channel, *Jimmy Hoffa: The Real Truth*.
41. Blakey and Billings, *Fatal Hour,* 234.
42. Provenzano obituary, *New York Times*, December 13, 1988.
43. Ragano and Raab, *Mob Lawyer*, 361.
44. Paul Guzzo, "Tampa Holds Clues in Mystery of Hoffa's Disappearance," *Tampa Tribune*, July 10, 2015.
45. *Detroit News*, "Jimmy Hoffa Disappeared 40 Years Ago," July 30, 2015.
46. "Jimmy Hoffa FBI File," FBI Records: The Vault, Accessed May 14, 2017, https://vault.fbi.gov/jimmy-hoffa.
47. Scott Bernstein, "NJ Crime Capo: Tony Pro Was in Detroit Hours before Hoffa Was Killed, Says FBI Informant," Gangsterreport.com.
48. Lester Velie, *Desperate Bargain: Why Jimmy Hoffa Had to Die* (New York: Reader's Digest Press, 1977).
49. Jeff Gerth, "Nixon and the Mafia," *Sundance*, December 1972.

50. Dan Moldea, *The Hoffa Wars* (New York: Shapolsky Publishers, 1993), 105.

51. Feldstein, *Poisoning the Press*, 80.

52. James Rosen, *The Strong Man: John Mitchell and the Secrets of Watergate* (New York: Doubleday, 2008), 491, based on newly discovered notes of Bob Haldeman.

53. Davis, *Mafia Kingfish*, 399.

54. Neff, *Mobbed Up*, 199.

55. *The New York Times*, July 6, 1973, 20.

56. *The New York Times*, July 20, 1973, 13.

57. The source for most of "Mob Favors" is Sid Blumenthal, ed., *Government by Gunplay: Assassination Conspiracy Theories from Dallas to Today* (New York: Signet, 1976), 134–37.

58. Jerry Zeifman, *Without Honor: Crimes of Camelot and the Impeachment of Richard Nixon* (New York: Thunder's Mouth Press, 1996).

59. Samuel P. Jacobs, "'Assange Is in Some Danger,'" The Daily Beast, June 11, 2010. Accessed April 30, 2017. http://www.thedailybeast.com/articles/2010/06/11/daniel-ellsberg-wikileaks-julian-assange-in-danger.html.

60. Moldea, *Hoffa Wars*, 351–52.

61. Ibid.

62. Ronald Goldfarb, *Perfect Villains, Imperfect Heroes: Robert F. Kennedy's War Against Organized Crime* (New York: Random House, 1995).

63. Robert Sam Anson, *Exile: The Unquiet Oblivion of Richard M. Nixon* (New York: Simon and Schuster, 1984).

64. Scheim, *Contract on America*, 303.

Seven: The Most Violent Man in the Oval Office

1. Christopher Hitchens, *The Trial of Henry Kissinger* (London: Atlantic Books, 2014).

2. Summers, *The Arrogance of Power*, 334.

3. Mark Feldstein, NPR interview, September 30, 2010.

Eight: The JFK Assassination and the Warren Commission

1. Mark Lane, *Plausible Denial: Was the CIA Involved in the Assassination of JFK?* (New York: Skyhorse Publishing, 2011).

2. Ibid.

3. Ibid.

4. In 2016, Sloyan discussed Ford's comments while lecturing for my "Who Killed JFK?" course at American University in Washington, DC.

5. Summers, *Not in Your Lifetime.*

6. This tape is mentioned in Jim Marrs, *Crossfire: The Plot That Killed Kennedy* (New York: Carroll and Graf, 1989).

7. Tim Weiner, "A Blast at Secrecy in Kennedy Killing," *New York Times*, September 9, 1998.

8. The Associated Press, "Ford Made Key Change in Kennedy Death Report," *The New York Times*, July 2, 1997.

9. Ehrlichman, *Witness to Power.*

10. Gerald Ford, *A Presidential Legacy and the Warren Commission* (Clarksville, TN: Flatsigned Press, 2007), xxii.

11. In a separate comment, John Connally said, "There were either two or three people involved, or more, in this—or someone was shooting with an automatic rifle."

12. Web version based on the Report of the Select Committee on Assassinations of the U.S. House of Representatives (Washington, DC: United States Government Printing Office, 1979), 256.

13. From a quarterly publication of Britain's Forensic Science Society.

14. George Ladner Jr., "Study Backs Theory of Grassy Knoll, New Report Says Second Gunman Fired and Kennedy," *The Washington Post*, March 26, 2001.

15. Richard Nixon, *The Memoirs of Richard Nixon* (New York: Grosset and Dunlap, 1978).

16. This memo is contained in the Report of the President's Commission on the Assassination of President John F. Kennedy, 1964. (Hereafter known as the Warren Commission Report.)

17. The *Washington Post* disclosed the memo in 1991. *Newsweek* had earlier described Ford as "the CIA's best friend in Congress."

18. This tape is mentioned in Marrs, *Crossfire.*

19. William Sullivan, *The Bureau: My Thirty Years in Hoover's FBI* (New York: Norton, 1979.

20. Gerald Ford, "Piecing Together the Evidence," *Life,* Oct. 1964, 41.

21. "Report of the President's Commission on the Assassination of President Kennedy," (Washington, DC: United States Government Printing Office, 1964).

22. Kantor, *The Ruby Cover-up*, 179.

Nine: Nixon and Ford

1. Henry Kissinger, *Years of Upheaval* (New York: Simon and Schuster, 1982).

2. Ehrlichman, *Witness to Power*.

3. Jules Witcover and Richard Cohen, *A Heartbeat Away: The Investigation and Resignation of Vice President Spiro T. Agnew* (New York: Bantam, 1974).

4. Ibid.

5. Spiro T. Agnew, *Go Quietly . . . Or Else* (New York: William Morrow, 1980).

6. Spiro T. Agnew, interview with ABC's Barbara Walters, 1980.

7. During this period, in a self-pitying remark about his potential legal problems, Nixon told Haig: "Some of the best writing is done from prison."

8. Bob Woodward and Carl Bernstein, *The Final Days: The Classic, Behind-the-Scenes Account of Richard Nixon's Final Days in the White House* (New York: Simon and Schuster, 1976).

9. Robert T. Hartmann, *Palace Politics: An Inside Account of the Ford Years* (New York: McGraw-Hill, 1980).

10. Bob Woodward, *Shadow: Five Presidents and the Legacy of Watergate* (New York: Simon and Schuster, 1999).

11. Ibid., 9.

12. Bryce Harlow and Charles Colson's comments are quoted in Seymour Hersh, "The Pardon," *Atlantic*, August 1983.

13. Ehrlichman, *Witness to Power*.

14. Hersh, "The Pardon."

15. Clark R. Mollenhoff, *The Man Who Pardoned Nixon : A Documented Account of Gerald Ford's Presidential Retreat from Credibility* (New York: St. Martin's, 1976).

16. Hersh, "The Pardon."

17. Woodward, *Shadow*.

18. DeFrank, *Write It When I'm Gone: Remarkable Off-the-Record Conversations with Gerald R. Ford,* (New York: Berkeley, 2008).

19. Dan Moldea, email to author.

20. Debra Conway, email to author.

Ten: Nixon and J. Edgar Hoover

1. Burton Hersh, *Bobby and J. Edgar: The Historic Face-Off Between the Kennedys and J. Edgar Hoover That Transformed America* (New York: Basic Books, 2007).
2. Summers, *Not in Your Lifetime.*
3. Michael Benson, *Who's Who in the JFK Assassination: An A to Z Encyclopedia* (New York: Citadel, Press, 1993), 191.
4. Ragano and Raab, *Mob Lawyer.*
5. Mark North, *Act of Treason: The Role of J. Edgar Hoover in the Assassination of President Kennedy* (New York: Carroll and Graf, 1991).
6. Summers, *Not in Your Lifetime.*
7. Mel Ayton, "The Truth about J. Edgar Hoover," *Crime Magazine*, July 19, 2005.
8. Anthony Summers, *Official and Confidential: The Secret Life of J. Edgar Hoover* (New York: Open Road Integrated Media, 1993).
9. "J. Edgar Hoover," a biography with no date posted on YouTube.
10. Fawn M. Brodie, *Richard Nixon: The Shaping of His Character* (New York: W. W. Norton, 1981).
11. Thomas Craughwell, *Presidential Payola: The True Stories of Monetary Scandals in the Oval Office that Robbed Taxpayers to Grease Palms, Stuff Pockets, and Pay for Undue Influence from Teapot Dome to Halliburton* (Beverly, MA: Fair Winds Press, 2011), 114.
12. Helmer Reenberg, "May 4, 1972—Eulogy by President Richard Nixon at Funeral Services for J. Edgar Hoover (color)," YouTube, Accessed May 14, 2017, Uploaded May 1, 2013, https://www.youtube.com/watch?v=vy3jT4ssr44.
13. Tom Wells, *Wild Man: The Life and Times of Daniel Ellsberg* (Basingstoke, UK: Pakgrave Macmillan, 2001), 498.
14. CSPANJUNKIEd0tORG, " 'Terminate with Extreme Prejudice' Daniel Ellsberg Talks About CIA Plot to Assassinate Him," YouTube, Accessed May 14, 2017, Uploaded Apr 28, 2015, https://www.youtube.com/watch?v=7wu6cTq_Wu8.
15. "Liddy Tells of Plot to Kill Columnist," *Newark Star-Ledger*, wire reports, April 14, 1980.
16. Talbot, *Brothers.*

17. YouTube.
18. JFK Facts.
19. Tim Weiner, *Enemies: A History of the FBI* (New York: Random House, 2012), 159.
20. All quotes transcribed from author's tape recording.
21. Weiner, *Enemies*, 283.
22. White House tape transcripts, October 8 and 25, 1971, as reported in Michael Wines, "Tape Shows Nixon Feared Hoover," *New York Times*, June 5, 1991.
23. Summers, *Official and Confidential*, 415.
24. Ibid., 409.

Eleven: Nixon, Sparky, and Ozzie

1. These were Ruby's words according to Russo. Russo, *Live by the Sword*.
2. Richard Billings, interview, Houston paper, 1998.
3. Michael Benson, *Encyclopedia of the JFK Assassination* (New York: Facts on File, 2002), 43.
4. Jim DiEugenio, "Rose Cheramie: How She Predicted the JFK Assassination," *Probe*, July–August 1999.
5. Ibid.
6. Benson, *Encyclopedia of the JFK Assassination*, 43.
7. Dan Moldea, *The Hoffa Wars: Teamsters, Rebels, Politicians, and the Mob* (New York: Paddington, 1978).
8. Marrs, *Crossfire*.
9. Mark Lane, *Plausible Denial: Was the CIA Involved in the Assassination of JFK?* (New York: Skyhorse Publishing, 1991).
10. Carl Oglesby, *The Yankee and Cowboy War: The Astonishing Link between the JFK Assassination and the Deposing of Nixon* (New York: Berkley Pub Group, 1976), 161.
11. Dan Moldea, *Hoffa Wars*.
12. Summers, *Official and Confidential*, 162.
13. Dated October 13, 1970, the memo is found in Bruce Oudes, ed., *From: The President: Richard Nixon's Secret Files* (New York: Harpercollins, 1989).
14. Robert Sam Anson, *Exile: The Unquiet Oblivion of Richard M. Nixon* (New York: Simon and Schuster, 1984).

15. In 1993, the PBS TV program *Frontline* showed a group photo—taken in 1955—of 16 men and boys on a picnic. Ferrie and Oswald are at opposite ends of the group.

Twelve: Did Oswald Know Ruby?

1. Scheim, *Contract on America*, 264.
2. Christian Jose, "Roger Stone Thinks LBJ Had JFK Offed," *Daily Caller*, November 4, 2013.
3. Sam Giancana and Chuck Giancana, *Double Cross*, 297–307.
4. Marrs, *Crossfire*, 269.
5. Brad Lewis, *Hollywood's Celebrity Gangster: The Incredible Life and Times of Mickey Cohen* (New York: Enigma, 2007), 286.
6. Ibid., 287.
7. *New York Times*, November 30, 1963.
8. Benson, *Encyclopedia of the JFK Assassination*, 122.
9. Ibid, 122.
10. Gary Cartwright, "Who Was Jack Ruby?," *Texas Monthly*, November 1975.
11. *The Man Who Killed Kennedy*, The History Channel, Nigel Turner Productions, 1988–2003.
12. Joe Nick Patoski, "The Two Oswalds," *Texas Monthly*, November 1998.
13. Coverthistory.blogspot.com, September 19, 2007.
14. Mark K. Colgan, "When a Mysterious Death Is no Longer Mysterious," JFK Lancer, http://www.jfklancer.com/pdf/Jada_mark.pdf.
15. "Beverly Oliver: Babushka Babe? Or Bamboozling the Buffs?," http://mcadams.posc.mu.edu/oliver.htm.
16. Gary Mack, email correspondence with author, January 10, 2009.
17. Gaeton Fonzi, *The Last Investigation* (Ipswich, MA: Mary Ferrell Foundation, 2008), 60–65.
18. "Interview with Jim Garrison," *Playboy*, October 1967.
19. Malcolm Macdonald, "Where Was Carlos Marcello?," *Anderson Valley Advertiser*, December 11, 2013.
20. *New York Post*, January 10, 2009, as well as various book reviews.
21. "Warren Commission Exhibit No. 1761," History Matters, https://www.history-matters.com/archive/contents/wc/contents_wh23.htm.

22. "Warren Commission Exhibit No. 1251," History Matters, https://
www.history-matters.com/archive/jfk/wc/wcvols/wh22/pdf/WH22
_CE_1251.pdf.

23. Kenneth Lawry Dowe, "Testimony of Kenneth Lawry Dowe," Office
of the U.S. Attorney, Dallas, Texas, July 25, 1964. Mcadams.posc.mu
.edu/russ/testimony/dowe.htm.

24. G. Robert Blakey and Richard N. Billings, *The Plot to Kill the President*
(New York: Times Books, 1981).

25. Robert Blakey, "Murdered by the Mob," *Washington Post*, November 7, 1993.

26. "Ex-flame Says Jack Ruby 'Had no Choice' but to Kill Oswald," jfk-
facts.org. August 14, 2016, http://jfkfacts.org/ex-flame-says-jack-ruby
-had-no-choice-but-to-kill-oswald/.

27. Letter from Lieutenant Dyson to Police Chief J. H. Curry, November 25, 1963, http://whokilledjfk.net/JackRuby.htm.

28. *The Man Who Killed Kennedy*, The History Channel, Nigel Turner
Productions, 1988–2003.

29. Obituary of Ralph Harris, *Liverpool Daily Post*, January 21, 2009.

30. http://www.youtube.com/watch?v+TUiZBmm9xUA.

31. Talbot, *Brothers*, 21.

Thirteen: Mob Assassination Connections

1. Ragano and Raab, *Mob Lawyer*.

2. Hinckle & Turner, *Deadly Secrets*, 1992.

3. In 1979, House assassination investigators found that Oswald's uncle
and father figure, Charles Murret, had "worked for years in an underworld gambling syndicate affiliated with the Carlos Marcello crime
family." Oswald was also an apparent associate of David Ferrie, a
Marcello employee believed by many researchers to be a key figure in
the JFK assassination that brought the new tapes to light. In cooperation
with the archives, Kutler hired professional court reporters to tran-
scribe the tapes. In 1997, many of the transcripts—reviewed and edited by Kutler—were published in Kutler, *Abuse of Power*, 528.

4. This tape is among 200 hours of Watergate Abuse of Power conversations released by the National Archives in 1996. Nixon strongly fought
the release of all tapes—beyond those made public in the 1970s—right
up until his death in 1994. But a lawsuit filed by historian Stanley Kutler

and the advocacy group Public Citizen led to a 1996 settlement with the Nixon estate that brought the new tapes to light.

5. Assassination Records Review Board, 1995 Releases, RIF #104-100-15-10440 (11/28/63) CIA #201-289-248.

6. Warren Commission Report, 801.

7. George Crile, "The Mafia, the CIA and Castro," *Washington Post*, May 16, 1976.

8. Sam Giancana and Chuck Giancana, *Double Cross*.

9. Melvin M. Belli, *Dallas Justice: The Real Story of Jack Ruby and His Trial*, 1964.

10. Jack Anderson, from a column in the *Washington Post*, September 7, 1976. In a January 23, 1978, article in *New Times* magazine—"The Secret Life of Jack Ruby" by William Scott Malone—Rosselli and Ruby were reported to have met in hotels in Miami during the months before the JFK assassination.

11. Warren Commission testimony, Volume 5.

12. Marrs, *Crossfire*.

13. Summers, *Not in Your Lifetime*.

14. Dan Moldea, "Why Does Hollywood Turn Thugs into Heroes?" *The Washington Post*, December 27, 1992.

15. Valentine, *Strength of the Wolf*, 253.

Fourteen: The Watergate-Assassination Connection

1. This tape, made public on August 5, 1974, has come to be known as "the smoking gun." It hastened Nixon's resignation, which came several days later, by showing that he began leading the Watergate cover-up shortly after the break-in.

2. Haldeman, *Ends of Power*.

3. Ehrlichman, *Witness to Power*.

4. Haldeman, *Ends of Power*, 39.

5. Ehrlichman too undoubtedly knew what was behind the "Bay of Pigs" code, but—unlike Haldeman—he never publicly spilled the secret. In a post-Watergate novel titled *The Company*, however, Ehrlichman spun a tale about a president and a CIA chief trying to blackmail each other over a previous assassination plot that involved both men.

6. This tape is among 200 hours of Watergate Abuse of Power conversations released by the National Archives in 1996.

7. Kutler, *Abuse of Power*, 490.

8. Ibid., 89–91.

9. *New York Times*, February 5, 1964.

10. Stephen E. Ambrose, *Nixon: Ruin and Recovery, 1973–1990* (New York: Simon and Schuster, 1991).

11. Daniel Schorr, *Clearing the Air* (New York: Houghton Mifflin, 1977).

12. Matthew Smith, *JFK: The Second Plot* (Edinburgh: Mainstream Publishing, 1992), 303.

13. Hersh, *Bobby and J. Edgar*.

14. Summers, *Not in Your Lifetime*, 219. "Oswald allegedly given envelope," Earl Golz, *Dallas Times Herald*, 8/7/78.

15. Ragano and Raab, *Mob Lawyer*.

16. Mark North, *Act of Treason: The Role of J. Edgar Hoover in the Assassination of President Kennedy* (New York: Carroll and Graf, 1991).

18. Summers, reported his find in *Not in Your Lifetime*.

19. HSCA Report, vol. iii, 471–73.

20. Valentine, *Strength of the Wolf*, 271.

21. House Committee on Assassinations Report, 249–50.

22. St. John Hunt, *Bond of Secrecy: My Life with CIA Spy and Watergate Conspirator E. Howard Hunt* (Walterville, OR: Trine Day, 2008).

23. Erik Hedegaard, "The last Confession of E. Howard Hunt," *Rolling Stone*, April 5, 2007.

24. Martin Shackelford, "Garrison's Case Finally Coming Together," *Fair Play*, Nov.–Dec. 1998. Accessed at www.oocities.org/garrisoninvestigation/garrison.htm.

Fifteen: "The Bay of Pigs"

1. Richard D. Mahoney, *Sons and Brothers: The Days of Jack and Bobby Kennedy* (New York: Arcade, 1999).

2. Richard M. Bissell Jr., "Response to Lucien S. Vandenbroucke, 'The "Confessions" of Allen Dulles: New Evidence on the Bay of Pigs,'" *Diplomatic History*, Vol. 8, No. 4, October 1984.

3. Matthews, *Kennedy & Nixon*.

4. In fact, a further declassified version of the final report, issued in 2000, reveals that the CIA went ahead with the invasion despite the

agency's apparent knowledge that the Soviet Union had learned the exact date of the amphibious landing in advance. An account of the newly declassified report is contained in the *Washington Post*, April 29, 2000.

Sixteen: Blackmailing the CIA Chief

1. Hunt's recollections are from a CBS New Special on Watergate, June 1992.
2. *Washington Post*, September 21, 1975.
3. The affidavit, dated March 21, 1978, was filed in the case of *Jack Anderson v. Richard Nixon*.
4. "Gordon Liddy on Sex, Drugs and Rock 'N' Roll," *High Times*, June 1981.
5. Charles W. Colson, *Born Again* (Grand Rapids, MI: Chosen, 1976).
6. From the "smoking gun" tape that, when released in 1974, quickly led to Nixon's resignation.
7. Haldeman, *Ends of Power*, 61.
8. Ehrlichman, *Witness to Power*, 350.
9. An Ehrlichman novel, *The Company*, features a president named "Monckton"—an obvious play on "The Mad Monk," Ehrlichman's favorite nickname for the erratic and reclusive Nixon.
10. John Ehrlichman, *The Company* (New York: Simon and Schuster, 1976).
11. Kutler, *Abuse of Power*, 528.
12. *Nixon: An Oliver Stone Film*, Eric Hamburg, ed. (New York: Hyperion, 1995).
13. Richard Ben-Veniste and George Frampton, *Stonewall: The Legal Cases Against the Watergate Conspirators* (New York: Simon & Schuster, 1977).
14. David, Scheim, *Contract on America: The Mafia Murders of John and Robert Kennedy* (New York: Shapolsky Books, 1988).
15. Scheim, *Contract on America: The Mafia Murder of President John F. Kennedy*, 300, 301.
16. Salinger made the disclosure during a 1977 interview with Anthony Summers, quoted in *Arrogance of Power*, 196–97.
17. John Dean, *Blind Ambition* (New York: Simon & Schuster, 1976).
18. Ragano and Raab, *Mob Lawyer*.

19. Sam Giancana and Chuck Giancana, *Double Cross*.

20. "Frank, Sturgis, The CIA's #1 Assassin-Spy," April 1977, 3, *High Times*; Malcolm Abrams, "Reds Are Framing Me as JFK's Killer," *Midnight Globe*, November 29, 1977.

21. E. Howard Hunt, *Give Us This Day* (New York: Arlington House, 1973).

22. L. Fletcher Prouty, *The Secret Team: The CIA and Its Allies in Control of the United States and the World* (Upper Saddle River, NJ: Prentice-Hall, 1973).

23. Hunt, *Give Us This Day*.

24. Mention of the landing-day leak and the Dulles quotes are from a final, and nearly deletion-free, version of the report. Issued by the National Archives in April 2000, it was originally sent to President Kennedy in June 1961. A story about the document was published in the April 29, 2000 edition of the *Washington Post*.

25. From Szulc's obituary in the *Washington Post*, May 22, 2001.

26. Ehrlichman's notes were turned over to the Senate Watergate Committee and are found in committee documents.

27. Kutler, *Abuse of Power*, 528.

28. Haldeman, *Ends of Power*.

29. Kutler, *Abuse of Power*, 255.

30. Haldeman, *Ends of Power*.

31. Drosnin, *Citizen Hughes*.

32. *Parade*, 2001.

33. Drosnin, *Citizen Hughes*.

Conclusion

1. Jeff Gerth, "Nixon and the Mafia—Conclusion," *Sundance*, November-December 1972.

2. Jefferson Morley, "Judge Tunheim says JFK files were 'probably unlawfully withheld' by CIA," March 17, 2017, jfkfacts.org.

3. Shawn McCreesh, "Is the American Mafia on the Rise?," *Rolling Stone*, November 22, 2016.

INDEX